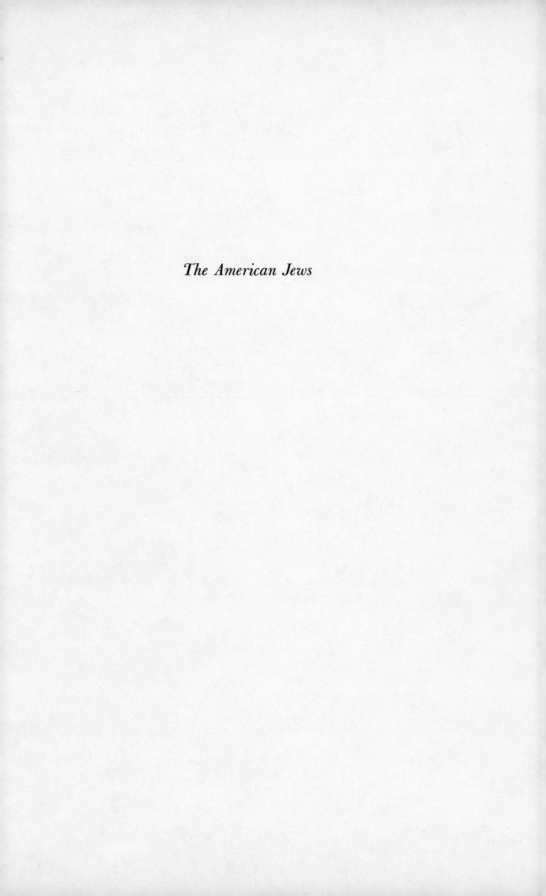

The American Jews

The
American
Jews

by
JAMES YAFFE

RANDOM HOUSE
New York

TO DEBORAH ANN AND REBECCA ELIZABETH,
MY CHILDREN, THIS BOOK IS
LOVINGLY DEDICATED

Preface

In gathering material for this book, I read hundreds of books, magazines, and newspapers, and conducted formal interviews with over two hundred people; I have also not hesitated to make use of casual conversations with friends, family, and acquaintances. Ultimately, however, the opinions expressed in this book are completely personal. In many cases my interpretation of the facts may be upsetting and even offensive to the people who provided me with those facts. And so, in thanking some of the organizations and individuals whose kindness and cooperation made this book possible, I hope I won't be adding insult to injury.

I received invaluable help from the following organizations: The Rabbinical Council of America, the Union of Orthodox Jewish Congregations, Young Israel, Yeshiva University, Torah Umesorah, the Central Conference of Rabbis, the Union of American Hebrew Congregations, Hebrew Union College, the Rabbinical Assembly of America, the United Synagogues of America, the Jewish Theological Seminary, the Reconstructionist Foundation; the American Jewish Committee, the American Jewish Congress, the Anti-Defamation League, the Jewish Labor Committee, the National Conference of Christians and Jews, the National Council of Jewish Women, the American Council for Judaism; B'nai B'rith, the Jewish War Veterans, the Hillel Society (especially its chapters at Yale, CCNY, and the University of Michigan), the National Community Relations Advisory Council; Hadassah, the Zionist Organization of America, the Theodore Herzl Foundation; the United Jewish Appeal, the Council of Jewish Federations and Welfare Funds, the Jewish Welfare Board, the Federation of Jewish Philanthropies of New York, the Jewish Board of Guardians, the Jewish Family Service, the Louise Wise Adoption Agency; Brandeis University, the *Jewish Daily Forward, Women's Wear Daily.*

Among the individuals who were kind enough to let me interview them, I would like to thank the following: David Amram, Mr. and Mrs. Morton Asch, Mr. and Mrs. Stephen Baker, Rabbi Bernard Bamberger, Harry Baron, Abraham Beame, Frances L. Beetman, Burt Bilski, Nathan Belth, Mac Benoff, Rabbi Elmer Berger, Graenum Berger, Rabbi William Berkowitz, Mickey Bernardik, Leonard Bernstein, Rabbi Jack Bloom, Lawrence Bloomgarden, Prof. Alvin Boderman, Sterling Brown, Clarence Burger, Rabbi Judah Cahn, Brant Coopersmith, Annette Daum, Rabbi Stanley Dreyfus, Prof. Ronald Dworkin, Prof. Daniel Elazar, Milton Ellerin, Representative Leonard Farbstein, Prof. Stanley Feingold, Leo Filers, David Finn, Harry Fleischman, Bruce Jay Friedman, Rabbi Herbert Friedman, Dr. Iago Galdston, Alexander Garfinkel, Mr. and Mrs. Steven Gerson, Rabbi Neil Gilman, Dr. Jerome Goldsmith, Prof. Abraham Goldstein, Rabbi David Goldstein, Rabbi Harold Gordon, Rabbi Sheldon Gordon, S. William Green, Chaim Gross, George Gruen, Sam Hartstein, Rita Hauser, Adolph Held, Rabbi Arthur Hertzberg, Rabbi Joseph Herzog, Louis Hilford, Milton Himmelfarb, Dr. Morris Hinenburg, Carol Horne, William Horowitz, Rabbi and Mrs. Richard Israel, Dr. Herman Jacobs, Rabbi Leon Jick, Prof. Gilbert Johns, Marcia Johns, Dr. Joseph Kaminetski, William Katz, Howard Katzander, Rabbi Wolfe Kelman, Rabbi Israel Klavan, Rabbi David Kline, Dr. Sidney Koenig, Mrs. Mignon Krause, Milton Krentz, Nathan Kroll, Rabbi Norman Lamm, Mr. and Mrs. Judah Lando, Mrs. Edna Lauscher, Rabbi Robert Lehman, Abram Lerner, Irving Levitas, Raphael Levy, Dr. Charles Liebman, Prof. Irving Linn, Walter Lurie, Rabbi Bernard Mandelbaum, Rabbi Julius Mark, Milton Marks, Will Maslow, Steve Max, Rabbi Allen Miller, Rabbi Israel Miller, Isaiah Minkoff, Emanuel Muravchik, Rabbi Judah Nadich, Mr. and Mrs. Robert Nangle, Joel Ollander, Harvey Platt, Norman Podhoretz, Joel Pomerantz, Dean Jacob Rabinowitz, Rabbi Emanuel Rackman, Alex Redein, Dan Rosenberg, Rabbi Leonard Rosenfeld, Mr. and Mrs. Daniel Roth, Dr. Abram Sacher, Neil Sandberg, Rabbi Melech Schachter, Dore Schary, Abraham Schenker, Representative James Scheuer, Rabbi Alexander Schindler, Rabbi Arthur Schneier, Albert Shanker, Morton Sheinman, David Sidman, Charles Silberman, Isaac Bashevis Singer, Prof. Erwin Smigel, Prof. Fred Sondermann, Rabbi Malcolm Stern, Mrs. Richard Stern, Rabbi Ephraim Sturm, Mr. and Mrs. Gerald Subak-Sharpe, David Susskind, Rabbi Marc Tannanbaum, Rabbi Harvey Tattlebaum, Miriam Taub, George Tobias, Jacques Torczyner, Jerome Weidman, Prof. Paul Weiss, Rabbi Joseph Wernik, Sue Wimpfheimer, Mr. and Mrs. Leonard Wolfe, Marjorie Wyler, Morton Yarmon, Walter Zand, David Zeff, Rabbi Martin Zion, Rabbi Arthur Zuckerman, Prof. Felix Zweig. My apologies to all those whom I have inadvertently omitted from this list, and my thanks to many others who requested that their interviews with me should not be publicly acknowledged.

A special debt of gratitude is due to my editor, Hal Scharlatt, with whom I took pleasure in disagreeing about everything except the important things. His insight, taste, and patience have given me a new respect for his much maligned profession.

Finally, let me express my gratitude to my wife, Elaine, for providing me with criticism, suggestions, and moral support, and above all for bearing with me during a hard two and a half years.

Table of Contents

Part One

Building

I.

"A Peculiar Element"

There is a tendency on the part of many people to describe American Jewish life today in the most glowing, optimistic terms. The struggles and frustrations are over; at long last the Jew has found a society in which he feels entirely at home, to which he has perfectly adapted himself. At the same time there is another tendency, equally prevalent, to look upon the Jew in America as "alienated." In much contemporary American literature, in fact, he is presented as a symbol of the Alienation of Modern Man.

This book is an attempt to account for this paradox, to show that it arises from certain deep contradictions within the American Jew. It is also an attempt to trace those contradictions through many different areas of American Jewish life, to describe their effect on the organized Jewish community and on the individual Jew, whether he embraces that community or rejects it. Finally, this is an attempt to see where these contradictions are leading the American Jew, whether he's heading toward disaster or glory, or simply toward oblivion. Underlying this attempt is the belief that what the Jew is going through today isn't unique. Many others—Christians, Americans, all the people of the Western world—are engaged in the same struggle.

But each in a different way. The American Jew's way is emphatically his own.

Like many complex historical phenomena, American Jewish life began in a deceptively simple manner.

In 1654 the first group of Jews in North America landed, along with many other settlers, in New Amsterdam. These twenty-three people founded a congregation, Shearith Israel, which still exists, located now on West Seventieth Street in New York. In the next hundred years, all through the Colonial period, Jews came in small groups from Spain, Portugal, the Netherlands, and other parts of western Europe. This is sometimes referred to as the Sephardic wave of immigration (Sephardic Jews have a special ancient form of worship which differs from that of most Jews), but in fact most of these early settlers were not Sephardic. They settled primarily in New York, Pennsylvania, and Maryland, where they found an atmosphere of religious and political tolerance. Some went South —Charleston, Savannah, and Charlotte had groups of them; the first white child born in Georgia was Jewish. Others tried to settle in New England, but the Puritans were opposed on principle to the existence of any religious groups besides their own—and opposed with equal fervor to the existence of any business competitors.

The "wave" was really no more than a trickle. These early Jews drifted in as individuals and never formed close-knit communities. At the time of the Revolution there were only three thousand Jews in America.

In the late 1840s the second wave of Jewish immigration began. This is usually called the German immigration, but it also included many people from Austria, Hungary, Bohemia, and even North Italy. They were escaping from the reactionism which swept Europe after 1848 and which encouraged, as all reactions do, a resurgence of anti-Semitism. Many of these German Jews became peddlers. Because he had to keep moving, preferably where the competition wouldn't destroy him, the German-Jewish peddler, his pack on his back, became a familiar figure all over the country.

Some German Jews went to New England but, like their counterparts a century earlier, found it impossible to get a foothold. They were caught between the long-established Yankees and the Irish immigrants who had been driven to America by the potato famines. The sympathy of the Jews was with the

Irish, alone and uprooted like themselves; but in education and manners they were much closer to the Yankees.

In the Southwest and Far West they had better luck. The Jews got there at the same time as everyone else and found no entrenched establishment to bar their way. For example, they helped build the city of Galveston, Texas; it had a Jewish mayor in the 1850s, and during its terrible yellow-fever plague of 1867 six Jewish funerals took place in one day. Few descendants of those original German Jews remain in Galveston, but their influence hasn't faded away. The thousand or so Jews in Galveston today live on an equal footing with the gentiles. In San Francisco, where Jews had an analogous history, they occupy a similar place in the highest social and political circles.

Again, because Jews went out West no later than anybody else, they led lives there which Jews traditionally don't lead. Temple Emanu-el in San Francisco was founded during the Gold Rush; somehow a *minyan* (a quorum of ten men, without which services can't be held) was gathered together among the prospectors. In New Mexico a rabbi named Jim Harper traveled from town to town, serving small communities who couldn't afford a rabbi of their own, and incidentally earning extra money as a rider in a Wild West show. Colorado contributes one of the great characters of American Jewish history— Otto Meers, known as the Pathfinder of San Juan. He was a gold prospector, Indian fighter, railroad builder, horse trainer, and mountain climber. He also founded a synagogue and had a reputation as a Talmudic scholar. He is also the only hero of the American West who spoke the Indian languages with a Yiddish accent.

But the German Jew, a man of the middle class in a middle-class world, flourished best in the Middle Atlantic States. While he seldom denied being Jewish, he felt himself much more to be a German, and indeed that was how the society considered him. Political tracts, circulated in German Jewish neighborhoods, invariably made appeals to the "German vote." He read German newspapers, conducted his synagogue services in German, and looked forward to giving his son a good bourgeois education. And some of these German Jews, like their Yankee and Scotch-Irish contemporaries, did very well for themselves in the boom years following the Civil War. The great German Jewish fortunes, those of the Schiffs, Warburgs, Lewisohns, Lehmans, Guggenheims, Strausses, Morgen-thaus—families that made incalculable contributions to American public life and business life—were established then.

By 1880 there were two hundred and fifty thousand German Jews in the United States,[1] and while very few of them were Schiffs or Warburgs, a large majority of them had managed to make comfortable niches for themselves on the American scene. Few of them realized that a bomb had been thrown in their midst.

———————

The bomb came from East Europe, where millions of Jews were living in city ghettos and village *shtetls* under conditions of appalling poverty. The *shtetl* was a collection of ramshackle houses and mud streets in which several hundred or several thousand people huddled together, excluded, prevented by law from engaging in almost all the normal occupations, yet rubbing elbows with the local peasants, who might be huddled in their own ramshackle houses just a street or two away. *Shtetl* culture had existed for a thousand years, but in the last decades of the nineteenth century it was suffering tremendous pressure around the edges. The emancipation in West Europe, though it reached the East European Jew as a faint faraway echo, suggested the possibility that life might be lived another way. And the very existence of the United States of America provided, for the discontented adventurous minority who wanted another way of life, a place in which to live it.

The first rumblings began in the 1870s, when a tightening of discriminatory laws sent some Jews from Rumania, Hungary, and Austrian Gallicia to the United States. In 1881 they were joined by Jews from Russia and Poland. Ten years later pogroms in Rumania and Lithuania further swelled the tide. In 1903 a massacre in Kishinev slaughtered thousands and sent tens of thousands out of the country. A few years later, in search of a scapegoat for the disaster of its war with Japan, the Russian government encouraged further pogroms, and further emigration too. A small number of these emigrants chose the pioneer life in Palestine, but most headed for the United States. They entered the country through the ports of Boston and Baltimore; they came down from Quebec to settle in the northern Midwest and founded Jewish communities in towns like Ypsilanti and Ann Arbor. The majority, however, sailed into New York harbor, crowded the decks of the steerage to get a glimpse of the Statue of Liberty, then cooled their heels on Ellis Island until an immigration inspector, who spoke not a word of their language, was ready to try to cope with them. The ferry from Ellis Island then spit them out to the streets of New York, and they found their way down to the Lower East Side.

For some this was only a temporary stop. Maybe there was a brother or a cousin or an uncle in another part of the country. And maybe, for the lucky ones, there was some kind of job waiting there. So they left the Lower East Side, rode hours or days on stuffy trains, and settled in a small replica of the Lower East Side in Chicago or Detroit. Or maybe they ended up sleeping on a cot in the room behind Cousin Mendele's little dry-goods store in a small town like Davenport, Iowa, or Sharon, Pennsylvania. Cousin Mendele didn't do enough business to pay salaries to hired hands, but at least there was food and a roof, while the "greenie" learned, more or less, how to speak the language of this strange, big, lonely country.

Most of the immigrants never saw anything like Davenport or Sharon—or Staten Island, for that matter. They stayed on the Lower East Side, an area that stretched from the East River to Broadway, from the Brooklyn Bridge up to Fourteenth Street—approximately twelve square miles, much of it occupied by other immigrant groups. It is difficult to estimate how many people lived in this area at any one time. In 1880 there were eighty thousand Jews in New York City; in 1910 there were one and a quarter million. Between 1899 and 1914 one and a half million Jews entered the United States. Statistics can only begin to indicate the congestion, the dirt, the noise, the rats, the tuberculosis.

The East European wave was the last big wave of Jewish immigration into the United States. It was cut off abruptly in 1921 by the passage of the first Immigration Quota Law. The law provided that the number of people of any particular nationality which might be admitted to the country must not exceed 3 percent of the number of people of that nationality already in the country ten years before. In one stroke Congress succeeded in limiting the Russians who could come here to a few thousand, while leaving plenty of room for Englishmen and Scotsmen—who didn't want to come here.

There was nothing Congress could do, however, about the

East European Jews who were here already. All through the twenties and thirties they, or their children, set about the task of breaking through the boundaries of the Lower East Side, of moving "uptown," of spreading all over the country. It has been estimated that 95 percent of the Jews in America today are descended from these East European immigrants.[2] What the American Jew is now, his style of living and thinking, comes to him from the *shtetl*, tempered in the furnace of the lower East Side, moulded and refined and strengthened—or weakened?—by the experience of the last thirty or forty years.

———●●———

Later immigrations were small, minuscule even, compared to the tidal wave from East Europe, but they have had their influence on American Jewish life. One hundred and forty thousand or so German and Austrian refugees from the Nazis arrived in America between 1933 and 1940.[3] Many were professionals who had been fairly well-to-do, but were forced to leave their countries without much money. This influx has enriched the American scene with great scientists like Albert Einstein and great musicians like Bruno Walter; with author Franz Werfel and political scientist Fred Sondermann; with most of that marvelous collection of actors who played Nazis in Hollywood movies during the war (Conrad Veidt, Ludwig Donath, Otto Preminger, Martin Kosleck, etc.); and with the fussy little man who owns the stationery store on the corner.

After the war a new group of Jewish immigrants came to America, the people who had somehow managed to survive the concentration camps: about one hundred fifty thousand came between 1945 and 1954. Twelve thousand or so from East Europe settled in the Williamsburg section of Brooklyn. These are the Hasidic Jews, most Orthodox of all the Orthodox; they can be seen from time to time on the New York subways, with their earcurls (*paes*) and black hats. Several thousand Arabic-speaking Sephardic Jews from Syria, Greece, Egypt, Yugoslavia, Turkey, and Egypt have found their way to America too. The most recent group of immigrants has come from an unexpected direction—Cuba. These Jewish refugees have formed a sizable colony in Miami, where so far they have kept very much to themselves, mingling neither with other Cubans nor with American Jews.

Finally there are about ten thousand Negro Jews, the

so-called Black Jews, most of whom live in Harlem. They have their synagogues and celebrate the Jewish holidays; many eat kosher food. Yet there is some question among Orthodox authorities whether they are legitimately entitled to call themselves Jews, whether their claim to be descended from certain Jewish tribes in Ethiopia is a valid one. And so, while the argument goes on, they are largely cut off from the rest of the American Jewish community.

———— •◦• ————

Nobody really knows how many Jews there are in America today. The *American Jewish Yearbook,* a highly regarded collection of statistics, learned articles, and assorted facts, gives the figure of 5.7 million. But because the U.S. Census Bureau is not permitted to ask any questions about religion, the *Yearbook* must depend on reports from local Jewish community relations councils around the country. And the methods used to gather this information are, to say the least, haphazard.

One of the most popular tactics is to get membership figures from local synagogues. Since many Jews, especially in larger communities, don't belong to any synagogue, this method would seem to lead to a drastic underestimation of the Jewish population. On the other hand, some Jews belong to more than one synagogue; anyway, synagogues are notorious for padding their membership figures, so perhaps the one inaccuracy counterbalances the other. Then there is the Cemetery Factor. The annual proportion of Jewish deaths to Jewish lives is considered to be mathematically stable; so all you have to do is find out from Jewish cemeteries in town how many burials they've had, and multiply. And then there is the Cohen Factor: count the number of Cohens in the local phonebook and multiply by the assumed ratio of Jews-named-Cohen to Jews-not-named-Cohen.

Let us assume that there are 5.7 million American Jews. They represent somewhat less than 3 percent of the population. Eighty percent of them live in cities with over 100,000 people. Only 200,000 of them live in cities with under 5,000 people. In cities under 50,000, less than 1 percent are Jewish. Most American Jews live in the Northeast, from Washington, D.C., and North Virginia up to Boston and Southern New Hampshire. Yet there are Jews everywhere. Seven hundred and twenty-eight communities are in touch with the Council of

Jewish Federations and Welfare Funds—an umbrella organization for local charities—and another two to three hundred
communities have some kind of religious organization. Every
town in the United States with over 5,000 people has at least
one Jewish family.

New York City has the largest Jewish population—2,381,-
000—representing 25 percent of the city and nearly half of all
American Jews. The second largest Jewish population is in
Los Angeles, with 500,000. The next eight cities, in descending
order, are Philadelphia, Chicago, Boston, Newark (and the
Essex County area), Miami, Washington, Cleveland, and Baltimore. Among these, some can expect to change their places on
the list in the next ten years. Miami, for instance, is the new
Promised Land, while Chicago, once second on the list, is
losing Jews rapidly. The South is also losing its Jews. It now
has about 150,000 in nine states, but this number will dwindle
in the next decade. Partly this is the result of a phenomenon
which is occurring all over the country. Young Jews who are
born in small towns as a rule don't go back to those towns after
college. They go to the big cities.

But the most important geographical fact about American
Jews today is not the move from small towns to big cities but
the move from big cities to suburbs. Jews have this in common
with all other middle-class Americans, but with a vengeance.
There is one famous statistic which tells the whole story: In the
last four years the Cleveland Public High School, located in the
center of the city, hasn't had a single Jewish graduate.

The more closely we examine these various waves of
Jewish immigration, the more struck we are by a curious coinci-
dence. Despite many obvious differences, the American
experience of all these immigrant groups has had one thing in
common: in each case it has been full of paradoxes. The early
Sephardic settlers, for example, left practically no descendants
who are still Jewish. (A few old aristocratic Sephardic families
still exist, proudly maintaining their ties to Judaism despite
their secure place in the highest social circles.) Some married
Christians or converted to Christianity, but this was not the
main reason for their disappearance. They disappeared not
because they intermarried but because they refused to intermarry—and so, without sufficient choice among their own,

they remained unmarried and died out. What was their purpose in coming here then? At the very least they must have been looking for a new life. Yet they ended up choosing extinction rather than assimilation.

The German-American Jews—those dull, stolid, unimaginative burghers—were just as paradoxical beneath the surface. This is proved by their reactions to the invasion from East Europe. On the one hand they despised the "Russians" (a name they scornfully applied to all East Europeans, no matter where they came from), because they were poor, wore strange clothes, had loud, coarse manners, and spoke English, if at all, with ugly accents. And they feared the Russians even more than they despised them. They feared that the presence of this horde of "barbarians" would cause a reaction of anti-Semitism which might eventually be turned against Germans as well as Russians. They trembled at the thought that they might be confused in the public mind with "those people," that their comfortable position in American society might be threatened.

This was why the Germans were especially galled by the fact that the Russians spoke Yiddish. For many centuries Yiddish had been the language of the *shtetl*, but it hadn't been born there. Originally it was a German dialect which Jews in the Middle Ages, fleeing before the armies of the Crusades, brought into East Europe with them. Anybody who understood German, therefore, could do reasonably well at understanding Yiddish. Every time one of "those people" spoke the hated language, it seemed to the Germans that he was crying out, "I'm just like you!"

The Germans did set up numerous philanthropic activities to help the new immigrants, but their motives in many cases were dubious. Finding that they could neither check the flow of immigration nor persuade the newcomers to go back where they came from, they took the only course left to them; they poured money into the project of scrubbing the faces of those dirty Russians, putting decent American clothes on them, teaching them table manners and English, making them as presentable as possible in gentile eyes. They did this out of fear and embarrassment, and because they thought the gentiles would criticize them if they didn't do it; and they took their revenge by treating the helpless immigrants as contemptuously as possible, by doling out soup and disinfectant and jobs with large doses of condescension.

Letters, memoirs, and German Jewish newspapers of the period are full of illustrations of this kind of fear and snobbery. German parents, for example, inveighed against their wayward daughters who had the ingratitude to "intermarry" with East Europeans. It was the German Jews who invented the word kike, deriving it from the "ki" ending of many Russian names. The great Rabbi Isaac Mayer Wise, the unofficial spiritual leader of German-American Jewry, tried to influence the government to pass an immigration quota law years before it was finally passed—and when that didn't work he flirted with the revolutionary idea of Zionism for a while, in the hope of diverting the immigrants from New York to Palestine.

This snobbish attitude lasted for many years, long after the immigrants had stopped being a threat. As late as World War II the teen-age daughter of an old German Jewish family in New Orleans refused to go to dances sponsored by the USO or the Jewish Welfare Board, for fear that she might be forced to dance with East European servicemen.

On the other hand, though all this is true, it isn't the whole truth. It is too easy to dismiss offhandedly the philanthropic activities of the German immigrants. These activities couldn't have been prompted solely by fear and embarrassment; they were carried on with too much diligence and imagination, often with a devotion that bordered on self-sacrifice. The best proof of this is the settlement houses, which sprang up on Lower East Sides all over the country. They began as nothing more than "de-lousing stations," but they quickly developed into complex beehives where almost all of the immigrants' educational and social needs could be met. The most famous of them, the Educational Alliance on the Lower East Side— founded in 1891 by the solid German money of the Guggenheims, Morgenthaus, Schiffs, and Lewisohns—provided everything from English lessons to medical care to books to Orthodox services. It sponsored free chamber music concerts, lectures, art lessons, and play groups for the children. It serviced a million immigrants between its opening and the beginning of World War I.

Among its graduates were such men as David Sarnoff, George Gershwin, Zero Mostel, Chaim Gross—the list would have to include hundreds of the most distinguished American Jews today. Very few of them have ever had anything bad to say about the Educational Alliance, or about most of the other set⁺lement houses built on its model. It is hard to see how an institution, if created only in a spirit of bitterness and condescension, could have turned out so well, could have been so perfectly adapted not only to the material needs but to the deepest feelings of the people it served.

Many of the other welfare organizations created by the German Jews and many individual actions won't submit, under close examination, to a completely cynical explanation. The American Jewish Committee, rigidly restricted in its early years to snobbish wealthy German Jews, came into existence in response to the Russian pogroms of 1904—and part of the help given to the pogrom victims was passage money to the United States. The same thing is true of HIAS—the Hebrew Immigrant Aid Society—which was founded in 1882 by the Union of American Hebrew Congregations, the official body of German Reform Judaism. What these instances and thousands more indicate is that the traditional ideal of *Zedakah,* of Jewish charity given in a spirit of loving-kindness, of "taking care of one's own," was not dead in the Germans. I have talked to some of those old-timers who still survive, and in every case they say, "We had to help them, didn't we? They were Jews."

Yet when pressed a bit, they are likely to add, "To tell the truth, I didn't really *like* those people much." And this, I think, is the real truth about the way the German Jews treated the East European Jews: both sets of motives, the snobbish and the compassionate, existed in them at the same time. This coexistence reveals itself in the behavior of many leading personalities and influential organizations of the period. The Educational Alliance, with all its splendid achievements, refused to keep Yiddish books in its free library. For a while, in fact, the New York Public Library down the street attracted business by putting up a sign in Yiddish which said, "If you want to read *your* kind of books, come in here." And the same wealthy Germans who founded Beth Israel Hospital so that young East Europeans would have a chance to be trained as doctors, refused to allow any East European doctors on the staff of their own Mt. Sinai Hospital uptown.

The East European reacted to all this in the traditional manner of the underdog. He hated the Germans and invented contemptuous names for them, like "yahuda" and "allrightnik." He laughed at their pretensions, but always with an edge of resentment. One man, an East European immigrant's son who was brought up in the midst of this conflict, said to me recently, "The only difference between Germans and Russians is that one fellow's father was peddling twenty-five years before the other fellow's father." And something of the old bitterness crept into his voice as he said it. But at the same time, the East European envied the Germans, and tried to emulate them as soon as he had the money to do so. He Germanicized his name and invented German ancestors for himself; it was said that any Russian Jew who had passed through the tip of Austria on the way to his boat felt he had the right to call himself a German. Even today, Jews of an older generation will instinctively have difficulty admitting their East European background. I asked one lady where her parents came from, and she answered, "They came from Austria!" Then she lowered her eyes a bit guiltily and added, "The part that's almost like Russia or Poland—you know?"

And it must be admitted that if the German Jews invented the word kike, the East Europeans who made money and moved uptown never hesitated to apply the word to their compatriots who were still trapped on the Lower East Side.

The feud took an ironic twist a generation later in the thirties, when the East Europeans were presented with an unexpected opportunity to take revenge for their earlier humiliations. The refugees from the Nazis began to arrive in America. Suddenly Germans were the newcomers who had no money or jobs and spoke with thick accents, and the East Europeans were the uptowners, the "allrightniks." They were human: they took advantage of the situation. They scorned the newcomers, called them "arrogant" and "pushy," condescendingly dispensed castoff clothing to them. Throughout the thirties a whole series of German-refugee jokes were current in Jewish communities. (*German dachshund to American cocker spaniel:* Back in Germany I used to be a Saint Bernard.) But the East Europeans also set up emergency funds to help the newcomers, and poured large sums of money into the effort, pitifully meager compared to the need, to get more of them out of Germany and into the United States. The double motive was operating in them as surely as it had operated in their persecutor-brothers a generation earlier.

But it's all over now. Time, the American educational system, and Adolf Hitler have dealt a death blow to the whole tired conflict. In the thirties a German Jew in Chicago informed my parents that his family back in Germany was in no danger from the Nazis. "They may put some of those foreigners in jail," he said, "but not *our* people." Five years later he learned that every member of his family there had been wiped out. The discovery that the Nazi was a rough democrat —to him all Jews were Jews, all went into the ovens impartially —persuaded this acquaintance to reexamine his prejudices against the Russians. A few years later his daughter married a boy whose father was born in Lithuania.

The dreaded "intermarriage," which filled so many Germans with horror, inevitably took place on a large scale. Today there are very few German families which aren't tainted with a heavy dose of Russian blood. But even intermarriage became irrelevant. The sons, or at least the grandsons, of the Russian immigrants started going to the same prep schools and colleges as the sons of the Germans. They all emerged with the same even polish. You can no longer tell a German from a Russian. As a final blow, the great organizations which the Germans created to make the East European presentable—the federations, the hospital boards, the American Jewish Committee— have mostly been taken over by the descendants of the East Europeans. And hardly anybody cares.

Today, in fact, it's rather chic to have a grandfather who came from the *shtetl*. We read Sholom Aleichem and Isaac Bashevis Singer; we applaud *Fiddler on the Roof*. And we tell jokes, like this one, which appears on a current record of Jewish humor: *First woman at Hadassah luncheon:* My husband and I are going to Europe next week. *Second woman:* Europe—big deal! I was born there!

The greatest paradox of all was in the soul of the East European immigrant from the very beginning. The Germans are often blamed for his Americanization. They are accused of making him shave off his beard, wear American clothes, and stop talking Yiddish. The implication is that the East European submitted to these indignities against his will. This charge couldn't be farther from the truth. The Germans may have helped the process along, but it would have taken place without any encouragement from them at all.

Superficially the American ghettos that the immigrants moved into were much like the *shtetls* they came out of. There was the same poverty, dirt, crowding, noise; undoubtedly some of the same lice and rats came over with them on the boat. The real difference between the *shtetl* and the Lower East Side was psychological, not physical. The *shtetl*, after all, had a positive system of values, a long cultural and religious tradition. Most of the people who lived in it weren't willing to leave; they preferred the horrors of poverty and pogrom, even of conscription into the czar's army, to the risk of giving up their culture. Those who left, therefore, were by and large those who were willing to take that risk. Not surprisingly, the great majority of them were young—young unmarried men, young couples with small children. The old rabbi with a long white beard—that standard figure of sentimental slum fiction—was there all right, but he was in the minority. He was likely to be elbowed and jostled by the mavericks, the malcontents, the hopeful or the desperate young. It would never have occurred to these people to be sentimental about the *shtetl*, in the manner of young intellectuals today.

It would never have occurred to them to be sentimental about the Lower East Side either. They had no intention of creating in America a duplicate of the world from which they had escaped. That wasn't why they had submitted to the miseries of an ocean voyage that would live in their nightmares for years after. Here was the big psychological difference between the *shtetl* and the Lower East Side: The *shtetl*, for most of its inhabitants, was a place to live in; the Lower East Side, for most of its inhabitants, was a place to leave.

But leave for what? There was only one world out there, and it was called America. The immigrants started out with only the dimmest notion of what this world was like, but they kept their eyes open and learned quickly. They found that it had many attractive features. There were no laws to keep you from living where you pleased, worshiping God as you pleased, eating what you pleased. Above all, the good things of this world were apparently available to Jews as well as Christians. The newcomers observed how well the German Jew had done for himself. If that "yahuda" could get ahead in America, why couldn't they?

And so the German Jew didn't want to Americanize the immigrant any more fervently than the immigrant wanted to do so himself. In Harvey Swados' phrase, he had "a frenzied mania to make it in America." [4]

This frenzy showed itself in many strange ways. People went to almost any length to learn English. The Educational Alliance and other organizations sponsored many lectures, some on highly intellectual subjects; the hall was usually packed with young men who couldn't follow a step of the argument, but who thought that the long words would help them develop an ear for the language. Maurice Hindus, in an account of his immigrant boyhood, tells how a friendly teacher gave him a thick book on which to practice his English. The book was Eliot's *Adam Bede*. Somehow the poor bewildered boy plowed his way through that ocean of archaic Midlands dialect and learned to speak and write very good English.[5]

All of these young scholars were desperately poor, of course, and had to work, many of them in the garment factories that filled the area. They did their reading and attended their classes at night, after twelve hours at the machine, or on their one day off each week. Novels with immigrant heroes seldom show them going to sleep. And the women often had the same ambition. With half a dozen children to bring up in a couple of rooms, many of them managed to go to night school once or twice a week.

The frenzy to become a "real American" showed itself also in the immigrant's intense patriotism. As one of them, now a dapper little man in his seventies, said to me, "We were good Americans already before we got off the boat." This patriotism was not restricted to the naïve or the simple-minded. Felix Frankfurter felt it—it accounts for the disturbing opinion he delivered from the Supreme Court during World War II, that the children of Jehovah's Witnesses could be expelled from public school for refusing to pledge allegiance to the flag. Professor Paul Weiss of Yale, the gadfly of American philosophy, a man who could hardly be more intellectually sophisticated and irreverent, describes how he and his brother saved up money, when they were small boys on the Lower East Side, to buy something for their tenement apartment—and what they finally bought was an American flag.

The immigrant's patriotism was essentially emotional, an outburst of affection for the country that treated him comparatively well. However, certain sociologists have tried hard to give it a rational basis. America was peculiarly fertile soil for the Jewish genius to grow in. It was a middle-class country; the Jews are a middle-class people. It valued education and hard work; so did the Jews. Its orientation was essentially urban; Jews have been forced for thousands of years to develop an urban mentality. All very plausible—but one word of warning is necessary. Jews have had a tendency to discover this peculiarly fertile soil in any country which would give them a measure of freedom and security. Heinrich Heine once said, "The character of the Jewish people always had a strong affinity to the character of the German race." [6] And Disraeli claimed, "The Jews are a race essentially monarchical, deeply religious, and essentially Tories." [7]

But the urge to be American wasn't the only thing that drove the East European immigrant. If it had been, Jewish life in America would be very different today; perhaps it wouldn't exist at all. He was driven in the opposite direction by an equally strong urge to hold on to his old traditions. In Abraham Cahan's *The Rise of David Levinsky,* still the best novel of immigrant life ever written in America, the young hero shaves his earcurls, burns his greenhorn clothes, and becomes American with a vengeance. But the strength of the counterurge is measured by the intensity of his guilt feelings; they prevent him from ever being entirely at peace with himself, and make him wonder, in the loneliness of his middle age, whether by giving up his life as a Talmud student in the *shtetl* he didn't lose something infinitely more valuable than what he gained.

To what extent is David Levinsky typical of the East European immigrants? To what extent was his inner conflict mirrored in them? They did hold on, as long as they could, to their *landsmanschaft* groups, small social clubs composed of people who had come to America from the same *shtetl;* they did read their Yiddish newspapers with almost religious fervor; they did follow the events in Russia, and especially the Revolution, with as much interest as if they themselves were still involved. (In many instances members of their families were involved.) But all of this might be explained as the normal loneliness and homesickness of the stranger making the painful adjustment to his new home, no different from what the Irish or the Italians experienced.

Many observers thought that it *was* different. One of the most perceptive was the young journalist Hutchins Hapgood, who wrote about the Lower East Side from 1898 to 1902 and collected his articles in a book called *The Spirit of the Ghetto.* Because Hapgood was not a Jew, not part of the world he described, his analysis of the typical immigrant boy may have more objectivity than most:

> If this boy were able entirely to forget his origin, to cast off the ethical and religious influences which are his birthright, there would be no serious struggle in his soul, and he would not represent a peculiar element in our society. He would be like any other practical, ambitious, rather worldly American boy. The struggle is strong because the boy's nature, at once religious and susceptible, is strongly appealed to by both the old and the new. At the same time that he is keenly sensitive to the charm of his American environment, with its practical and national opportunities, he has still a deep love for his race and the old things.

What Hutchins Hapgood discovered, in short, was that same strain of paradox, that self-contradiction, that split personality which runs through all of the American Jew's history.

If this paradox characterized the earliest settlers, the German peddlers, the East European immigrants, we shouldn't be surprised to find it in the American Jew today. It *is* in him, as powerfully as ever. Though it no longer reveals itself in a conflict between ambition and tradition, it has taken on many strange new forms, all of which the American Jew has built into his institutions, his manners, his hopes and his achievements. This split personality is the key to understanding American Jewish life.

II.

Body and Soul

There are Jewish traditions, of course—charity, piety, learning—which have been handed down consciously from parent to child for many generations. But there is also a Jewish cast of mind, a characteristic attitude toward life, an instinctive strategy for dealing with the world, which has arisen unconsciously out of four thousand years of common experience. When the East European immigrants came to America, this attitude was as much a part of them as the peasant clothes they wore. Sooner or later they burned the clothes, but they carried their peculiar cast of mind uptown with them, and passed it on to their children, who passed it on to their grandchildren in the 1960s. Today it gives a special color and flavor to Jewish life in America. It may even explain certain things about that life.

The Jew is an idealist, but he is also a materialist. He believes in spiritual things, in the unknowable and the ineffable, in sacred values that come from God—but he also believes that you have to be practical in this world. Man must reach for the stars, he says, but while doing so must take precautions, so that he doesn't fall flat on his face. These two contradictory attitudes coexist within the Jew. Unlike the Russian, for instance, who often wallows in mysticism at the expense of reality, or the Swiss, whose mind is untroubled by anything he can't see and count, the Jew seldom resolves his feelings in one direction or the other.

This mixture of the spiritual and the material has ancient antecedents. It is set forth in the Torah (the first five books of the Bible, which are the sacred cornerstone of Judaism) and in the writings of the prophets. It is further developed in the Talmud, a collection of commentaries on the Torah, and commentaries on the commentaries, which was compiled over the centuries by great rabbis, and which has to the pious Jew almost the authority of Torah itself. The world, say the Bible and the Talmud, was made for man, not man for the world. And the prophet Elijah proclaimed "that God is 'the place of the world,' and that yet he dwells within it."

It follows that the pleasures of life are here to be enjoyed; our flesh was not given us to be mortified. The Baal-shem, the great mystic who founded the Hasidic sect, says, "One shall not undertake mortification; he who does harm to his body does harm to his soul; and ecstasy arising from ascetical practices comes from 'the other side,' they are not of divine but of demonic character." [1] On the other hand, the Jewish religious tradition also makes it clear that God is our father, and our chief duty is to obey His commandments. That, in fact, is why men should take pleasure in material things—because He has commanded us to. And he has also commanded us not to become too attached to these things, not to forget where our chief duty lies.

Out of this double attitude come a number of curious paradoxes of Jewish behavior. There are few Jewish teetotalers. Yet according to many studies made over the last twenty years, there are even fewer Jewish alcoholics; Michael Harrington writes in *The Other America* that during the years he worked with derelicts on New York's Bowery he never encountered among them a single Jew. Similarly, there are few Jewish vegetarians (If God hadn't wanted us to enjoy meat, would he have given us teeth?). But there are practically no Jews who go in for hunting. To kill a living creature may sometimes be necessary, but it is not a Jew's idea of sport.

Jews love to eat, no question about it. Jewish country clubs, according to *Sports Illustrated* magazine, consume almost twice as much food (and half as much liquor) as gentile country clubs. [2] Yet gout is a disease almost unknown among Jews, and dieting is a favorite pastime. Furthermore, Jews buy more medicine than other people and visit doctors more often. Statistics suggest that Jews live longer than most other Americans. To make up for this, of course, the birth rate is somewhat lower.[3] Yet Kinsey says that married Jews have sexual intercourse more often than the national average.[4] He doesn't say if they enjoy themselves more.

The mixture of spiritual and material is reflected also in Judaism's attitude toward death and the afterlife. It is often said that Jews don't believe in heaven or hell, or in life after death. This isn't quite accurate. Talmud and Torah are ambiguous on the subject. Resurrection and the afterlife are mentioned, but not often. The general view seems to be that they exist, but that it isn't good for us to speculate about them too much. Our job is to make the best life we can for ourselves right here, and let God worry about the rest of it. The Kaddish, the Hebrew prayer for the dead, is concerned mostly with praising God for our lot on this earth. It tells us that our loved ones live on in the hearts of those who remember them.

Judaism, therefore, is impatient with excessive mourning. Moses, in the Torah, tells his people to mourn his death for thirty days, then to stop their weeping and get back to the job of entering the Promised Land. The real sin, he says, is to waste one's life. For this reason the Talmud prohibits us from making too elaborate and ornate an occasion out of the funeral. The dead must be buried in unadorned caskets; no flowers are permitted; particularly obnoxious is the morbid custom of "viewing the body." The extent to which American Jews actually obey these injunctions varies considerably, but the injunctions are there.

What they reveal is a curious attitude toward religious ritual. Judaism is full of ritual; a truly pious Jew could accompany every one of his daily actions with a blessing. But Torah and Talmud give severe warnings against any ritual which involves worshiping material objects, what the Second Commandment calls graven images. God is God, and the world is the world: each has its own nature, its integrity. You enjoy material things because God created them, but you don't pretend that He lives in them. Converts to Judaism who were brought up as Christians are troubled by this idea more than by any other. In the synagogue they find no cross, no statues, no images of saints—only the Torah, which can be touched with reverence but must not be worshiped. This absence of concrete symbols bewilders them. Rabbis training prospective converts tell me that the most common question they ask is, "What do I pray to?"

There is a tendency in the Jew not only to shun graven images but to mistrust all ritual that seems to be carried too far. The Jew believes, of course, that the pious man exists. Yet how can he exist? To be genuinely pious, to obey all of God's commandments, is clearly impossible. Consequently the man who seems to be unaware of this, who expresses his piety too easily and too often, is suspect.

This attitude is embodied in a very old story about two brothers: one prays constantly, day and night; the other never prays at all. But the pious one is a failure at everything he does, and the indifferent one is hugely successful. Finally the pious brother confronts God and demands to know why his devoutness isn't being rewarded. "Because you nudge me too much," God says.

------◆◆------

This mixed view carries over from religion to everyday life. It is the basis of a morality which causes the Jew to seem at one moment tough and hard-headed, at the next moment soft and sentimental. Should men make moral judgments according to strict justice, or according to mercy and compassion? The Old Testament never makes up its mind on the point. Sometimes it presents a just and exacting God, sometimes a merciful and yielding God.

We see the paradox all around us in America. Jews like to proclaim their toughness. David Sarnoff, the president of RCA, makes this statement about his career: "I'm grateful only to my enemies. They alone can help me."[5] A young Jewish Congressman, Representative James Scheuer of New York, scorns another Congressman for doing things "the nice genteel way"; he praises one of his colleagues as "a nice tough Jew." Sophie Tucker delivers the following words of consolation to a close friend whose husband has just died: "Peggy, don't expect anything from anybody, and if someone does do something nice, it will come as a pleasant surprise."[6] And the grief-stricken widow, instead of howling with horror, remembers the incident admiringly and says, "I never heard any truer words."

Yet David Sarnoff is a generous contributor to charity; Congressman Scheuer is a fearless fighter for civil rights; and Sophie Tucker was famous in show business as a soft touch.

This ambiguity goes all the way back to the *shtetl*. People were very quick to shed tears in the *shtetl;* even men were permitted to cry under certain circumstances. But the tears were supposed to dry up quickly too—and they usually did. The Lower East Side produced equally impressive examples of such self-control. In an interview in the New York *Post*, Zero Mostel told a story which illustrates the point. His mother used to say to him, "I'll be happy when you show me a bankbook with ten thousand dollars in it." One day, when he showed her his bankbook with ten thousand dollars in it, she said, "You call that a lot of money!" [7] The story is funny, but the basic ambiguity of her feelings remains unresolved.

It would be a mistake to think that this ambiguity doesn't exist in many young Jews today. One day I visited a Sunday School class for twelve-year-olds. The teacher presented them with this dilemma: In order to build a middle-income housing project for four hundred people, the city must first condemn a block of run-down tenements and evict forty old people who have lived in them for years. The city will, of course, find them another place to live, but even so, the change is liable to be disastrous; how can these people in their seventies and eighties adjust to new surroundings, a new way of life? The class' reactions were very emotional. One girl cried out, "You just can't do it to them!" One boy answered her, "You have to make room for progress. You can't let four hundred go stranded for forty." The argument raged for awhile, and in the end a consensus was expressed by that same compassionate girl who had started things off: "I don't think it should be this way—but I guess it *has* to be! Only I wish it wasn't!"

This conclusion, I think, is very Jewish.

Many small as well as large quirks of American Jewish life become explicable as soon as we understand this mixture of spirituality and practicality. Often it comes out as pure low comedy. For example, the Jewish Theological Seminary gave a dinner recently to honor the men who had contributed large sums of money toward its new building. It was a very serious occasion. The names of the donors were called out, and solemnly, one by one, they made their way up to their places in front of the crowd. What the orchestra played, as each donor made the trek for which he had paid at least one hundred thousand dollars, was "Mademoiselle from Armentières." Nobody seemed to be struck by the incongruity.

This comic note is sounded every day in the pages of the New York *Post*, that bible of middle-class American Jewry. The resort and restaurant section of the *Post* must be a total enigma to anyone who hasn't got the key. Half a dozen pages are crowded with advertisements for resort hotels in the Catskills, Miami Beach, Lakewood, New Jersey, for catering establishments in Brooklyn and on Long Island, for kosher restaurants all over the city. One catering establishment recommends its "circular temple with three hundred theatre-type seats," another its "total catering concept, uniting the dignity of the Temple with the gratifying joyous spirit of elegant catering." The ads for resort hotels are usually built around the upcoming religious holiday—and there always seems to be an upcoming religious holiday. The hotel has its "temple" too, of course, with plenty of room for all worshipers, and a beautiful eighteen-hole golf course for relaxation between services. Whether the holiday be Hanukkah, which is joyful, or Yom Kippur, which is sad, or Passover, which is a little bit of both, the hotel guarantees you a pleasant, reverent, food-filled weekend—or, as one of the largest establishments puts it, "ageless traditions amid up-to-the-minute luxury." And to back up the guarantee, many of these ads include the picture of the "famous" rabbi or "world-renowned" cantor who will preside over the services. (The cantor usually gets top billing over the rabbi.)

The point is that nobody minds. Nobody feels that something sacred is being profaned, that the dignity of the occasion is being compromised. Nobody feels any incompatibility between "ageless traditions" and "up-to-the-minute luxury."

Still, the effort to avoid attenuated or hypocritical spirituality sometimes leads to appalling tactlessness and bad taste. It leads to rabbis giving testimonials for kosher products. It leads to the Met Food Stores featuring, in their ads, "The Ten Commandments of Good Business." (First Commandment: Our customers are the most important persons.) It leads to the "Manna About Town" ads in the *Post*—chatty little discussions of such subjects as the Israeli-Arab war, religious freedom, the meaning of Yom Kippur, and the Nazi holocaust, building up to a pitch for Chase and Sanborn coffee or Planter's peanut oil.

All too often, in fact, in their eagerness to avoid those "ascetical practices" that the Baal-shem warned against, Jews are unable to see the distinctions that do exist between the spiritual and the pragmatic. This blind spot accounts for the presence on the obituary page of the Essex County *Jewish News*—among the announcements of deaths and memorials, the ads for funeral parlors and tombstones—of this little box: [8]

Bragman's Deli and Restaurant
Trays of Delicatessen
Turkey, Chicken—Trays of Sandwiches
Hot Foods Available

And this same blind spot accounts for an incident which I have on authority of Rabbi Wolfe Kelman, an executive of the Rabbinical Assembly of America. A young rabbi in a small community was asked to marry the son of the synagogue's president to a gentile girl. Like most rabbis he refused to perform the ceremony unless the girl converted to Judaism— and she was quite willing to do so. She entered conscientiously into the spirit of the thing. She attended services regularly. She studied all the books. She learned Hebrew and ate only kosher food. She became far more devout, in fact, than most of the Jews in town, including her prospective father-in-law. But the conversion hit a snag. The girl confessed to the rabbi that there was only one thing she couldn't bring herself to do—she simply couldn't give up her belief in the divinity of Jesus Christ. She had no trouble accepting everything else, so if the rabbi would only let her go on believing in Jesus she would gladly become a Jew. The rabbi, of course, refused to convert her.

There was an immediate and violent reaction from her fiancé's father and the other members of the synagogue. They were furious at the rabbi's decision. The girl sincerely wanted to be a Jew, didn't she, so what right did he have to stand in her way? What business was it of his what she believed in? A person's beliefs are his own affair, aren't they? Isn't this a free country? It took many months, and the intervention of a distinguished rabbinical authority from New York, to persuade the congregation that their rabbi had a point.

The down-to-earth approach to the spiritual aspects of life could hardly be carried any further.

◼●◼

The peculiar Jewish cast of mind shows itself also in the attitude toward freedom and authority. Again the attitude involves certain contradictions, and again these can be found in the Torah and the Talmud.

What they tell us is that all authority comes from God. No man can usurp it. The Torah lays down all the rules we need for life, and no mere human being can ever change them or add to them. There is a problem, however. Difficulties sometimes arise on the meaning of God's law; two men may disagree on what Torah is saying. If no man has any more authority to interpret God's words than any other man, it would seem that the disagreement can never be resolved.

Logically it can't, but Jewish tradition finds a way out. Some men, it says, do have more authority to interpret Torah than others. This authority comes not from some mystical power implanted in them by God but from superior learning, piety, and reasoning ability which they have demonstrated to everyone's satisfaction. As to the vexing question of how we are to know these men when we see them, how we can recognize their superior abilities—apparently we just do. It happens that way. The great rabbis of the past, the Hillels, the Baal-shems, never had any official status; there has never been a Jewish pope. The community submitted to them voluntarily, spontaneously, and always with the unspoken proviso that they could be superseded by an even greater authority.

These great rabbis, of course, were in turn obliged to submit to those of equal stature who had lived and written before them. This is how the Talmud evolved. Theoretically anybody could (and still can) add to it, but only by dealing painstakingly with the wisdom already set down in it. God has laid down his rules for all time, but he wants us to find legal ways of handling them, manipulating them, adapting them to new circumstances. Doubt, controversy, even hairsplitting are part of our obligation to God. No better illustration of this attitude exists than the Book of Job, with its overwhelming pessimism, its shattering doubts which it never resolves. Only the Jews would have put Job in the Bible.

In the *shtetl* this attitude led to a form of Talmudic disputation known as *pilpul*. The scholars, young and old, of the community would gather daily at the synagogue and endlessly analyze and re-analyze the smallest points in the Talmud. An old saying describes this process as two Jews arguing three sides of a question. Sometimes the "analysis" would grow very loud and heated. Much of the energy and passion of the community was thrown into *pilpul*. Irving Howe suggests that it existed partly as an escape valve.[9] Frustrated by day-to-day problems that couldn't be solved (like the anti-Semitic policeman on the corner), the *shtetl* dweller relieved his feelings in the effort to solve "eternal" problems. Whatever his motivations, he passed on to his American descendants, on the Lower East Side and today, a style of life in which the *pilpul* influence is clear.

From his earliest days the Jewish child is bombarded with talk. He grows up in a family in which there is continuous conversation, constant weighing of the pros and cons of every major and minor point. And the talk always leads to arguments —let's face it, sometimes to fights—and the fighters are constantly making up, which of course leads to more talk. The pressure of what a Jew wants to say is so great that his voice isn't enough; he must also use his shoulders, his eyebrows, his head, and above all his hands, to say it. The first thing that a mother who is ashamed of being Jewish says to her child is, "For heaven's sake, stop talking with your hands!"

The passion for argument, the reluctance to accept any kind of final authority on any question, characterizes the American Jew today. The history of almost any small Jewish community in America reveals the truth of Winston Churchill's famous remark, "One Jew is a Prime Minister. Two Jews are a Prime Minister and a Leader of the Loyal Opposition." In "Yankee City," subject of a famous postwar sociological study, the committee that found a suitable building for the synagogue deliberately submitted a negative report—knowing that then everyone in the congregation would be in favor of the building, including the faction that had previously opposed it.[10]

Anybody who has ever attended a lecture before a Jewish organization will recognize the same principle at work. As soon as the lecture has ended and the floor is thrown open to questions, certain familiar types inevitably appear. There is the little elderly man with a slight accent, whose question turns out to be the rambling, apparently endless story of his life. There is the sharp-faced, shabbily-dressed iconoclast who begins by announcing, "This meeting has been a terrible disappointment to me! The speaker completely avoided the issues, and all of the questions have been beside the point!" There is the shaggy-haired young intellectual who launches into a long, incoherent speech expressing his personal philosophy but having no apparent connection with the subject at hand. Jews simply love to talk.

The supreme folk hero of Jewish disputatiousness is, of course, the Jewish waiter. He has apparently always existed, that little man with a surly look on his face and a towel over his arm, determined to prevent you from ordering what you want to order, never reluctant to join in on your conversation and disagree with you, uncannily proficient at arriving with the soup just as you've come to the point of your favorite story. Jokes about him are legion, and go back very far in Jewish tradition:

> *Customer:* Waiter, what time is it?
> *Waiter:* I'm not your waiter!
>
> *Customer:* Shut the window, waiter, it's cold outside.
> *Waiter:* So if I shut the window, will it be warm outside?

But he isn't just a legend, he is a living reality. Only last year John Steinbeck apparently encountered him in Israel, where he brought the wrong order and suggested a better ending for *Of Mice and Men.*[11]

These hoary waiter stories suggest another aspect of the Jewish penchant for argument. According to an old saying, "If you ask a Jew a question, he'll answer you with another question." Faced with this accusation, the Jew has a classic retort: "What do you mean, I'll answer you with another question?" But in fact this Talmudic habit of thought, this trick of seeing life as a series of questions, has given a peculiar rhythm and intonation to Jewish speech. It explains why the Jew—not only the average one, but even the intellectual—peppers his conversation with rhetorical questions, sometimes with whole strings of them.

Read *The New York Times* carefully for a while and you'll find this particular speech habit popping out at you all over the place. A delicatessen owner, describing his passive attitude toward the hoodlums who robbed him, says, "Isn't it better to lose a salami than lose your life?" The president of a leading department store, in an address to members of his industry, says, "Are buttons harder to sew than computers to make?" A New Yorker who was phoning her boss during the transit strike to tell him she couldn't get to the shop, produced a whole fireworks display of questions: "How can I make it? Even if someone took me downtown in a car, how would I get back? Where would I sleep, the Port Authority?" The chances are that none of these people has ever looked into the Talmud, but *pilpul* has its grip on them all the same.

The intensity of the Jew's devotion to his intellectual independence is revealed every decade or so when somebody tries to "organize the Jewish community." Many such attempts have been made in America. B'nai B'rith was founded in 1843 (when there were less than twenty-five thousand Jews in America) because its founders believed there was too much factionalism in Jewish life. In 1906 Judah Magnes of the American Jewish Committee tried to form a Jewish Kehilah (community organization) so that unified measures could be taken to combat poverty and crime among the immigrants. The American Jewish Conference tried it again in the early forties, as a response to the threat from Hitler. And in 1951, on the strength of a report from sociologist Robert McIver, the National Community Relations Council almost succeeded in forming an "umbrella organization" of Jewish organizations—but several of the largest, including B'nai B'rith and the American Jewish Committee, refused to join.

Recently the agitation started again. It was triggered by a statement, issued by the commander of the Jewish War Veterans, that President Johnson had suggested to him that Jews ought to support his Vietnam policy in return for the government's support of Israel. There was much hue and cry from many Jewish organizations and from individual Jews. U.N. Ambassador Arthur Goldberg appointed himself unofficial mediator, met with the heads of several organizations, and told them that the President hadn't really meant what he was supposed to have said. There was another outburst, but this time the ground had shifted. What right did Ambassador Goldberg have to act as a representative for American Jewry? And why were some organizations invited to meet with him, while others were left out? If American Jewry were only unified, this kind of fracas could be avoided.

But nothing has come of the agitation, and probably nothing will. The habit of independence, the instinct to form a rival congregation, is simply too strong. And this is just as true of those who support the idea of a unified Jewish community as it is of those who oppose it. As one wise old observer put it, "Even those who speak loudest about oneness don't believe they're the ones who should do the sacrificing."

The deeper point is that this diversity isn't necessarily incompatible with Jewish unity. When an issue arises about which most Jews feel the same—Hitler in the thirties, for instance—they manage to come together and act with considerable, if not perfect, efficiency. They cooperate more effectively when they feel they're doing so of their own free will.

———— •• ————

There is another reason why Jewish unity isn't likely to occur in the near future. Who would bring it about? A leader of immense personal influence would be required, and Jews have an instinctive suspicion of such leaders. Irreverence for the great and powerful is the natural consequence of the prophet's injunction, "Thou shalt not follow any man." Partly this is involved with the fear of anti-Semitism. Jews are afraid because demagogues can so easily arouse the mass—and the aroused mass has a way of taking its fury out on Jews.

But mostly, I think, Jews just have a natural cantankerous desire to puncture balloons, to find clay feet on idols. During the last election, when David Dubinsky, the union leader, showed President Johnson around the garment district—a scene teeming with reporters, photographers, policemen, excited crowds—an elderly Jewish woman pushed up to Dubinsky and shouted, "Stop making faces for the camera already and start doing something for the workers!"

The spirit of the Old Testament lives in that lady. But it isn't really as simple as all that. The stern biblical injunction against worshiping false gods inevitably sets up its own reaction. There's something lonely and frightening about a God who never embodies himself in material things, who gives you no guarantees for a future life, who won't even let you indulge in a bit of pomp and circumstance now and then. It isn't only the converts to Judaism who feel the need of "something" to pray to. For this reason, American Jews are among the world's greatest celebrity-worshipers.

For the Hasidim this is a religious act. Hasidic sects are built around their rebbeh, an awesome, inspiring, half-divine figure who intervenes between his disciples and God. Hasidim of the *shtetl* used to travel miles to attend the rebbeh's "court," to hang on his holy words. Most of those great Hasidic rebbehs were killed when the Nazis overran eastern Europe, but two important ones survive in Brooklyn today—the Satmar Rebbeh and the Lubavitcher Rebbeh. Their disciples are as devoted as they ever were.

Other Jews find their gods in the political arena. Every

decade seems to have one political figure who is supremely popular with American Jews, sometimes for reasons which defy logic. Franklin D. Roosevelt had two decades during which he could do no wrong in Jewish eyes. A Jew, asked why he liked FDR, could always find plausible answers: "He's against Hitler." "He's in favor of the Jews in Palestine." In fact, until circumstances combined to push him, FDR took a highly cautious, almost lenient attitude toward the Nazis, and he was known to be distinctly cold toward the idea of a Jewish state in Palestine. But the Jews liked him and projected their own feelings and opinions on him. When he died, Eleanor Roosevelt filled the gap as Jewish folk hero for a while—until Adlai Stevenson came along. Stevenson was in turn replaced by John F. Kennedy.

And again, the precise nature of Kennedy's opinions was less important than the mere fact of his appeal. The Herzl Foundation, a Zionist cultural organization, has published a book called *John Kennedy: On Israel, Zionism, and Jewish Issues.* Sandwiched between lush expensive photographs are ornately printed quotations from statements Kennedy made on Israel, both as Senator and as President. The statements are friendly enough, but not unusually so; they are rather mild, in fact, compared to those of certain other American politicians. When Harry Truman was President he did a lot more for Israel than John F. Kennedy ever did; but the Herzl Foundation isn't likely to publish an expensive photograph book about Harry Truman. For the American Jew, Truman simply never had the magic.

But one superhero a decade is hardly enough to satisfy this voracious appetite for celebrities. A steady diet of sub-heroes must be provided, mostly by Jewish organizations trying to raise money or create good will. Appropriately, much of this celebrity-consummation is done at dinners. Every organization has its own honorary award, its bronze plaque or engraved scroll for the outstanding something-or-other of the year, and this award is invariably presented at a hotel banquet hall after the coffee is served. The celebrity, of course, is merely bait. Or, as one public-relations man told me, "Even though he's a distinguished man, from our point of view he's a fan dancer."

Nobody understands this trait better than the resort hotels, and nobody takes advantage of it more adroitly. This is why Grossinger's, the famous kosher resort in the Catskills, lines its walls with signed photographs of every famous person who has ever occupied a room there: Chaim Weizmann is there, right next to Yogi Berra, and Jonas Salk hangs between the Gabor sisters. The chances are slim that we'll see any of those celebrities during our weekend at Grossinger's, but their spirit is presumed to hover over us.

And yet, underneath all this, that sneaking irreverence for the great and powerful never quite disappears. Sometimes it shows itself in the most unexpected places. A few years ago some followers of the Satmar Rebbeh broke a mirror in his wife's bedroom. This was their way of telling their beloved leader that it was unbecoming for a Rebbeh's wife to care about her appearance.[12]

───────※───────

The Jews are sometimes called optimists, sometimes pessimists. Both descriptions are accurate, for the Jews' peculiar cast of mind produces a double attitude toward the future. Throughout their lives they seesaw endlessly between hope and despair.

As always, the paradox can be found in the Torah and the Talmud. They tell us that God will fulfill our love for Him and justify the evil and suffering of our lives. But they also tell us that the future of the human race is still undetermined, that we're not saved yet. This explains the Jewish attitude toward the Messiah, which puzzles and sometimes exasperates Christians. The Jew believes that the Messiah will come. But that is precisely what he believes: the Messiah always *will* come, the Messiah never *has* come.

Obviously such an attitude gives a certain emotional coloring to the Jewish style of life. This comes out clearly in Jewish rituals, and especially in the pattern of religious holidays. The solemn holiday of Yom Kippur is followed by the happy holiday of Succoth; the wild antics of Purim are hardly over before preparations must begin for the more sober pleasures of Passover. And within each holiday, though it may have its overall character of gaiety or gloom, there are always mixed feelings. The prelude to Purim is a day of fasting (though only the extraordinarily pious ever remember it); and the epilogue to the fasting of Yom Kippur is a feast of chopped liver, matzoh ball soup, pickles, and cold meats that becomes the occasion for a raucous family party. This alternation of fasting and feasting —this sense that the one ritual, even while it's going on, is already tinged with the atmosphere of its opposite—is ingrained in the Jewish cast of mind.

It gives rise to a peculiar ambivalent notion about fate. The Jew, because he's an optimist, doesn't believe in submitting to fate. He believes he can improve himself, he can get ahead, he isn't forced to accept his lot if he doesn't like it. This is why he cares so much about education for his children and supports so strenuously schemes of social and political improvement; both these values require a faith that the future can be changed. At the same time that he has this faith, however, the Jew doesn't have complete faith in it. In a corner of his mind is always a haunting fear that something will upset the applecart; all his life he is more or less in a state of anxiety.

Oddly enough, the optimistic side of his nature will assert itself most strongly at those times when things look blackest. Something called Yiddish luck is often invoked when dire circumstances occur. But as soon as things start to get a little better—as soon, in short, as there is some logical reason for being optimistic—Jewish pessimism will take over. This was demonstrated several years ago by a survey made in veterans' hospitals.[13] It compared wounded Jews with wounded Italians. It found that both groups complained loudly when in pain— more so than the "old Americans"—but behaved quite differently after sedation had ended the pain. The Italian then leaned back, satisfied, willing to enjoy life while he could. The Jew immediately became anxious about the future and pestered the doctor with questions—"What have I got, doctor? Am I going to be all right?" In the words of a distinguished psychiatrist (a Jew with many Jewish patients), "Jews just won't let themselves, or anybody else, be."

This optimistic pessimism—or pessimistic optimism—is at the heart of that homely, prickly, yet somehow exotic plant known as Jewish humor. It has been analyzed many times, mostly by Jews, and there are many different theories about it. Isaac Rosenfeld, for instance, says that it is based on the incongruity between man's ambitions and his impotence to achieve them.[14] And Irving Kristol says that it makes us laugh because of the "circularity" of its logic.[15]

More interesting than why Jewish jokes are funny is why Jews are almost obsessively driven to tell them. This obsession may be more evident to non-Jews than to Jews. An official in one of the foundations, a Midwesterner who is not Jewish, puts it this way: "When I started in on this job, I found that I had to learn how to communicate with Jews, and at first it was confusing. We'd be having an important meeting, and one of the Jews on the staff, a distinguished scholar or an important scientist, would be talking on a high level about some abstruse and complex problem. Suddenly he'd say, 'Let me illustrate my point by telling you an old Jewish story.' He'd tell the story, and as a gentile I wouldn't know what he meant half the time!"

This trait, which every Jew must candidly recognize in himself, is an expression of his mixed optimism and pessimism. Complex problems, whether they concern the manufacture of hydrogen bombs or zippers, are potentially frightening; they could lead to disaster. Somehow they must be reduced to everyday terms. They must be shown to have their funny side. Somewhere in the long canon of Jewish stories there's bound to be one that will do the trick.

It isn't simply a case of smiling through our tears; rather it is a kind of whistling in the dark. The joke often has a disturbing edge to it; it makes us laugh at our complex problem, but after we've stopped laughing we find that we feel even uneasier than before. The reason is that the Jew wants to find comfort for the sufferings and inadequacies of his life, but also doesn't want to find comfort. He has a yearning to evade reality and an itch to face it. His yearning leads him to make a joke, and his itch leads him to make it with his eyes wide open.

Jewish humor is uncomprisingly realistic. It faces the absurdities and weaknesses and venalities of its heroes without batting an eye. Yet it makes us feel not only pity or affection for those heroes, but also a kind of admiration. And we feel this not in spite of their foibles, but because of them. A good example is the beggar in a famous story by Sholom Aleichem. He leaves the *shtetl* in the little Russian town of Kasrilevka and somehow finds his way to Paris, where he calls upon the great Rothschild. For a sum of money he offers to tell Rothschild a guaranteed method of living forever. Rothschild is interested and pays him the money. The beggar then gives him the formula for eternal life: "Come to Kasrilevka, Mr. Rothschild. In the entire history of that town no rich man has ever died there." [16]

Our first reaction is to laugh at the beggar's cleverness in

outsmarting Rothschild. Our second reaction is to become uneasily aware of what a miserable life people must lead in
Kasrilevka. Our final reaction is to admire the beggar on a
deeper level for his ability to snatch some kind of partial
triumph out of his own wry awareness of his misery.

An even older story arouses the same complicated feelings
in us. It consists of a dialogue between two poor, gaunt shab-
bily dressed Hebrew teachers in a *shtetl:*

> *First teacher:* If I had Rothschild's money, I'd be richer
> than Rothschild.
> *Second teacher:* What kind of a crazy thing is that to say?
> If you had Rothschild's money, how could you be richer
> than Rothschild?
> *First teacher:* I'd do a little teaching on the side.

This story, like the one before, uses the circular logic
Irving Kristol mentions—the inheritance Jewish humor gets
from Talmudic *pilpul*. It also shows that lack of reverence for
the great and powerful which we have noticed already as part
of the Jewish mentality. Rothschild was the subject of hundreds of stories in the *shtetl*, second in popularity only to God;
just as today no institution can be too sacred and no individual
too exalted to escape the attention of some sharp-eyed Jewish
wit. But in the end the effect of the joke depends not on its
irreverence or its mad logic, but on the compassion and grudg-
ing admiration it makes us feel for its hero.

It follows, then, that genuine Jewish humor can be neither
too sentimental nor too brutal. Sam Levenson and Harry
Golden have many of the right characteristics, but their humor
is diluted with a softness, a mushy nostalgia, an unwillingness
to face the full horror of what they see. There isn't enough
pepper in their work to qualify it as vintage Jewish humor. On
the other hand, they come closer than the humorists who deni-
grate their subject. Put-down humor or "sick" humor isn't Jewish; there is nothing Jewish about "camp." Nor is the true
tradition being preserved by tasteless parodies like *What Is a
Jewish Girl?* or *How to Name Your Jewish Baby,* or *My Son,
the Folksinger:* the basic joke in all of these is that Jewishness
itself is somehow ludicrous.

The true tradition is being preserved, however. The torch,
which was carried by Sholom Aleichem, was passed on to the

Marx Brothers; nothing could be more Jewish than their desperate, zany insults, designed to deflate their pompous enemies but eventually making nothing but trouble for themselves. And this torch is now in the capable hands of men like Mel Brooks and Neil Simon, who use wisecracks to turn ordinary life upside down, and especially Bruce Jay Friedman, the poet of Jewish anxiety. And of course the fountain of anonymous Jewish jokes gushes forth as prodigally as ever.

We shouldn't be surprised at this. Jewish humor, after all, is an expression of the contradictions in the Jewish character, and these contradictions persist in spite of changed circumstances. Mere logic is no match for them at all.

III.

The Ancient Enemy

Before he could fulfill any of his ambitions in America, the Jewish immigrant had to fight one major battle—the same battle that Jews through the ages, in many different ways, had been fighting. The enemy was anti-Semitism. It isn't possible to understand the American Jew today without determining to what extent he won this battle, and without examining the scars it left on him.

American anti-Semitism has always been different from the European variety. European governments have often made it an instrument of state policy, a means of diverting the attention of their citizens from internal problems; hereditary monarchies used it in the name of Christianity, Hitler used it in the name of cultural purity, and the Soviet Union is using it today in the name of proletarian unity. But in America anti-Semitism has never had any legal status. It has always been sporadic; an impulsive, sometimes highly virulent outburst of hate by fanatics, like Father Coughlin before the war and George Lincoln Rockwell in recent years. It never had official sanction.

This doesn't mean that large numbers of people haven't *felt* hostile to Jews. They have, and their hostility has most often taken the form of social and economic discrimination. The cruelty of such discrimination should not be underestimated. It may not be as brutal as open persecution, but it has horrors of its own. Because it is so elusive, it can often be more damaging to the feelings of its victims. The immigrant boy, mysteriously rejected by a medical school for which he knew himself to be qualified, or politely turned down for a job before he could even present his credentials, was filled with a baffling frustration with which it was hard for him to come to terms. He was bitter at the injustice, yet he was impotent to protest. If he shouted "anti-Semitism," those who had rejected him would simply raise their eyebrows and make it clear that his aggressiveness, his pushiness, proved how right they were to avoid contact with "the children of Israel."

This kind of anti-Semitism didn't become a problem for American Jews until late in the nineteenth century. It is often considered to have begun—symbolically, perhaps, rather than actually—in 1877, when the German Jewish banker Joseph Seligman and his family were refused accommodation at a resort hotel in Saratoga Springs. From then on the "gentleman's agreement"—extending to country clubs, fraternities, business groups, and more important, to college admissions and to jobs —became a part of American life. The date 1877 is significant. The anti-Semite began to flourish exactly when the American Jew was being transformed from a negligible minority into a conspicuous one.

By the turn of the century the problem was big enough so that the Jews were moved to do something about it. In 1906 wealthy German Jews founded the American Jewish Committee—AJC—to help the victims of pogroms in Russia, but soon it extended its activities to America. Its method was to go behind the scenes, in what it referred to as a "statesmanlike" manner, and persuade important gentiles to use their influence against discrimination.

In 1913 B'nai B'rith formed its extraordinary organization known as the Anti-Defamation League—ADL—which still gets money from the parent organization but operates with total autonomy. ADL's methods were more aggressive and open than those of AJC. It was willing to apply pressure, not merely persuasion. For example, major movie companies in the early 1900s used to turn out two-reel melodramas in which a popular feature was the Jewish villain. Rosenstein, the miser and jewel fence, appeared in many of them, rubbing his hands together and grinning evilly as he bilked poor Christian widows and orphans out of their life savings—an edifying spectacle for Jewish children at Sunday matinées. There were few

Jewish movie producers in those days, but many Jewish theater owners; so ADL organized them to boycott the companies, and in a short time Rosenstein and his ilk faded into oblivion.

In 1916 the most militant of the so-called "defense agencies" was founded. The avowed purpose of the American Jewish Congress was to break the "monopoly" which German Jews exercised over American communal life through the American Jewish Committee. Its guiding spirits were East European Jews whose instincts were naturally more radical and belligerent. From the beginning Congress scorned AJC'S tactics of "quiet persuasion in high places." Partly, no doubt, this was because those high places were closed to members of Congress. But also Congress genuinely felt that these tactics were undignified; they smacked too much of the old European institution of the "state Jew," the canny, groveling intermediary whose privileged position at court enabled him to beg crumbs for the ghetto.

The truth, however, is that all of the defense agencies hardly existed, except on paper, until the early thirties. They were small, poorly organized, and poorly financed; but the threat of the Nazis made them strong. Resurgent anti-Semitism has always produced miracles among Jews. It has invariably strengthened and unified those who haven't been destroyed by it. In the thirties, as we have seen, it performed the miracle of making German Jews feel kindly toward Russian Jews. It also miraculously extracted large sums of money from a community that was, after all, as hard hit by the Depression as the rest of America.

The money was used on two fronts—to help the persecuted Jews of Germany and to counteract anti-Semitic activities at home. The three agencies operated, of course, in their characteristic ways. ADL held public meetings and marches, urging church people, newspapers, and politicians to express horror at the Nazis and to clamp down on the likes of Father Coughlin, Gerald L. K. Smith, and the Nazi-financed German-American Bund. AJC tried to achieve the same effect by private negotiations with gentile leaders. Congress led in the boycott of German goods, and showed its radical bias by the emphasis it put on economic discrimination.

———◆◆◆———

The end of the war, with the full revelation of the horrors of the concentration camps, forced American Jews to change their tactics in fighting anti-Semitism. What Congress, a small minority, had been saying all along now seemed clear to almost everybody—conciliation and persuasion weren't going to make a dent; action was needed. Congress pioneered with the new formula: prejudice can't be controlled, but discrimination can; you can't change people's feelings, but you can change their behavior. The way to deal with anti-Semitism, therefore, is not, like AJC, to plead with influential people behind the scenes; nor, like ADL, to sponsor public-relations campaigns to improve the image of the Jew. Instead, the laws must be changed, discrimination must be legally outlawed, and constant litigation and agitation must be carried on.

Congress began by mounting a full-scale attack on quotas in medical schools. Its great leader, Rabbi Stephen Wise, threatened to sue Columbia University, on the grounds that its Jewish quota was a violation of its Federal tax exemption. The suit never actually went to court; it was never intended to. "He did it just to shake them up a little," says an official of Congress. But the new attitude of defiance was symptomatic. One of its earliest victories was the passage by the New York State legislature, in 1948, of an effective Fair Employment Practices law. This proved that the new strategy could work, and soon it was adopted by the other defense agencies. At first, of course, they wouldn't quite admit that they were modifying their old methods; but today they make no bones about it.

Besides, the old methods weren't completely moribund. In 1949 ADL mixed them with some of the new aggressiveness and came up with a victory of its own. It decided to attack the problem of Jewish quotas in colleges. It conducted a series of meetings with college administrators; the position that many of them took was, "There are no such things as quotas. Other schools may have them, but not us." In the words of one ADL official, "Some of them were lying in their teeth, but some of them really believed it." ADL had made studies and had the facts, but it knew that the colleges wouldn't accept them. So it hired Elmo Roper, the country's leading public-opinion analyst, to conduct an "independent" survey of the situation. Roper came up with the same statistics that ADL already had in its files, and the colleges were unable to dismiss his findings as biased. "It was both laughable and sad," says that ADL official, "to watch the reactions of those dignified academicians to Roper's facts." Once they got over the shock, the colleges instituted corrective measures.

Today the aggressive approach is so taken for granted that ADL, AJC, even Congress sometimes, find themselves criticizing certain groups or individuals for being too aggressive. The Jewish War Veterans is often the recipient of such criticism. When speakers from the John Birch Society address public meetings, it sends people to heckle them. The defense agencies deplore this; they believe in ignoring such speakers. A few years ago the Jewish War Veterans tried to organize a boycott against American firms who, under Arab pressure, refused to do business with Israel. The defense agencies wouldn't cooperate. "Boycott is a dirty word to them," say the War Veterans.

On the other hand, as a result of the new aggressiveness, there is one group that everybody now jumps on—the National Conference of Christians and Jews. The NCCJ was founded in response to the vicious anti-Catholic propaganda against Al Smith in the 1928 election campaign. Wealthy German Jews were immediately attracted to the organization; Roger Williams Strauss was one of its founders. They liked its basic assertion that change in the long run will be brought about only by education and persuasion. It still operates according to the same principle. Instead of picketing and suing, it organizes teachers' workshops on prejudice and recruits high school sophomores and juniors for youth institutes at thirty colleges around the country; the theory is that these young people will return to their respective schools and spread the message of tolerance. In 1943 it invented the idea of public functions at which a priest, a minister, and a rabbi all appear on the same platform—an idea which has now become an accepted part of American mores. Its leadership, in accordance with its fundamental philosophy, has always been carefully divided among the three denominations. Its executive director has never been a Jew, a policy which has the full support of the Jews on its board.

Because it has stuck to its guns despite the changes going on around it, the National Conference comes in for a lot of ridicule from the more militant agencies. They are especially scornful of its most famous invention, Brotherhood Week. "Giving away blotters," say its critics, "accomplishes nothing except to let the bigots off the hook easily." The NCCJ officials are aware of these criticisms and respond to them with patience and forbearance—though one of them did let a slightly acid note come into his voice when he suggested to me that "if we dropped Brotherhood Week tomorrow, all the Jewish defense organizations would start scrambling for it."

It is a bit too easy, I think, to jump on the National Conference. Admittedly its approach seldom produces spectacular results. In certain states, like New York, where the climate is favorable to liberal ideas, it may have an insignificant impact. But there are many areas of the country, notably in the South, where ADL has an uphill fight, where AJC is largely a club for rich Jews, where Congress has never succeeded in establishing a foothold at all. In such areas the National Conference is often the only channel of communication between minority groups and the establishment.

A case in point is provided by Fort Worth, Texas. It used to be run by Amen Carter, a millionaire and a virulent anti-Semite; he wrote editorials for his newspaper in which he referred to the rival city of Dallas as "Jew-town." For a long time the National Conference couldn't organize in Fort Worth because the other gentiles were intimidated by Carter. Finally it hired a hearty hail-fellow Rotary Club type to head its tiny branch. He moved around town, meeting everyone, shaking hands, flattering the power people—using all the tactics, in short, which fill the American Jewish Congress with contempt. He finally jollied some of the gentile leaders into attending a twenty-five-dollar-a-plate brotherhood dinner. As guest of honor he chose the most influential gentile among them—a man who was far from being a paragon of brotherhood. But this man was flattered, and others hoped to be given the same honor in the future—and so the brotherhood dinner became an annual affair.

In a few years things had changed in Fort Worth. Anti-Semitism disappeared from public speeches, Jews were taken into local clubs, rabbis were invited to speak at schools and churches. Amen Carter is dead now, and his son, Amen Carter, Jr., was chairman of a recent brotherhood dinner.

————◆•◆————

There is no question that the defense agencies could never have been as successful as they have been without the active cooperation of the Christian world.

In the past Christian churchmen have mostly looked upon anti-Semitism as something the other fellow indulged in, a crackpot marginal feeling at worst. The Nazi holocaust was a shock to them, not only because of its brutality, but because that brutality broke loose in a modern, educated, Christian nation, with the blessing and support of most of its Protestant and Catholic clergymen. That this support was no accident was further proved by ADL's recent study of anti-Semitism and Christian belief. It showed that 25 percent of American Christians have anti-Semitic opinions which they have drawn solely from their religious training; another 20 percent blame their religious training for at least some of their anti-Semitic prejudices. This kind of unpleasant fact has forced many Christian churchmen to reexamine their religious suppositions, including their picture of the Jew as Christ-killer.

Extraordinary things have already come out of this reexamination. The World Council of Churches fired the opening gun in 1948 by passing a resolution to improve Jewish-Christian relations. Catholic and Protestant religious textbooks are being edited to eliminate negative references to Jews. New textbooks are being issued with the specific purpose of explaining Judaism to Christian children. On the higher educational levels, institutes on Jewish-Christian relations are constantly being held at seminaries around the country. In 1966 AJC arranged an international colloquium on Christianity and Judaism at Harvard; it was attended by one hundred leading theologians and scholars from all over the world. Courses on Judaism and chairs of Jewish studies have been established at dozens of colleges—in fact, there aren't enough qualified Jewish scholars to fill them all. Fordham University just announced the appointment of a rabbi to teach its first course in Judaism.

It isn't only among churchmen that the Nazis made anti-Semitism disreputable. Senator Joseph McCarthy's reactionary anticommunism would automatically have been accompanied by anti-Semitism in an earlier era. Many of his supporters did, no doubt, tell each other privately that all Jews were Communists. But in public the Senator bent over backward to avoid the stigma, even going so far as to appoint two young Jewish lawyers as his chief investigators. The Senator shrewdly recognized the temper of the time—and in fact, the McCarthy era, with all its hysteria, failed to produce any significant resurgence of anti-Semitism.

The new atmosphere has created a phenomenon which is especially evident in intellectual circles and on college campuses. Jewishness is now acceptable, sometimes even fashionable. At the opera and other important cultural battlegrounds in New York, socially prestigious women are constantly seen with Jewish escorts. Their mothers would never have dared. Yiddish—that symbol of the hated *shtetl*—is no longer an outcast. A recently published Yiddish dictionary has been expensively advertised. Yiddish words pepper the speech of television personalities from Jerry Lewis, who is Jewish, to Johnny Carson, who isn't. The story is told of the representative of a graduate school who came to Harvard to interview candidates for a fellowship. He wanted to find out which of the candidates were Jewish, but it is now illegal to ask such a question directly. The only method the interviewer could think of was to ask the candidates if they spoke Yiddish. He tried this on the first boy, who looked him in the eye and said, "Just enough, sir, to get along in the Yard." The story may be apocryphal, but the attitude it conveys is real.

To some Christians the new sympathy for Jewishness has produced deeper effects than a taste for Yiddish jokes. Since 1956 thirty thousand Christians in America have converted to Judaism. The Union of American Hebrew Congregations, which maintains regular classes for converts in several cities, estimates that enrollment has increased 25 percent in the last ten years.

Why do they convert? Most of them, 85 to 90 percent, do so because they are about to marry Jews. Yet a generation ago even marriage wouldn't have led them to such a drastic step. Today, while some of them are admittedly pressured into conversion (the husband feels uneasy if his wife refuses to be Jewish, the grandparents offer bribes or threats in order to ensure Jewish grandchildren), a kind of good feeling about Judaism seems to be an important factor. The sentiment expressed by one Italian boy is common: "I've gone with Jews all my life. I like them. I decided I want to be one. Let's say it's my declaration of manhood."

What makes these conversion statistics especially remarkable is the fact that Judaism has never been a proselytizing religion. It doesn't refuse converts, but it definitely discourages them. The rabbi is required to explain to the prospective convert, in detail, all the burdens and obligations and dangers involved in being Jewish. If this doesn't discourage him, he is sent home to think it over; when he returns, the explanation is given to him all over again, with fresh details. Three times this must be done, and then, after a period of intensive study, the convert will be accepted.

The Orthodox add extra refinements to the process of discouragement. For example, if the Orthodox rabbi really wants to make it hard on the prospect, he can invoke all sorts of ancient and humiliating rituals. According to strict law, a woman convert is supposed to sit up to her neck in ritual water while two learned men stand outside the bathhouse giving her instruction in some of the major and minor commandments. No wonder that converts, according to most rabbis, turn out to be more faithful synagogue-attenders and Sabbath-observers than the majority of born Jews.

———————◄●►———————

Still another symptom of the new Christian sympathy for Judaism is the tremendous increase in recent years of interfaith dialogue. An interfaith dialogue is almost any kind of discussion between Christians and Jews on matters of religion, any attempt by the two groups to get together and explain their beliefs and behavior to each other. Such a discussion can take many different forms—three girls from a Catholic college having dinner with four Jewish students in a cafeteria; a dozen married couples meeting once a month in somebody's living room; an audience of two hundred listening to two rabbis and two ministers in a church auditorium; a group of influential prelates and rabbis spending a weekend together at a country retreat. All these types of dialogue, and many others, have been sponsored by organizations ranging from the Synagogue Council to AJC.

The demand from Christian leaders is so great that "there aren't enough Jews to go around," says Rabbi Marc Tanenbaum, AJC's expert on interreligious affairs.

Rabbi Arthur Hertzberg, one of the most enjoyable mavericks on the scene today, points out a significant and ironic fact about the dialogues. The secular establishment, the defense agencies, pursue them far more strenuously than the religious establishment. This leads him to conclude that the present craze for dialogue is little more than a ploy on the part of the defense agencies to ensure their continued existence. Now that the fight against anti-Semitism is almost won, they must find some other justification for getting money from American Jews. They used to say, "We exist because we can *defend* you from 'them' "; now they hope to say, "We exist because we can *talk* to 'them' "!

A more serious, even bitter, attack on dialogue comes from Orthodox Judaism. The Synagogue Council, made up of representatives from all branches of American Judaism, worked for several years with Christian groups to set up high-level dialogues, only to have its Orthodox members walk out at the last moment. Their ostensible reason was that the publicity the dialogues were receiving gave the impression that theological differences between Jews and Christians could somehow be ironed out, eliminated. No truly pious Jew, they said, could allow such an impression to remain.

The irrepressible Rabbi Hertzberg points out that the Orthodox walkout is itself a symptom of the changed atmosphere. Twenty years ago, he says, the Orthodox would never have walked out. Their fear of anti-Semitism would have prevented them from doing so; they would have held on tenaciously to any means of creating better relations with the gentiles. Today, however, the Orthodox know perfectly well that their hostility won't keep the dialogues from taking place. By condemning the dialogues they are expressing their confidence in Christian sincerity.

It is still too early to determine the effect the dialogues are having on the individual Christians and Jews who participate in them. They contain, I think, both a promise and a danger. The promise lies in the genuine good will, and even more important, the good sense of the participants. By and large they are planned carefully and intelligently; there seems to be very little trailing off of interest after a session or two.

The danger lies in the fact that the Jew and the Christian enter into dialogue for entirely different motives. The Christian wants to learn more about Judaism and Jewish life. His sense of guilt has made him dissatisfied with his present view of Christianity; he hopes to find values in Judaism which will help him rethink his Christian ideas. But the Jew's motive is much simpler. He wants Christian anti-Semitism to come to an end. He wants the Christian to admit the harm he's done and stop doing it. He may not be conscious that he has this motive. He may sincerely believe that he has joined the dialogue in order to exchange ideas, broaden his horizons, learn more about Christianity. But once the formalities are over, anti-Semitism is the only subject he really wants to discuss.

This attitude is understandable. Jews have been hurt, and are still too absorbed in their pain to take an objective interest in the philosophy and theology of those who inflicted it. Nevertheless, we must wonder about the ultimate effectiveness of a "dialogue" in which one party has little desire to listen.

———•••———

There are many heartening things about the new Christian attitude, but the most spectacular, to many people, is the Catholic participation. This participation was initiated by Pope John and given its highest official sanction in Pope Paul's famous statement on the Jews, hammered out over several years by Vatican II. This statement declares that "what happened to Christ cannot be attributed to all Jews, without distinction, then alive, nor to the Jews of today . . . The Jews should not be presented as rejected by God or accursed . . . The Church . . . deplores hatred, persecutions, displays of anti-Semitism, directed against Jews at any time or by anyone."

Much has been written about Jewish influence on Vatican II: how ADL and AJC both sent lobbyists to Rome; how Cardinal Cushing of Boston set up an audience with the Pope for Rabbi Heschel of the Jewish Theological Seminary; how an audience was granted to the wife of a millionaire who had just given a large endowment to Pro Deo University; how an audience was granted to Ambassador Arthur Goldberg; how Rabbi Tanenbaum was the only Jew left in the Vatican when the statement was finally issued. It's a good story, a kind of theological James Bond adventure. It will be told many times, in many different versions.

It is quite impossible for an outsider—or even, I suspect, an insider—to determine what effect these lobbyists actually had. The Orthodox rabbinate, which advised a strictly hands-off policy, says they had a pernicious effect. The American Jewish Congress says they would have been more effective if they had filed a brief but did not show up in person. And the argument still goes on as to whether the Vatican's statement was strong enough. An earlier draft used the word "condemns" in addition to the word "deplores." Doesn't this revision indicate that the final statement was watered down?

To understand all this argument we must understand the American Jew's attitude toward the Catholics, which is even more complex than his attitude toward other Christians. It is

another example of his ability to hold simultaneously two contradictory feelings.

On the one hand, many Jews are anti-Catholic. They justify this in a number of ways. They disagree with Catholic
opinion on important issues—abortion, divorce reform, birth
control, separation of church and state. Beyond the disagreement itself, they are disturbed by the Church's tendency, as
they see it, to use its political power to impose its views on
others: for example, not only are Catholics prohibited from
practicing birth control, but in a state like Connecticut, which
is under Catholic influence, it is illegal to dispense information
about contraceptives. Catholic views on censorship are particularly obnoxious. Imagine drawing up a list of books that people
aren't allowed to read!

On theological matters, too, Catholic ideas are alien to Jews.
Catholics genuflect, cross themselves, pray to pictures and use
beads. To the Jew, with his severe approach to religion, this is
all so much image-worshiping, a plain violation of the Second
Commandment. Worse, it's superstition. And there's nothing a
Jew, who may knock wood ten times a day to ward off bad
luck, despises more than superstition.

On a more pragmatic level, Jewish and Catholic interests
in America have often collided. Both groups are essentially
urban, with great concentration in the Northeast. The largest
waves of Catholic immigration were somewhat earlier than
those of Jewish immigration, so the Jews often found Catholics
barring their way. The Democratic party on the Lower East
Side was controlled by Catholics when the Jews arrived, and
they were not anxious to yield their political power to the
newcomers; this struggle continues in Tammany Hall to this
day. A few years ago, when Sanford Garelik became the first
Jew to be appointed Chief Inspector of the New York Police,
injured howls went up from many Irish policemen, who felt
that this job should continue to be their personal property; this
reaction did not endear the Catholics to the Jews. Today both
Catholics and Jews have moved to the suburbs in large numbers, and are treading on each other's toes.

Finally, many Jews are convinced that Catholics are more
anti-Semitic than other Christians. It is unfortunate that the
most highly publicized American anti-Semite of the thirties
was Father Coughlin. For many New York Jews over forty, one
of their earliest memories of anti-Semitism is connected with

those elderly Irish women who used to hawk Coughlin's magazine, *Social Justice*, on the streets of New York. The salestalk always included a string of obscenities directed at Jews. Burdened by similar memories, Jews are puzzled by the occasionally ambiguous behavior of Catholic churchmen. Why, for example, during his good-will tour to America, did Pope Paul allow one of his seminarians to read the phrase "gathered together for fear of the Jews" on national television?

Nevertheless, Jewish belief in Catholic anti-Semitism has something irrational about it. Jews cling to it in spite of any evidence to the contrary. Most authorities agree, for instance, that Protestant anti-Semitism, because it is social as well as religious in nature, is more widespread than Catholic anti-Semitism; but few Jews I have talked to are willing to believe these authorities. A Jewish religious leader told me about a study which suggested that anti-Semitism is no worse in parochial schools than in other types of schools. His reaction was, "That proves what hypocrites they are! If they practiced what they preached, there ought to be *less* anti-Semitism in their schools!"

This kind of inverted logic suggests that many Jews have an emotional reaction against Catholics which goes deeper than logic. I. B. Singer writes about the twinge of uneasiness he used to feel as a boy whenever he passed a nun on the street.[1] Few Jews are unfamiliar with this twinge. And Bruce Jay Friedman, American-born and much younger than Singer, says that the Catholic school across the street from him, when he was a boy, seemed like "the battlefield—a scary mysterious place." Yet he admits that he never got into any fights with the Catholic boys—in fact, nothing ever actually happened.

The underlying cause for these irrational feelings, I think, is that to most Jews Catholics are the *real* Christians. They go to church more than Protestants. They pray more—or at any rate, they pray louder, with more elaborate gestures. They "really believe that stuff." Therefore, they are potentially more dangerous.

And so, Jews are anti-Catholic—but they are also pro-Catholic. In spite of themselves, they have a certain fellow feeling for the Catholic because he too is a member of a religious minority, a victim of prejudice. Anti-Catholic movements in America have often been anti-Semitic too. In the twenties, when the Ku Klux Klan was active not only in the South but in

New England and the Midwest, it attacked Catholics and Jews indiscriminately; a bond was formed between the two groups which many Jews feel to this day.

Explosions of anti-Catholic propaganda in political campaigns have always boomeranged among Jewish voters. Jews opposed the Know-Nothing party in the nineteenth century, supported Al Smith overwhelmingly, and proved that John F. Kennedy wasn't the "Catholic candidate" by giving him 88 percent of the Jewish vote (the Catholics themselves gave him only 81 percent of their vote). And in Catholic cities like Baltimore and Boston, Jews have always been able to work well with the political and religious power structure. Elderly Baltimoreans still remember the days when Cardinal Gibbons and the senior rabbi ruled the city jointly. These good friends often took long walks together, during which they decided questions of public morals, what plays and movies could be shown, and who would be appointed to the school board.

Under the circumstances it isn't surprising that the Jewish reaction to Vatican II has been ambivalent. Nobody believes that the Catholics mean what they say, yet everybody would be shocked if it turned out that they didn't mean it. On the one hand is the man who said to me, "They'll never change just because the Pope tells them to. If he tells them they can eat meat on Friday, *that* they'll do in no time flat—but they'll never give up the anti-Semitism." On the other hand is the man who said, "I get along better with Catholics than with other gentiles. Let's face it, we talk the same language."

Curiously, it was the same man.

———•◦•———

Most of the experts believe that anti-Semitism is staggering at the moment. None of the experts believe that it is down for the count. Certain random statistics tell much of the story. College quotas are largely a thing of the past. Ten percent of the total college population are Jewish; 15 to 20 percent of the faculties of leading universities are Jewish. And this includes English departments, traditional bastions of anti-Semitism, where the theory used to be held that only a man with an Anglo-Saxon background could have a genuine understanding of English literature.

In the Ivy League schools the figures are even more

impressive. Eighteen percent of the students at Yale are Jewish; 25 percent of the students at Harvard are Jewish. At Columbia it's 40 percent, and Princeton, whose Jewish quota was less than 2 percent in 1941, now has 15 percent. Nor are these Jewish students relegated to second-class citizenship on the campus. They are just as likely as not to hold high-status positions. In the last ten years a high percentage of the editors of the Yale *Daily News* have been Jewish. (The first Jewish managing editor of the *News,* incidentally, was appointed to his job by his editor-in-chief William Buckley.) At Harvard the faculty, dominated by Jews, makes a special effort to hire qualified non-Jews. At Brown a few years ago the Jewish editors of the newspaper ran an editorial urging non-Jews to join, assuring them that they wouldn't meet with prejudice.

Medical schools, once particularly difficult for Jews to get into, have also succumbed to the new spirit. In 1948 10 percent to 15 percent of the medical students in New York State were Jewish. By 1954 this had risen to 50 percent—in some schools it was as high as 80 percent. Restrictive want ads are outlawed in most states now. Jobs are open to Jews in banking, public utilities, large corporations—industries which used to be almost totally restricted. Wall Street law firms have started hiring Jews at a great rate, and creating incentives for them by appointing Jewish partners.

Another area where there are few opportunities under any circumstances has now opened up to Jews. Bruno Walter, before the war, could never get a permanent orchestra appointment because he was Jewish. Serge Koussevitzky, Eugene Ormandy, and Pierre Monteux, all Jews, had to convert to Christianity in order to reach the top in the symphony world. But after the war Leonard Bernstein broke the barrier, and today many conductors—Georg Szell and Erich Leinsdorf, to mention the best known—are Jewish.

Needless to say, the more vicious and blatant forms of anti-Semitism barely manage to keep alive. Rockwell's American Nazi party had a few hundred members. Gerald L. K. Smith still distributes his magazine, but his subscribers are all elderly people, living in the past. Cities notorious for their anti-Semitism have long since become tame and tolerant. Minneapolis, once known as the capitol of anti-Semitism, was put on the road to reform in the mid-forties by its mayor, Hubert Humphrey. For a few years after the establishment of Israel, the Arab states helped finance right-wing anti-Semitic groups, but they gave it up when they found it didn't pay.

Though social anti-Semitism is much harder to eradicate, of course, even here there has been progress. Jewish fraternities still exist, but there is much interchange of membership; the Jews take some gentiles, and vice versa. At Yale the secret societies have opened up to Jews. Three Jews recently turned down invitations from Skull and Bones, the most prestigious of all; they preferred the competition. Country clubs and businessmen's clubs, traditionally closed to Jews, have relaxed their restrictions. In recent years the AJC has devoted much of what remains of its behind-the-scenes negotiation to this project—on the grounds that Jews who are excluded from clubs are perforce excluded from certain business opportunities. It urges Jews not to refuse personal invitations to have lunch or play golf at such clubs, but to use their influence to prevent organizations they belong to from holding official functions there. For example, the Bar Association of Kansas City, under pressure from AJC members, stopped holding its annual dinners at a restricted club—and this club is no longer restricted. In 1960 only two of the twenty-eight University Clubs accepted Jews. By 1965 seven accepted Jews, another was about to, and five more were engaged in discussions with AJC.

And AJC is quick to point out that clubs which have lifted their restrictions need not feel inferior. The Century Club of New York, described by Cleveland Amory as "easily the most distinguished in America from both a *Who's Who* and *Celebrity Register* point of view," [2] has had Jews on its rolls for years.

The gentleman's agreement is breaking down in the real estate world too. There are still some townships which won't sell houses to Jews; there are even cooperative apartment buildings in New York which won't sell apartments to Jews; but they are harder to find all the time. One of the main reasons for this is the tremendous expansion into the suburbs since the end of the war. Jews were as much a part of this expansion as anybody else. They moved into most new neighborhoods at the same time as gentiles, bought houses next-door to gentiles. Often they all formed neighborhood associations at the beginning and started their first suburban social life together. In many suburbs these habits remain.

Yet the experts won't let out that third cheer and start ringing the victory bells. There are still some flies in the oint-

ment. In the industries that really count—the power industries
—Jewish participation is minuscule. For example, only five of
the fifty largest banks in America have any Jews at all among
their senior officers. Four of these have only one Jew.

Social club discrimination, though decreasing, is still widespread. According to a 1962 survey 67 percent of all such clubs
practice religious discrimination.[3] In New Orleans the Mardi
Gras clubs are closed to Jews, despite the fact that it was a Jew
who started the Mardi Gras. In Cleveland the two largest
businessmen's clubs will take no Jews; until recently Christian
members of one of them couldn't even invite Jewish guests. In
one small town in South Carolina the country club started
letting in Jews after the war, but with the proviso that none of
them could have parents who were alive. The club didn't want
any embarrassing old people with accents being brought
around.

More important, even in towns where the country club is
open to Jews, the old social cleavage probably remains. For
every city like Galveston or Dallas where Jews and gentiles
mingle freely, there are dozens like Kansas City and Chicago
and Norfolk, where the famous "six o'clock shadow" still exists.
Until six o'clock Jews and gentiles meet together at business, at
ladies' luncheons, in backyard gossip sessions; after six o'clock
they move into their separate corrals just as obediently as if
they had been herded there. This is true even in a town like
Ann Arbor, where the Jews are proud of the fact that no street
has more than three Jewish families on it.

New York is the one big exception to this rule. Here Jews
can mingle with gentiles, or be by themselves, as much as they
please. Here the ads for Levy's rye bread—"You don't have to
be Jewish to enjoy it"—can be seen in every subway station, to
the amazement of Jews from out of town. But it has often been
said that there are two kinds of Jews in America, New York
Jews and all the rest.

Though discriminatory behavior has been greatly reduced
in recent years, it is unclear how much anti-Semitic feeling
remains. There are indications that the old disease is still in the
blood. Law firms are hiring Jews, but according to a Yale Law
School study, only the ones at the top of the class; Jews in the
middle are still at a tremendous disadvantage compared to
gentiles with the same class standing.[4] The same trend appears
to be true of colleges. An AJC survey shows that Jewish high

school students must have higher scores on their aptitude tests than non-Jews if they wish to get into the Ivy League; the average Jewish score is 675, the average non-Jewish score is 625.[5]

Some of the old superstitious ignorance about Jews persists. A young rabbi who spoke at a Methodist church in Michigan recently was asked by one woman to explain just how Jews went about making matzohs out of blood. Another lady called up a rabbi down South and asked if her Sunday School class could visit the synagogue when the sacrifices were taking place.

And the old thoughtless viciousness breaks loose from time to time. "Kike" and "yid" are not yet incomprehensible words, even to Jewish teen-agers. The beach outside Norfolk is still lined with signs saying "Gentiles Only." The Rat Finks, a group of Young Republicans in New Jersey, sang anti-Semitic songs during their caucuses. All over the country there are incidents every year of synagogues being defaced by swastikas. The culprits, when they're caught, seldom turn out to belong to organized groups; they are usually middle-class college students whose vandalism is a spontaneous outburst of hate.

The John Birch Society follows the pattern clearly. Officially it isn't anti-Semitic, but it attracts the typical middle-class anti-Semite, the respectable, frustrated bank clerk or small businessman. Before the meeting the Birchers swap nasty anti-Semitic remarks. During the meeting itself there is no anti-Semitism at all, but as soon as the meeting ends, the anti-Semitic remarks begin again.

Perhaps the greatest danger of the present situation lies in the unwillingness or inability of many Americans to recognize an anti-Semitic incident when they see one. In the town of Wayne, New Jersey, in 1967 a member of the school board named Newton Miller urged his fellow townspeople to vote against certain other board members because they were Jewish. There was a furor, and Miller apologized—for "hurting the feelings" of the Jews. But he refused to modify or withdraw his original remarks. Not surprisingly, one would think, the Jewish members of the board weren't eager to accept Miller's apology. But the electorate saw it differently. They voted overwhelmingly against the Jewish candidates, because they had churlishly "turned away the hand of friendship when Newton did the Christian thing."

The perverseness of this reasoning is almost incredible. It forces a Jew to ask himself how many other people in America are as blind and insensitive as the citizens of Wayne, New Jersey. If there were a depression tomorrow . . . If another Hitler came along . . .

This kind of speculation leads us to consider the effects of anti-Semitism on Jews themselves. The time has come to examine the scars.

IV.

Battle Scars

It isn't easy to find a Jew whose personality hasn't been warped by his feelings toward gentiles. Sometimes the damage is great, sometimes slight; many individuals succeed in overcoming it, or in learning to live with it, or even in making something valuable out of it. But the damage, in one form or another, is almost always there. To classify these forms at all is to oversimplify them, and very few Jews are the victims of each one of them; yet there are even fewer to whom some of them don't apply. The vast majority of American Jews will find themselves somewhere in the catalog that follows.

Let's begin with an obvious example—the way a large number of Jews today feel about Germany and the Germans. The basic attitude can be expressed very simply: all Germans are Nazis. This applies just as much to those who were in their teens or younger during the war, to those who weren't even born when Hitler died, and to generations of Germans yet unborn.

This generalization has a corollary: no Nazi ever stops being a Nazi. The poison has no antidote—neither time, nor remorse, nor religious conversion. For this reason Germany must be watched from now until the end of time, and every smallest hint of neo-Nazi sentiment must be greeted by cries of warning. I was interviewing a group of CCNY students when Kurt Kiesinger, who belonged as a boy to a Nazi youth organization, succeeded Adenauer as Chancellor of West Germany. A white-faced young man came rushing in to announce the news: "They've just elected the Nazi!" Not the ex-Nazi. Kiesinger's liberal record, his repudiation of that incident from his past, his extreme youth when it took place—none of this counted for anything. He was still and always would be "the Nazi."

Similarly, this feeling surfaces whenever a German concert performer, presumed to be a Nazi collaborator, comes to America. For many years after the war artists like Walter Gieseking, Kirsten Flagstad, and Elisabeth Schwarzkopf were unable to appear in this country. When they finally did, the pickets showed up. Admittedly much less of this goes on now, yet in Chicago recently, when the symphony considered hiring Herbert von Karajan as its permanent conductor, protests poured in from Jews.

The idea expressed by these protests is that "we mustn't give our money to those Nazis." The same idea underlies the feeling of many Jews that it's immoral to buy German products. Some mothers won't buy German toys for their children. Milton Himmelfarb, in an article in *Commentary*, confesses that he always looks twice when he sees a Mercedes or a Volkswagen in a synagogue parking lot.[1]

This feeling is so intense that it exists in people who are well aware of its irrationality. The *Atlantic* sent a number of intellectuals to West Germany and published a symposium of their reactions. The Jews among them all reveal a struggle between their prejudice and their urge to overcome it. Some, like Diana Trilling and Stanley Kauffmann, found what they expected to find; some, like Harvey Swados and Irving Kristol, bent over backward to be fair; but none of them was comfortable on German soil.[2]

Obviously one of the underlying reasons for this feeling is the desire for revenge. Jewish leaders, in their public pronouncements, often make no attempt to conceal this feeling. At a meeting of Nazi death camp survivors in New York, Nahum Goldmann, the president of the World Jewish Congress, said, "Not only must Jews always remember, but the Germans must always be reminded."[3] It's almost as if some symbiotic relationship now exists between the Jews and the Germans. We can never break loose from them; we're doomed to go through the ages together, tied to them by our hatred.

But the deeper reason for this is the Jew's own sense of

guilt. He feels guilty over the six million Jews who were killed by Hitler. What more could he have done to help them? Perhaps nothing, but his guilt stems from his sense that he might so easily have died instead of them.

This sense of guilt underlies the eagerness of a few Jews to accuse the six million of passivity, of going to the gas chambers like sheep instead of fighting back. Thus the popularity of Hannah Arendt's *Eichmann in Jerusalem*—in which Miss Arendt, a refugee from Germany, congratulates herself on her cleverness in getting out in time. And sometimes the sense of guilt produces tragic symptoms. It fills certain people with despair, makes them doubt the meaning of life and the existence of God. Rabbi Richard Rubenstein of Pittsburgh University expressed the feelings of many Jews when he said, "After Auschwitz I find I must reject a transcendent God entirely." [4]

Antipathy to the Germans is strong even among young people who can't remember the war years. Many rabbis have told me that the college students in their congregations are bored by sermons about "the six million." "Oh no, rabbi, not that again!" Yet these same college students are likely to react as one young man reacted when he visited the site of Dachau. "I felt," he wrote home, "as if I were buried with those people."

———◆◆———

Jewish feeling about Germany, however, must be seen in perspective. It is a special and extreme case of a feeling which Jews have had about gentiles for a long time, long before Hitler came along. It is expressed in an old folk saying which Jewish mothers have been passing on to their children for centuries: "Scratch a goy and you'll find an anti-Semite." Even Jews who reject this saying for its crudity, who demonstrate their enlightened views by insisting that "of course they're not *all* like that," will often produce a more sophisticated version of the same idea. "I have plenty of gentile friends," one woman told me, "and I'm very fond of them, but let's face it, even after years of friendship something will come up, and you'll know how they really feel!"

This suspicion that all gentiles are anti-Semitic at heart prompts many Jews to feel an instinctive fear and distaste for Christian religious symbols. Father Edward Flannery, a leader in the Catholic fight against anti-Semitism, felt the enormity of the problem for the first time when a Jewish girl said to him,

"The cross makes me shudder. It's like an evil presence to me."
Most Jews have had a similar reaction, often in their school
days, when they had to join in on hymns with the name of
Jesus Christ in them. How many of us can remember mouthing
those words or keeping our fingers crossed while we pro-
nounced them, as if we were in danger of betraying our people
to the enemy. Such habits die hard. A Jewish civil rights activist who recently spent a summer in Mississippi writes of his
uneasiness in a Negro church, when he had to sing the words
"And this we ask in Jesus' name." [5]

Out of this unreasoning fear comes an idea which many
American Jews secretly entertain—that any day now there will
be a violent outbreak of anti-Semitism in this country, a new
Hitler will take over, and Jews will be sent once more to the
gas ovens. The Wayne, New Jersey, incident provided proof of
this to many people. The day after the Wayne election a group
of Jewish lawyers gathered in the corridors of the New York
federal court building and exchanged their fears in solemn
whispers. These men were all under thirty-five, prep school
and Ivy League graduates, with hardly any experience of anti-
Semitism among them.

This same unreasoning fear of the gentile leads some
American Jews to overreact to crackpots like George Lincoln
Rockwell. AJC's expert on right-wing groups used to address
many Jewish organizations on the subject. He is a man not
prone to underestimate the dangers; yet whenever he made a
reference to Rockwell's impotence and insignificance, there
was always someone in the audience who cried out, "That's
what they said about Hitler!"

This point of view is not isolated or untypical. One undis-
puted fact proves this: Though there is less anti-Semitism in
America today than ever before, contributions to ADL from all
over the country are larger than ever before. Even in cities like
Galveston, the Jewish community has made no move to cut its
ADL budget. It has nothing to be protected against, but somehow it feels the need to be protected anyway.

What a man fears he will, of course, try very hard to
please and propitiate; he will be very careful about hurting its
feelings. So Jews are constantly concerned about the feelings of
gentiles. Above all, the hostile gentile world must never be
held to account for its sins—especially if the sin happens to be
anti-Semitism. Let a Jew who has been injured fight back, and

instantly there will be an outcry against him from other Jews. One lady I talked to was in a fury over the "unforgivable" behavior of a Jewish lawyer, as reported in *The New York Times*. He was filing suit against a cooperative apartment building which had turned down his application because he was Jewish. "He ought to be ashamed of himself!" This lady said. "*I* don't go places where I'm not wanted!"

This kind of timidity creates some ironic situations. Many of the most influential men in the movie industry, which still dominates the Los Angeles area, are Jewish. Yet the leading Los Angeles businessmen's club, the California Club, has never accepted Jews. The movie moguls have quite enough power to force this club to open its doors to them, but they have never made the attempt. To do so would mean to admit that non-Jews consider them inferior, and their shaky egos won't allow that—so they have dealt with the situation by pretending it doesn't exist. In Los Angeles, then, we have the spectacle of half a dozen of the most powerful business leaders being excluded from a club to which many of their subordinates and dependents belong.

In his efforts to placate the gentile, the Jew must not only avoid giving offense, he must avoid attracting attention altogether. "Don't make yourself conspicuous"—this is one of the earliest pieces of advice that the Jewish mother gives to her child. Almost any action a Jew performs might be condemned by other Jews on the grounds of its conspicuousness. For example, the Jews of Ann Arbor for many years have had the custom of burying their dead in nearby Detroit. But recently some of their leaders have started a campaign to reverse this trend. "How does it look to the goyim? As if we thought we were too good for a local cemetery!"

Any kind of conspicuous behavior is undesirable, but the worst kind is immoral or downright criminal behavior. A great many Jews live in terror of the banner headline that screams out the guilt of someone with an obviously Jewish name. If a Jew must commit a murder or an embezzlement, let him be named Smith or Robinson. But better still, let him keep his hands clean. Reprehensible conduct that gets into the public eye is doubly reprehensible, because—to use at last the phrase that all of us have engraved on our hearts—it's "bad for the Jews." The sensitivity of some people to this kind of thing can hardly be exaggerated. Every time they read that bookies have been arrested, draft dodgers have been exposed, building inspectors have been accused of taking bribes, they automatically check the list for Jewish names. Jews felt as grieved at President Kennedy's death as all other Americans; but I wonder how many of them, in the first hour after the assassination, didn't say a little prayer to themselves, "Please God, make it *not* be a Jew!"

Not only must Jews keep their own sins out of the gentile gaze; they must be careful not to expose the sins of their fellow Jews. This is the source of the friction which has existed from time immemorial between the official Jewish community and the Jewish writers. The writer feels that his first obligation is to deal honestly with the world he knows best. The official community feels that his first obligation is to make that world look attractive to the gentiles. So in 1917 Abraham Cahan was taken to task by a prominent rabbi for *The Rise of David Levinsky*. And in 1938 Jerome Weidman was informed by a committee of self-appointed civic leaders that he ought to withdraw *I Can Get It for You Wholesale* from the bookstores. (His reply to this group is unprintable.) And twenty-five years later the head of a large rabbinical group had Philip Roth on the carpet for his "unwholesome picture of Jewish life" in *Goodbye, Columbus*. The best Jewish writing, it would seem, has always been "bad for the Jews."

The most important principle in pleasing the gentile is to be whatever he wants you to be. Above all—or so many Jews believe—he obviously wants you to be sweet and safe and tame and weak. To satisfy this image, Jewish theater and film producers have created the wholly mythological figure of the gentle, inoffensive, philosophical, shoulder-shrugging Jew, ready to give the hero the benefit of his wise warm-hearted advice. Pauline Kael detects him in the kindly old pharmacist in *West Side Story,* and points out that his chief function is to convince the gentile world how harmless the Jew is.[6] He is, in fact, a kind of Jewish Uncle Tom—Uncle Max, perhaps.

And the Jew, desperate to propitiate the enemy, naturally welcomes all evidence that he is succeeding. This evidence can be pretty specious; he will lap it up eagerly just the same. Leonard Lyons, the New York *Post* columnist, is a good barometer for Jewish feeling on this matter. Every day he provides his readers with examples of famous gentiles who are on good terms with Jews and love Jewish things. Over the course of one year his column contained the following tidbits: Henry Fonda conducted a seder in New York; Brendan Behan sang Jewish songs; Maureen O'Sullivan visited a discotheque with a young man in a yarmulke; Cary Grant conducted a seder in London; Nathan's Famous ships salamis to the Queen Mother; Jan Peerce was given a kosher dinner by the Governor of Mississippi; Frank Sinatra conducted a seder in Hollywood; Princess Grace is crazy about bar mitzvahs; and Richard Tucker suggested to President Johnson that he conduct a seder in the White House. In an era when gossip columnists are biting the dust all around us, Lyons continues to hold his readers.

All the time, deep down in his heart, the Jew feels sure that his efforts to placate the gentile are doomed to failure. Many American Jews therefore take a more drastic step to protect themselves from the onslaughts of anti-Semitism: they isolate themselves as much as they can from the gentile world.

In the *shtetl* this isolation was pretty much enforced from the outside. Nevertheless, the majority seldom complained about it. Making a virtue out of necessity, they told their children that the goy was a "demon," and that they'd better stay out of his way for their own protection. In America today this isolation is not imposed by law, and in many places, as we have seen, it has ceased to be imposed by custom. Yet the six o'clock shadow is still the dominant pattern of American social life, and it isn't easy to decide whether the Jew or the gentile is most responsible for its continued existence.

As soon as they were affluent enough—beginning with the period following World War I—Jews started country clubs. Unquestionably they did so because they were prohibited from joining the gentile country clubs already in existence. In newer, more comfortable buildings, with the benefits of modern heating and air conditioning (often missing in the older, gentile clubs), Jews created an atmosphere and a form of social life which has nothing specifically "Jewish" about it at all. Their clubs, in fact, are replicas of gentile country clubs in almost every respect.

The original reason for Jewish country clubs continues to exist; in many areas Jews are still excluded from the gentile clubs. But in many other areas they aren't—yet the Jewish country club doesn't disappear. Nor does it open its doors to gentiles, as a rule. The fabulous Hillcrest Club in Hollywood, which was started by Jews in the movie industry, and looks a little bit like the setting for a production number out of a movie musical (its initiation fee is the highest in America, $22,000; each member becomes a shareholder in the club's private oil well), was rigidly closed to gentiles for years, though many applied. Recently it has relaxed this policy, and honorary Jews like Danny Thomas and Frank Sinatra belong, but the membership is still overwhelmingly Jewish.

Most Jews seem to feel like the members of a club in the Midwest whose admissions committee recently proposed to admit non-Jews. There was loud opposition and the proposal was turned down. One man expressed the consensus of opinion: "We'll be overrun by non-Jews. We won't feel comfortable here any more." But what was he expressing—a negative feeling, or a positive feeling, or both at the same time?

The waters become even muddier when we consider the Jewish resort hotel. These extraordinary institutions are located chiefly in two places—in the Catskill Mountains of upper New York State and in Miami Beach, Florida. The ones in the Catskills are very Jewish: the food is strictly kosher, there is always a synagogue of sorts, and business is good on the religious holidays. The Miami Beach hotels seldom serve kosher food, only occasionally have a synagogue, and use the sun, not the Jewish calendar, to lure their guests. They are much more expensive than the Catskills hotels.

Many people who go to the Catskills are Orthodox Jews who must eat kosher because of their religious commitment. But many more feel no such obligation. Most of the guests I talked to at Grossinger's were Jewish (though non-Jews often go there too), and most of them admitted that they never eat kosher outside of their own homes and seldom inside. What's more, they spend many vacations at non-Jewish places; they go skiing in New Hampshire, surfing in Bermuda, sightseeing on Lake Como. But from time to time they all come back to some place like Grossinger's—or to its biggest rival, the Concord, which caters to a younger, showier type of guest, but whose food is just as impeccably kosher. The Miami Beach hotels exert the same mysterious magnetic attraction. The civil rights law prevents them from turning down guests of any religion, yet their clientele remains mostly Jewish.

This same mystery surrounds many other aspects of American Jewish life. College fraternities have lifted the old restrictions; Jews can get into almost any of them—yet most campuses still have their "Jewish" fraternities, whose members may well have turned down bids from non-Jewish ones. When people with clearly Jewish names reply to stock, bond, and insurance advertisements, they are usually assigned to Jewish salesmen; almost always it turns out to be good business. Young Jewish associates in Wall Street law firms are more likely to share apartments with Jewish roommates. Jewish doctors in non-Jewish hospitals, no matter how prominent they are, get less involved in hospital affairs and speak less freely at meetings than Jewish doctors in Jewish hospitals. The Riverside Memorial Chapel, New York's leading Jewish funeral home, employs no gentiles as ushers or official greeters; even in their grief Jews feel more at ease if there are no gentiles around.

In 1962 AJC studied the Jewish community in Baltimore and came to these conclusions: Jewish employees are much more likely to work for Jewish employers; although most Jews claim they don't care what religion their doctor or lawyer professes, they nevertheless use Jewish doctors 95 percent of the time and Jewish lawyers 87 percent of the time; the great majority of them say that it doesn't matter to them if their children go to a school that has only a few Jewish pupils in it—yet 90 percent send their children to schools which are predominantly Jewish.[7]

Some Jews will allow this isolationism to push them into leaving the country completely, going to Israel, where they won't have to see any gentiles at all. A few years ago I sat at a hotel bar with a friend who was contemplating such a step. A firemen's convention was being held at the hotel, and suddenly a group of firemen, loud and hearty and Irish, came charging into the room. My friend watched them a moment, then said, "That's why I'm going to Israel—to get away from those firemen." According to Harold Isaacs, in his *New Yorker* series, my friend's motive is common among American Jews who have settled in Israel.[8] The tragic irony is that they feel just as estranged as ever, for in that world full of Jews, they are looked upon as Americans.

Most Jews don't have to go that far. They are able to isolate themselves effectively enough right here in America. But why do they do it—out of fear or out of inclination? It seems to me that both explanations are true. The two contradictory motives have become so mixed up with each other that it's no longer possible to disentangle them.

Whatever his motives, the self-isolating Jew seems to be content with his lot. Or is he? How many, I wonder, have moments of doubt—like a man in Cleveland, a lawyer in his thirties, with whom I talked? He had been born and brought up in Shaker Heights, a suburb which is almost entirely Jewish. All his friends, all his schoolmates, all the girls he dated, had been Jews. Finally he married a Jewish girl, went into a Jewish firm, and joined a Jewish country club. Now he was bringing up his children in exactly the same way. "My God," he said with a sigh, "I'm a Jewish George Apley!"

———————

There is another trait besides isolationism which the Jewish George Apley often shares with his Bostonian model. It is a trait which isolationism must inevitably give rise to. To justify his withdrawal from the gentile world, to hide from himself that he was motivated by fear, the Jew may tell himself that he is superior to that world. "We're the Chosen People."

I am not referring to the theological and ethical meaning of that difficult concept. The Jewish superiority complex that I'm talking about is a very different thing. It was expressed by many of the folk songs which used to be sung in the *shtetl,* songs which declared that all the goyim are drunkards and lechers and thick-headed muzhiks. By implication, of course, this made the Jews a finer breed; the element of contempt in the song was accompanied by an element of self-congratulation.

Though the *shtetl* is far behind American Jews, it's extraordinary how much of those old folk songs are still part of their consciousness. In one well-known study, in a city referred to as "Riverton," Jewish adults and teen-agers were asked to give their opinions of gentiles.[9] The following stereotype emerged: Gentiles drink more, fight more, care less about their children's education, have less close families. The teen-agers accepted this stereotype more reluctantly than the adults, but most of them did accept it.

It will be objected that the citizens of Riverton, like the inhabitants of the *shtetl,* were unsophisticated people with little experience of the gentile world. I can only say that in the course of my interviews, I found the same opinions held by people with wide experience of the gentile world. Even Jews who were openly hostile to Judaism at the start of an interview often let their chauvinism show when their guard was down. "All religions are absurd," one graduate student told me. "No religion should be allowed to survive." Half an hour later he said, "If any religion *does* survive, I hope it'll be Judaism. There's less absurdity in *it* than in the others."

The Jewish superiority complex is involved, I believe, with another common attitude. Many Jews feel a horror for those who convert to Christianity. To some extent this is a hangover from the ancient belief that converts are, by definition, traitors —they have joined the enemy, made common cause with the persecutors of their people. But mixed in with this horror, I think, is a large portion of astonishment and contempt. How could that convert have the bad judgment to prefer *them* to *us*? He's not only a traitor, he's also a damned fool!

Along with the contempt, the Jewish superiority complex may have an element of belligerence in it. It isn't enough for the Jew to feel superior to the gentile; he must let the gentile know it. Every time a Jew announces how proud he is to be Jewish—though nobody has accused him of *not* being proud —he is betraying this impulse. His hidden motive, I think, is the deep-seated Jewish fear of being thought cowardly. This is an unfortunate by-product of one of the best aspects of the biblical heritage—the conviction that physical violence is evil, that human beings can't settle their problems by fighting one another. In the *shtetl* this was looked upon as more than a moral imperative. It was believed that nonresistance, the passive acceptance of gentile persecution, had been responsible for the survival of the Jews.

Yet even in the *shtetl* many weren't quite comfortable with this belief. It made them ashamed of themselves; they felt like cowards. For this reason the Jew has always had a double view about the warrior, and by extension about the athlete. On the one hand he has despised him for his brawn. (Milton Himmelfarb speculates that American Jews loved Adlai Stevenson partly because he was so obviously *not* an athlete.[10]) On the other hand he has often bolstered his ego by identifying with that brawn. This is one reason why Jewish sports heroes have an irresistible attraction for the American Jew. Against his better judgment he is prouder of a Sandy Koufax or a Gary Wood than of a Marc Chagall or a Jonas Salk.

He yearns to take on the athlete's power, of course, so that he can beat the gentile at his own "physical" game—and sooner or later, in certain Jews, this stops being an amiable quirk and turns into a vendetta. The Lower East Side pushcart peddler who prided himself on his honesty wouldn't hesitate to sell damaged goods to the gentile housewife. "If the goyim don't keep their eyes open, let them suffer the consequences!" His son, the successful dry-goods merchant, has usually given up such unscrupulous methods. But as he scowls across his desk at the gentile salesman struggling to make an impression, he may very well be saying to himself, "In spite of all you've done to keep us down, we've licked you! Look at you now—and look at me!"

———◦•◦———

So far all of these attitudes—fear, obsequiousness, isolationism, belligerence—are variations on one basic conviction: the chasm between Jew and gentile can never be bridged; the Jew can never really belong to the gentile world. Most Jews have this sense of estrangement to some extent, but some make desperate efforts to ignore it. In one way or another they try to become part of the gentile world, despite their secret suspicion that it can't be done. Their struggles can be comic or pathetic. Sometimes they can be ugly.

On the comic side is a peculiar form of Jewish social snobbery based on the theory that a man's status is directly proportionate to the number of gentiles he knows. Gentile-name-dropping is as common among Jews as celebrity-name-dropping among everyone else.

The popularity of certain expensive little schools in New York is based on this form of snobbery. The Brearley School for girls and the Collegiate School for boys—to name two among many—are excellent educational institutions, but they have the special appeal to Jews of being "gentile schools." In fact, both schools have a high proportion (though not a majority) of Jewish pupils. This does not dispel the illusion that, being gentile, they endow their students with some mysterious aura of superiority. "My niece has so much better manners," I heard a woman say, "since she started going to Brearley last month."

In trying to establish contact with the gentile world, some Jews go much further than sending their children to gentile schools. Some, though not many, convert to Christianity, and some have found ambiguous refuges halfway between Judaism and Christianity. The Ethical Culture Society is one of these. By its own definition it isn't quite a religion, though it holds Sunday services (which it calls meetings) and some of its leaders are licensed to perform marriages. It claims to have extracted from Judaism and Christianity their common ethical content, which it packages for people who are looking for ideology without old-fashioned ritual. Theoretically, then, the Society is open to both Christians and Jews. In fact, its members are mostly Jews.

The Unitarian Church offers some of the same attractions to Jews who are looking for entrée into the gentile world. Its wares are even more tempting than those of the Ethical Culture Society, because contrary to popular belief, only 5 percent of all Unitarians are Jews.[11] Many Jews who become Unitarians are motivated, no doubt, by sincere religious conviction—but most seem to be looking for an escape from the stigma of Jewishness.

There are Jews who go all the way and convert to some full-fledged, unequivocal form of Christianity. The majority of these people marry into the gentile world, become active in their churches, surround themselves with gentile friends, and give their children more than the average amount of religious education. They are, in fact, amazingly similar to Christians who become converts to Judaism. Many of them seem to be happy with their lot, but many others feel just a bit uncomfortable in the gentile world. All they can do is hope that their children will be able to resolve the conflict.

———

The Jew's desire to be with the gentiles leads, by a natural transition, to his desire to be *like* the gentiles. If you can't join them, imitate them.

This passion has, of course, been a godsend to the creators of Jewish jokes. There are hundreds on the subject. One of the most familiar deals with the Jewish businessman who buys a yacht, wears a yachting cap at a rakish angle, and invites his old parents from the Bronx to visit him in his new gentile habitat. His mother looks him over for a while, then gives a shrug and says, "All right, sonny, by me you're a captain. By Papa you're a captain. But what are you by captains?" It isn't surprising that this classic joke should clearly recognize both the ambition and its futility.

A generation ago this ambition showed itself clearly in the matter of names. It was not uncommon, in the twenties and thirties, for a Jew to change his name. Often he rationalized this by saying that the name he had been born with was "ugly" or "funny-sounding." Maybe so, but the new name he chose invariably had, to his ears anyway, a gentile sound.

The results of all this name-changing were sometimes grotesque. My father knew a man named Mendel Garfinkel who changed his name to Hemingway Garfield. A friend of mine met a man named Elmlark and racked his brains to figure out what the name had been originally. Finally he found out: Mr. Elmlark had once been Mr. Fogelbaum—tree-bird. The most famous of American changed names is Belmont—nothing but a French translation of the solid old German Jewish name Schoenberg. Gallicizing, in fact, has been almost as popular among Jews as Anglicizing. The name Levine has lent itself particularly well to this. The New York telephone book is full of Le Viens and La Vines and, most imaginative variation of all, La Vignes. No matter how you slice them, they're all Levine.

Here too the Jewish jokester has, from the beginning, recognized the absurdity and futility of the effort. A very old story tells of a man named Cohen who changed his name to O'Brien—and then, a few weeks later, appeared before the judge to change his name to McDonald. Why? "Because people are always asking me what it was before I changed it."

The passage of time has only increased the futility, in many cases. So many immigrants took certain names, like Green, Harris, and Ross, that today they are automatically thought of as Jewish names. How often did the immigrants turn away from the old Jewish-sounding names like Abraham, Moses, Jacob, to give their American-born children fine gentile names with a genuine Anglo-Saxon ring—like Irving, Sidney, Morris, and Seymour, like Shirley, Marilyn, and Sylvia.

Jews who want to be like gentiles not only assume gentile manners and names, but sometimes try to assume gentile faces. The essential difference between the Jewish face and the gentile face is supposed to depend on the size and shape of the nose. A grandmother I know commented favorably on her new granddaughter's small un-Jewish nose. "But she *is* Jewish," said the baby's mother, "you might as well make up your mind to that." "I want her to *be* Jewish," said the grandmother. "I just don't want her to *look* Jewish."

This underlying assumption that gentiles are somehow better-looking than Jews explains a common foible—the intense delight that many people take in discovering that certain movie stars are Jewish. I talked to an elderly lady who thinks she knows them all—Kirk Douglas and Tony Curtis and Lauren Bacall, and dozens of others. Whenever a new star bursts on the scene, her first question is, "Do you think he's Jewish?" But it's only glamorous stars that arouse her curiosity, never character actors or comedians. What thrills her is the reassuring knowledge that Jews can be up there in the pantheon, among the beautiful people—that a lucky few can overcome the handicap of their Jewish looks.

Her distaste for Jewish looks is shared by an astonishingly large number of fellow-Jews. In the course of my interviews I was struck by how many people felt they had to tell me that they didn't look Jewish. A certain rabbi, in fact, makes this the basis of a kind of off-the-cuff lie-detector test. Whenever someone announces, "I'm Jewish, and I'm proud of it!" the rabbi says to him, "That's good, because you look it." A red face and a hollow laugh are the usual reactions. And in fairness to the rabbi, he admits that he had the same reactions when the test was first tried on him.

A man's physical self-image is the most revealing clue we can have to his total self-image. If he doesn't like his looks, then he probably doesn't like himself. The rabbi's little experiment suggests that many Jews don't like themselves much.

———◆●◆———

Self-hatred, in fact, is a word often used to describe a common phenomenon—Jewish anti-Semitism. Students of minority-group behavior have explained the psychological process many times. The minority comes to accept the majority's stereotype of it. The Jew believes all the epithets that the anti-Semite throws at him, even the ones that contradict each other. He believes that Jews are clannish and pushy, miserly and ostentatious, vulgar and excessively intellectual; he believes that they have an unfair advantage by being smarter than other businessmen, and also that they get ahead in business only by being dishonest. In his heart he applies these insults to himself. Openly, often angrily, he applies them to other Jews.

In his attitudes toward anti-Semitism, the self-hating Jew is especially confused. The subject is on his mind constantly. He is far more sensitive to so-called "Jewish traits" than most gentiles are. Jacques Torczyner, the president of the Zionist Organization of America, says that the gentile groups he addresses never mention his accent (which happens to be French), but there are always people in the Jewish group who are made uneasy by it and ask him about it.

And the self-hating Jew is convinced that the cause of anti-Semitism is the behavior of "other" Jews—the ones who fit the anti-Semite's stereotype. They are a constant torment to him, those "bad" Jews. He sees them everywhere. Sometimes they seem to be pursuing him, going out of their way to make his life miserable. Oddly, they are particularly in evidence whenever he happens to be with a gentile.

The psychiatrist Kurt Lewin tells a story which reveals devastatingly the truth about the self-hater's obsession. One of his patients went to a restaurant one evening with a gentile friend. At the next table she instantly became aware of a man and a woman who were laughing and talking with ostentatious loudness and vulgarity. Anybody could see that they were Jewish. And so for half the meal she was trembling with embarrassment, cursing those awful spreaders of anti-Semitism, and praying that her gentile friend wouldn't notice them. But eventually her friend did notice them. What's more, he recognized them; they were people he had met in business, and they definitely weren't Jewish. As soon as the woman found this out, she stopped feeling embarrassed and was able to enjoy her dinner. And the couple at the next table, she observed, started talking and laughing much less loudly and vulgarly than before.[12]

But with all his anxiety about anti-Semitism, the self-hating Jew is quick to condemn individuals and organizations who, in his opinion, are constantly making "a lot of unnecessary fuss" over the problem. He can't admit at any cost that some of this prejudice might be directed against him, and so he comforts himself by insisting that it doesn't exist. There is no anti-Semitism in this day and age, he declares. Anyway, it's greatly exaggerated. If only they'd all shut up about it, it would go away.

A professor at an eastern university got very upset recently when some Jewish faculty members wanted to organize a symposium on anti-Semitism. "The subject is dead," he said. "It's a thing of the past. Nobody's interested any more. If you hold a symposium like that, all you'll do is arouse anti-Semites." The man who produced this specimen of logic is one of our leading mathematicians.

But the self-hating Jew sometimes doesn't stop at expressing anti-Semitic opinions. Sometimes he himself engages in discrimination. Mostly this is harmless and a little pathetic—a Jewish serviceman, for instance, will join in with his buddies in telling anti-Semitic stories—but occasionally it goes much further and turns into extreme anti-Semitic behavior. A few years ago Daniel Burros, an organizer of the Ku Klux Klan in New York, was revealed by a *New York Times* reporter to be a Jew. Burros killed himself the next day.

Burros was a psychotic, and Jewish anti-Semitism is not a psychosis. Yet many Jews talk about it as if it were. We use the word "self-hatred" as a convenient club against anyone who disagrees with us. Zionists refer to anti-Zionists as self-hating. Pious Jews refer to unreligious Jews as self-hating. Girls who go out with gentile boys are accused by Jewish boys of self-hatred. The vehemence of those who hurl this accusation at every target in sight raises questions about their own self-image.

So why not recognize the truth? Hardly any Jews are entirely free from the effects of this disease. In AJC's Baltimore survey, two-thirds of the respondents admitted to believing that other Jews are pushy, hostile, vulgar, materialistic, and the cause of anti-Semitism.[13] And those were only the ones who were willing to admit it.

————◆◆————

I have described each of these symptoms separately, but in most people they seldom appear in splendid isolation. One moment the Jew may grovel at the gentile's feet, the next moment he hits him in the face; one moment he hates his fellow Jews, the next moment he vigorously defends the proposition that all the great men of the twentieth century have been Jewish. What about Picasso, De Gaulle, Sir Alexander Fleming? "Everyone knows they're really Jewish," he scornfully declares. He is, in short, a regular mishmash of inferiority complexes and superiority complexes when it comes to his feelings toward the gentile world.

Nothing is more likely to arouse every one of these complexes, and possibly some I've forgotten, than the subject of intermarriage. The opinions of Jewish parents on this subject have been measured by many surveys. Ninety percent of them don't want their children to marry gentiles.[14] But no survey can measure the intensity of many people's feelings on this subject.

In the *shtetl*, when a child married a gentile, his parents said he was "dead." They observed the one-week period of formal mourning for him; sometimes they had a burial service with an empty coffin. In America today we don't go to such extremes. Yet almost all rabbis refuse to perform mixed marriages; there are some who do, but nobody admits to knowing who they are, and they have underground reputations like abortionists. And an Orthodox rabbinical group a few years ago condemned interdating as sinful.[15]

The feelings of laymen tend to be just as emotional. When I discussed the subject with a group of suburban parents, one mother told me how her daughter one day announced she was going to marry a Catholic boy. The mother dragged the daughter up to her room, locked her in for the rest of the night, and went to her at hourly intervals to scream at her, slap her face, and throw things at her. Eventually the girl was cowed into giving up her wedding plans. She fell into her mother's arms, crying out, "I love you, I love you! I won't ever go to *them!*" "And today," her mother concluded, "she's married to a good Jewish boy and keeps a kosher home—which is more than *I* ever did!"

This mother was willing to tell her story proudly in front of all her friends. And none of them was appalled or even discomfited by it. They praised her for her iron will and hoped that they could "handle the situation as well if it ever came up."

It is easy to see how the psychological factors we've been examining—the fear, the contempt, the envy, the hatred of gentiles—enter into the reactions of these parents. But why, with anti-Semitism finally on the wane, with Jews and gentiles mingling more freely and amicably than ever, does the prejudice against intermarriage seem to be stronger than ever?

To answer this question, we must recognize that the changed atmosphere of the gentile world, its new openness to

Jews, has caused a revolution in the attitudes of Jewish young people. There are still psychological distortions, but they are far less pervasive in the under-thirty generation than in their parents and grandparents. It isn't difficult to find indications of this. The more commonplace they are, the more vividly they tell the story. On the Yale campus some zealous Christian boys formed a group to proselytize among the Jews, so four Jewish boys took out an ad in the Yale newspaper, "We'd rather fight than switch." A small boy, the son of a government official, attended the Easter egg-rolling on the White House lawn with a jar of matzoh balls. "After all, it's Passover too," he said. A rabbi expressed amazement that his daughter reads her Hebrew book on the bus every morning. "When I was a kid, I kept my Hebrew books under my coat, even if the bus was filled with Jews. You just didn't do things like that in America in those days."

The contrast between today and yesterday becomes overwhelming when we consider Christmas, which has always been a problem for American Jews. What policy do you adopt, if you have children, toward a holiday which everyone around them is celebrating, and which so clearly excludes Jews? Do you have a tree in the house? Do you give presents? Do you drag in Hanukkah to muddy the trail? Each family, except the most devout, worked out its own peculiar compromise—and some were peculiar indeed. In some families the Christmas tree was renamed the Hanukkah bush, and a star of David was placed on top of it. In another family a tree was permitted in the house, but no wreath on the front door. "Inside we can do what we want, but outside it wouldn't be honest to pretend we're something we're not." In another family the children got presents for each day of Hanukkah, and on the last day the present was a Christmas tree. In another family the father took his stand firmly on principle. "In this house," he said, "we'll only give *small* Christmas presents!" But there was one thing that happened in very few families—no Christmas at all. Years ago my aunt suggested this to her children, and my cousin protested bitterly, "If I can't have Christmas, I don't want to be a Jew!"

It would be unrealistic to suppose that no Jewish families today are tying themselves in knots with such equivocations. But it happens far less than it did a generation ago. AJC, ready as usual with a survey, claims that only one out of every twenty

American Jewish families now have Christmas trees. The lady who, as a child, was allowed to have a tree but no wreath on the door suggested the same arrangement to her own daughter. The girl said, "Don't be silly, Mother. Why should we have a tree? We're Jewish!"

The question is sometimes asked, how vulnerable is this new self-confidence of American Jewish youth? Suppose these young people were exposed to the kind of anti-Semitic attack which their parents and grandparents often had to face. Wouldn't the shock make them crumble quickly? In New Haven a few years ago there was an incident which suggests that this might happen. A group of Jewish parents petitioned the school board to eliminate Christmas celebrations from the public schools. The board held a public meeting in a large auditorium, and many Jewish high school students were in the audience. The meeting grew heated, tempers exploded, and a group of bigots in the crowd started shouting threats and obscenities at the Jews. The high school boys and girls had never had such things directed at them; they had read about them in books, but this was the first time they had ever been exposed to them. Many of them collapsed completely; some of the girls became hysterical; even the boys were close to tears.

It isn't a pleasant story, but it isn't a common one either. Most Jewish young people in America today will not have to face such a test. Their self-confidence will grow, and in many instances it will lead them to the abyss that their parents dread —to marriage with a gentile. This is the cause of the extraordinary state of mind which prompted that doting, overindulgent mother to slap and bully her child the whole night through. She felt instinctively that the danger is greater now than it has ever been.

The statistics seem to bear this out. There is disagreement over them, as there is over all statistics, and an authoritative national study of intermarriage has yet to be made. But subsidiary studies have been made in certain states, and a full-scale study has been made in Washington, D.C. They indicate that 13 percent of the American Jewish population are married to non-Jews. But this figure includes first- and second-generation marriages. If one excludes old people and concentrates on American-born Jews who have attended college—the majority now in their teens will belong to this category—the rate of intermarriage rises (in Washington, D.C.) to 37 percent.[16]

There are interesting variations in this picture. Two-thirds of these marriages are between Jewish men and gentile women; Jewish women, it seems, are more content to remain in the nest—or less courageous, perhaps. Iowa has far more inter-marriage than New York; clearly Jewish boys in Iowa have fewer Jewish girls to choose from. In only 22 percent of mixed marriages are the children raised as Jews, but to balance that somewhat, most of the children aren't raised as Christians either. And finally, in approximately one out of four cases, the gentile wife converts to Judaism.

Among official representatives of the Jewish community, even the wildest optimists have been able to interpret these statistics in only one way: at the present rate we're losing more Jews than we're gaining. And who says the present rate will continue? As the older generation dies off, as more intermar-ried couples exercise their influence on the younger generation, it's likely that the rate will increase—on the principle of a snowball rolling down a hill. Nor does it seem possible to alert the young to the danger. They listen politely, they nod, they say that they would certainly prefer to marry a Jew and make their parents happy—and then they talk about "love." "If I meet a gentile boy and fall in love with him, what am I supposed to do? I certainly can't tell him I won't marry him because I'm worried about the future of Judaism!"

And what exactly can their parents say to them? After all, they believe in "love" too. They were brought up on Holly-wood movies, just like their children.

———•◦•———

A few years ago the social scientist Marshall Sklare ad-dressed the annual convention of the Jewish Funeral Directors of America. His subject was Jewish survival.

A joke? Not if you think about it a while. Obviously Jewish survival must be a matter of great concern to the funeral directors. If there are no more Jews, there can hardly be Jewish funerals. And so their organization, like every other Jewish organization in America, is in the "survival business."

They have no choice. Like it or not, they must ask them-selves certain questions. Is the Jew, as Arnold Toynbee once wrote, merely a fossil, the desiccated vestige of a dead culture? How much truth is there in Sartre's provocative remark, "It is the anti-Semite who creates the Jew"? If the anti-Semite disappears, will the Jew disappear along with him? For thousands of years the Jews have survived persecution. Will they end up being killed by kindness?

But these questions can't be answered until we understand the kind of world that the Jew has made for himself here in America. For whether or not he *will* survive in the future, he definitely *is* surviving right now—not only surviving but thriving. He has complex organizations and institutions, all running at top speed. He has an energetic, often hectic family life. He makes money and loses it, cracks jokes, commits crimes, even writes books—many of them about himself. He has opinions on a wide variety of subjects, and expresses them vociferously. Above all, he has devised many ways, both official and personal, to tell himself and the world that he is a Jew.

He may be a fossil, but he certainly doesn't act as if he knew it.

Part Two

Praying

V.

The Religious Establishment

Judaism is more than a religion.

This is its crucial difference from Christianity, a much more important difference really than that nagging old question about the Messiah. You're a Christian by virtue of believing in Christ, going to church, and worshiping God; when you stop doing those things, you become an ex-Christian. It isn't that easy, however, to become an ex-Jew. You must openly and deliberately forswear Judaism and convert to something else. Even then, you never entirely lose your old status. According to Judaic law, for instance, the wife of a converted Jew is still required to get a religious divorce. In the eyes of that law she will be divorcing a Jew—whatever he may be in his own eyes. The majority of Jews no longer accept the supremacy of the Judaic law; yet most accept the idea that Judaism is more than a religion.

The source of this idea lies in the origins of Judaism, as described in the Talmud. God, we are told, went to all the peoples of the earth and offered to make a covenant with them. If they agreed to worship Him as the one God and to obey His commandments, He would give them the Torah and make them "a kingdom of priests and a holy nation." He was offering them, in fact, the concept which has transformed the modern world—monotheism. But all the peoples of the earth refused His offer, except for a small nomadic tribe in the land of

Canaan, the Israelites. And so they and all their descendants become His Chosen People. They have been grateful for this honor ever since, though sometimes dubiously. There is an old story that a deputation of Jews went to God after a particularly nasty pogrom and asked Him if they were indeed the Chosen People. He answered yes, and they said, "Look—why don't You choose someone else for a while?"

The covenant is known in Hebrew as the *b'ris,* and this is also the name for the religious ceremony which accompanies circumcision. When a Jewish baby is circumcised, he is symbolically introduced into the covenant. The adult male who converts to Judaism must be circumcised before his conversion can be considered final, for he too must enter into the covenant. And the Jewish boy who has somehow never been circumcised —there aren't many—must have the matter taken care of before he can be married to a Jewish girl. The physical nature of this rite is significant; it suggests that there is something irreversible about entering into the covenant, something that can't be affected by a mere change of belief.

Out of this concept of the covenant comes the feeling, which most Jews have to some extent, that they are involved with all other Jews. No two creatures could be less alike, it would seem, than the Jew of Scarsdale and the Jew of Morocco. Yet the Jew of Scarsdale contributes money for the welfare of the Jew of Morrocco; the two species, however reluctantly, feel a kind of interdependence. This interdependence, this peoplehood, isn't nationalistic in the usual sense. Without sacrificing any of it, Jews have managed to be good Americans, good Englishmen, good Frenchmen, and good Moroccans.

One reason why this feeling is so hard to explain is that it so often exists below the level of conscious understanding. The people in the resort hotel business, for instance, see a good deal of the phenomenon, and even they can't quite understand it. "People come here from all over the country," says the public-relations man for Grossinger's. "They're from all walks of life, all different economic levels. But if they're Jews, right away they're talking as if they've known each other all their lives. It's very mysterious."

Jewish celebrities often find themselves exposed to this mystery, and it can be a nuisance. Many of them echo Leonard Bernstein's complaint: "Jews think they have a vested interest in me." Jewish organizations are insulted if he doesn't accept their invitations; individual Jews are constantly writing to him, asking favors or giving advice for which they expect his thanks. The attitude seems to be, "Why shouldn't we approach him? After all, it isn't as if he's a stranger."

It's all very confusing really, as is well known by Jews themselves. Where does the religion end and the peoplehood begin? Can one exist without the other? What *is* Judaism anyway? Hundreds of books have dealt with these questions, and nobody seems to come up with answers that satisfy everybody else. Yet the many contradictory definitions often turn out to have one common characteristic: an acceptance of the fact that the Jew is real even though his nature can't be accurately described or his existence logically accounted for. And so one theologian has said, "A Jew is anyone who considers himself to be a Jew, and is so considered by other Jews." And another has said, "Judaism is the religion of the Jews." And Judaic law wastes no time on abstract discussion: "Anyone born of a Jewish mother," it says, "or who converts to Judaism, is a Jew."

———◆●◆———

Many American Jews pay no attention to their religion, but for those who do, there are three divisions to which they may belong—Orthodox, Reform, and Conservative. Each represents a different solution, or at least a different approach, to the problem of reconciling four thousand years of tradition with the special circumstances of modern American life.

For thousands of years there was one form of worship and one way of life—known today as Orthodoxy. The early Jews didn't call it that, of course, because there was no alternative philosophy from which they had to distinguish it. This was the faith held by the Jews of the *shtetl*, by the earliest Jewish settlers in America, and by all the observant Jews in this country until the middle of the nineteenth century.

It is based on the more than six hundred commandments, the *mitzvahs*, laid down by God and given to Moses in the Torah. This body of law, known as *halakah*, is intended to control every aspect of existence for the pious Jew, from the way he prays to the way he eats, from his ethical behavior to his sexual behavior. He is expected to obey each and every *mitzvah*. He is never justified in ignoring or stretching one simply because it isn't convenient or doesn't apply to the modern world or goes against his reason. If a law is reasonable, in fact, some Orthodox Jews seem to feel rather annoyed at it. Where's the credit in obeying a law that any atheist would be glad to obey? Rabbi Joseph Soloveitchik, the most respected Talmudic authority in modern American Orthodoxy, has put the idea in this way: "Reason is merely the flavoring to the food. It is just as nourishing, and must be eaten, even if the flavoring is absent."

Reform Judaism rejects this approach completely. It began early in the nineteenth century, when Napoleon brought emancipation to the Jews of western Europe. Absolute adherence to *halakah* was no longer possible for somebody who wanted to leave the ghetto and live in the outside world. Some Jews, like Heinrich Heine, solved this problem by converting to Christianity, but most of them took a more legalistic way out. They contended that the laws of Moses were not immutable and eternal, but had been devised to deal with a particular situation. When the situation changed, the laws could be changed too—or eliminated on account of irrelevance. And the test of a law's relevance, of course, would be the individual's own judgment and feeling.

Reform also played down, and in some cases abandoned, the idea of peoplehood. Clearly this idea represented an annoying obstacle to what the opponents of Reform have called its real purpose—to provide a philosophical justification for complete assimilation into the gentile world, to take the Jewishness out of Judaism. But defenders of Reform, while admitting the dangers inherent in its do-it-yourself approach, believe that this is exactly where it gets its strength. Reform commitment is deeper, they say, just because it doesn't hinge on external authority. It requires a kind of mystic identification which can only be achieved by voluntary means. No doubt many Reform Jews never succeed in achieving it, but the claim is made that those who do are stronger for it.

From the start Reform was essentially a movement of the bourgeoisie, and had little appeal to the East European masses or the lower classes. Its greatest popularity, therefore, was in that most bourgeois of European states, Germany. When the German Jews started immigrating to America in the 1830s they naturally brought Reform with them. By sheer weight of numbers it soon overshadowed what was left of the earlier Orthodoxy. But for a while Reform didn't know its own strength; it existed simply as a number of separate synagogues which had been transplanted from German to American soil. It wasn't until the seventies that it began to organize, under the leadership of Isaac Mayer Wise, the great hero-villain hypocrite-saint of American Judaism. In the next decade it established Hebrew Union College, its seminary in Cincinnati, for the training of Reform rabbis, and the Union of American Hebrew Congregations, which provided a basis for cooperation among the separate Reform synagogues. Its rabbinical organization, the Central Conference of Rabbis, was founded in 1889; the last-born of Reform's power structure, it partially represented a reaction against Wise's principles, which had become so extremely Reform that many of his own adherents couldn't stomach them.

By 1889 the East Europeans were pouring into the country, and Reform soon found itself facing both a threat and an opportunity. The East European Jews, if they professed any religion at all, were Orthodox; suddenly Reform was in the minority. That was the threat. But most of the East Europeans, as we have seen, were young people anxious to get ahead in America. Clearly they would have great difficulties if they clung to their Orthodoxy; just as clearly, Reform was the means by which the Jews before them had integrated themselves into American life. That was the opportunity. Sure enough, in the following years many East European Jews, especially those who made money and were able to move "uptown," switched to Reform.

Orthodoxy didn't disappear, however. There were still older people who held on to the faith out of principle or habit. And many younger ones who hadn't been as financially successful as their fellows developed a resentment against Reform. As late as 1920 Orthodoxy still held on to 80 percent of those American Jews who admitted to any affiliation at all—though it's impossible to say how many of those were already teetering on the brink.

Naturally Orthodoxy began to develop its own organizations and institutions. The most important of these was the Rabbi Isaac Elchanan Theological Seminary, the first large training center for American Orthodox rabbis, and the nucleus of Yeshiva University, Orthodoxy's greatest educational institution today. A number of rabbinical organizations sprang up too, and two important synagogual organizations, the Union of

Orthodox Jewish Congregations and Young Israel, an attempt to retain the principles of old Orthodoxy but dress them up in American clothes. The tenaciousness of Orthodoxy in those years was also dependent on geographical variations. For reasons we will discuss later, Orthodoxy can survive only in fairly large, close-knit communities. Where such communities existed, as in New York or Chicago or Baltimore, Orthodoxy held out much more successfully against the inroads of Reform.

These inroads not only displeased the devout Orthodox but were highly distasteful to many of the Reform leaders. The increasing strength of their movement was no compensation to them for the social disadvantages. Those vulgar Russians were not only competing with them in business and applying for membership in their clubs, but threatening to pollute their relations with God Himself! Certain German Jewish leaders decided that the way to prevent this disaster was to provide the East European Jews with a well-financed American Orthodoxy, an establishment of their own that would keep them out of the Reform establishment. With this purpose in mind, important German Jewish money in 1886 founded the Jewish Theological Seminary.

There are few cases on record of a Frankenstein monster which escaped so successfully from the control of its creator. Instead of pulling the East Europeans back to Orthodoxy, where they belonged, the JTS became the center for a whole new branch of American Judaism, the Conservative movement —a movement which grew faster than the other two and has ended up challenging Reform for supremacy in the American Jewish world.

Today it seems clear that something like Conservative Judaism had to happen. In order to enjoy the blessings of modern life without feeling cut off from the old ways, the East European Jew needed something more flexible and pragmatic than what Orthodoxy or Reform could offer him. The architects of Conservative Judaism provided him with a blueprint for compromise, complete with theological arguments and Talmudic precedents. They declared, just as the Orthodox do, that the Mosaic law can never be considered obsolete, because it was revealed to us directly by God; but they also declared that the law contains within itself certain principles which allow us to adapt it to changing circumstances—like the United States Constitution, which contains the machinery for its own amendment. When we amend the Mosaic law—even when we drop a *mitzvah* completely, as the Conservatives have sometimes done —we justify ourselves not by saying, "We're bigger than the law," but by saying, "We're obeying the law."

A further refinement of this philosophy was devised by Mordecai Kaplan, and led to his forming the one genuine splinter group in the movement. Kaplan took all the Conservative ideas—that Torah can be reinterpreted in terms of modern life, that Judaism is not only a set of laws but a "feeling"— and carried them to a logical conclusion which he called Reconstructionism. The Reconstructionists reject the belief that the law was revealed by God. God never actually spoke to the Israelites; they were a primitive people and had to invent that story in order to explain their world and justify their religious experiences. We, the descendants of that people, are permitted to do exactly what they did—explain the world *we* live in, and in *our* own terms. What the Israelites did hand down to us are certain texts, holidays, traditional heroes, rituals—Kaplan calls these sancta—whose significance changes at different periods of history. Our heritage from the ancient Hebrews is not *halakah,* but these sancta.

What this philosophy does is to remove Torah, and therefore God himself, from the center of Judaism, and put the people in His place. And in fact, it was Kaplan who popularized the now-ubiquitous word "peoplehood." He preached his ideas first to the Society for the Advancement of Judaism, which he founded in 1922. Its synagogue on the West Side in New York is still the center of Reconstructionism; Kaplan, in his eighties now, attends Sabbath services there every Saturday. Today the Federation of Reconstructionist Synagogues has ten members in the United States, three of them belonging at the same time to Conservatism's United Synagogues of America.

At a recent Hillel leadership conference it was the panel on Reconstructionism that drew the largest attendance and caused the most excitement among the college students. Yet it has never really caught on among rank-and-file Conservatives. It is too intellectual, too closely reasoned, too Talmudic even in its rejection of Torah. It sounds too much like what it is, the brainchild of a rabbi. Conservatism is designed to please laymen, not experts. It depends less on pure logic, more on instinct and feeling, than either of its competitors.

In its spectacular success over the last sixty years, Conservatism was helped along by several external factors. The snobbishness of some Reform leaders closed off that movement to many East Europeans who might otherwise have joined it. The stubbornness and fear of the old Orthodox rabbis prevented Young Israel from gaining a strong foothold in the crucial early years. And one completely fortuitous circumstance, that the JTS was located in New York and Hebrew Union College was located in Cincinnati, gave Conservatism a power base in the heart of American Jewry. Reform still hasn't recovered from this tactical disadvantage. But perhaps the most important factor was the organizational genius of Conservatism, Rabbi Solomon Schechter. It was he who took the JTS out of Reform German hands in the early 1900s. Later he breathed life into the Rabbinical Assembly, the organization of Conservative rabbis which had been formed in 1900. And in 1913 he helped to found the United Synagogues of America, the powerful Conservative synagogual body.

And so, by the early 1920s, when immigration from the Old World was choked off, Judaism in the New World had divided itself into three clear-cut parts. Each division had its own philosophy, its own organizational structure, and its own leaders. Each was ready to do battle for the souls of the American Jews.

———◆◆———

The battle is still going on. Statistically, as of this moment, it seems to be a stand-off. The theory (all Jewish statistics, as we have seen, are highly theoretical) is that over a million people are affiliated, either directly or through their families, with each division of American Judaism. This means that about 60 percent of the Jews in America belong to synagogues of one kind or another.

Despite statistical discrepancies, one thing is certain: affiliation is growing in all three movements. There are eight hundred Conservative synagogues, four times as many as there were in 1950; six hundred Reform synagogues, twice as many as in 1950; and according to the sociologist Charles Liebman, in his exhaustive study of American Orthodoxy for the *American Jewish Yearbook*, there are sixteen hundred Orthodox synagogues—a remarkable figure when we remember that, according to what all the experts said a few decades ago, Orthodoxy ought to be dead by now. Its eulogy was spoken over and over again, yet today it is not only alive but supports ambitious projects like the Albert Einstein Medical School and Yeshiva University, which raised $7.5 million in 1964.

The three movements in American Judaism draw their strength from somewhat different sections of the country and segments of society. Orthodoxy flourishes in those big cities which attracted many East Europeans early in the century. Its center, therefore, is New York. About nine hundred Orthodox synagogues are located in New York State; most of the money raised by Yeshiva was New York money. Another important center of Orthodoxy is Baltimore, the location of one of the largest seminaries that grants rabbinical ordination, a real competitor to Yeshiva's theological school. In San Francisco, on the other hand, where few East Europeans came, there is practically no Orthodoxy.

Socially and economically Orthodoxy has improved itself immensely since the war. Most of the Orthodox today are American-born and college-educated. They are likely to be young businessmen, lawyers, accountants, very Americanized in manner and appearance. There are some Orthodox millionaires now—Cleveland has two such families, the Ratners and the Stones, which may account for the unusual financial support which Cleveland Jewry gives to religious education. There are also Orthodox intellectuals now. The Association of Orthodox Jewish Scientists, with five hundred members, just held its tenth annual convention; Route 128 to Boston, the college circuit, is lined with Young Israel synagogues, many of them full of people from the academic world. One rallying cry of contemporary American Othodoxy was sounded by Rabbi Immanuel Jakobovits, of New York's Fifth Avenue Synagogue, when he resigned to become Chief Rabbi of Great Britain: "My challenge here has been to make Orthodoxy elegant and fashionable and to show that you don't have to live on the Lower East Side in squalor to be a strictly traditional Jew." [1]

As yet Orthodoxy hasn't quite achieved this lofty aim. In the social and economic rat race it still runs third. The average Orthodox young man may be a college graduate, but chances are he attended a city college, not an Ivy League school. And the offices of the various Orthodox organizations, most of them located in the unfashionable part of lower Fifth Avenue in New York, are shabby and slightly run-down, compared with

the opulence of Reform and Conservative offices. The Orthodox have more money today than they ever had, but still not
enough, apparently, to put up a front.

Reform also flourishes in big cities, does less well in the
suburbs, but really hits its stride in middle-sized communities
in the Midwest, the Far West, and the South. One reason is
that Reform came first to many of these communities and
established itself firmly among the oldest families. If a community has shown noticeable growth in recent years, then it may
have acquired a Conservative synagogue too; if its population
has remained fairly stable, then it probably can't support more
than the synagogue which happened to be there first. This is
especially true down South, where Reform has deep philosophical roots. Even in a city the size of New Orleans, Reform
domination has never been seriously jeopardized. The Orthodox there were unable to muster enough support to keep a day
school going, and Conservatism is still struggling to establish
itself.

Once Reform had all the money and all the social prestige.
It still has a lot of both. The old German families (what's left of
them) are Reform. The chief rabbi of Temple Emanu-el in
New York is very touchy when the wealth of his congregation
is mentioned to him; understandably he has grown tired of
hearing about the subject. In Los Angeles, though Conservative affiliation is growing and Reform affiliation is dropping,
the most prominent Reform temple is still unquestionably the
high-status social leader.[2] It is known as "the Hillcrest of temples," though it probably isn't as hard to get into as that highly
exclusive country club. In New Orleans the Reform Temple
Sinai has such rigid social standards that one lady, unable to
break into the hierarchy, became a Unitarian out of desperation.

Mostly, however, the East Europeans have taken over
Reform just as they have taken over everything else; their first
wedge was the Reform rabbinate, and now they are as likely as
not to be the presidents of synagogues. This mixture between
the new East European blood and what remains of the old
German blood is a volatile one, and sometimes causes small
explosions within the movement. Many of these have to do
with politics. Reform today is very liberal, on the whole: Reform rabbis marched in Mississippi; it was the first branch of
Judaism to form a social action committee; both the UAHC

and the Central Conference of Rabbis have issued strong statements opposing the war in Vietnam. Yet Reform in the old days, under German domination, leaned to the right; those solid substantial burghers never doubted the sanctity of private enterprise. And so, many of the most distinguished Jewish reactionaries today—Lewis Strauss and Lessing Rosenwald, for example—are active in Reform congregations.

Nevertheless, the financial and social supremacy of Reform has been challenged since the war by the Conservatives. Their power base is the suburbs, where the largest number of new synagogues have appeared; the first synagogue in a new suburb is almost always Conservative. If the population in a particular area has been growing, you may be sure that Conservatism is growing there too. And these new suburbanites, of course, are precisely the people who have made money since the war.

The Conservatives can point to some impressive figures to confirm their success story. The JTS in recent years has raised $35 million—not for buildings, but simply to increase its faculty and improve its facilities. Last year it started on its first building drive, and has collected $8 million so far. In 1964, before its present building drive, the JTS raised $4.5 million; in the same year the Combined Reform Campaign, which was raising money for all the institutions of Reform Judaism together, produced only $2.4 million.[3]

More significant than the money it can raise is the incredible bustling activity of the Conservative establishment. It publishes the best magazines; it produces the best radio and television programs; it snares the most exciting lecturers; it runs —as I can testify personally—by far the best dinners. And because it came on the scene late, unencumbered by internal rivalries from the past, it exercises the tightest control over individual synagogues and rabbis; there is less dissension in the ranks of Conservatism. As a result the Seminary Empire, as it is sometimes called, exudes a spirit of success and self-confidence that I have detected nowhere among the other two divisions. The Orthodox are dedicated, intense, exhilarated by their sense of fighting an uphill fight. The Reformers are earnest and just a bit weary. But the Conservatives are the ones who have destiny in their pocket—or seem, anyway, to believe that they do.

But it is easy, in the dazzle of all these organizational complications, to lose sight of the purpose behind them. What sets these organizations in motion is a large number of people striving to worship God. We must now examine some of the specific forms of worship which each branch of Judaism requires, and how its members put these requirements into practice—often a very different thing.

VI.

Halakic Smorgasbord

The Jewish laws that most people have heard about are those applying to food, the laws of *kashruth*. There is something mystifying about the pious Jew's drive to "eat kosher." None of the *mitzvahs* are more inconvenient to obey and more difficult to justify on logical grounds; yet they have held on stubbornly through the centuries, while many other *mitzvahs*, no more absurd than they, have fallen into obscurity. Technically *kashruth* is no more important than any other aspect of halakah, but in fact it has a special way of nagging at the pious Jew's intellect and emotions.

The main dietary laws are these: Certain foods are forbidden at all times, including any meat that comes from the pig and all kinds of shellfish. Meat and poultry that aren't forbidden must be ritually slaughtered in a kosher manner, a procedure that involves, among other things, the killing of the animal while it is insensible but not yet dead, and the careful draining of its blood. Finally, to eat meat and dairy products together at the same meal is highly un-kosher, or *tref*. After a pious Jew has eaten an egg or drunk a glass of milk, he must wait a certain number of hours before he dares to eat a steak.

Constant caution is required. Dishes, glasses, and utensils which have been used for meat cannot be used for dairy foods; they might absorb tiny particles of steak or milk, and these might still be there during the next meal, unseen, untasted, treacherously producing the forbidden mixture. A careful housewife always keeps two sets of dishes in her kitchen, and if by accident a dish should be used at the wrong meal, she must either throw it away or subject it to a complicated ritual purification.

Orthodoxy requires its adherents to obey these rules strictly. It offers no concessions, except for urgent reasons of health. This makes life for the Orthodox Jew often difficult and sometimes impossible. Traveling, for instance, is even more of a nuisance for him than for most people. Usually he must carry his food with him wherever he goes—including paper plates and plastic utensils.

The complexities of *kashruth* have much to do with the location of Orthodox synagogues. The reason why the Orthodox tend to congregate in big cities is that nowhere else are they likely to find kosher butchers. This difficulty has made Orthodox migration to the suburbs much slower than that of other Jews. Orthodox families who move into suburban areas where no community of their fellows exists are admired as pioneers. Their friends and relations couldn't be more concerned over them, couldn't worry more about the hardships they're enduring, if they were living in the wilds of Africa.

When we consider the sacrifices involved in the keeping of *kashruth*, it seems natural to wonder how many Orthodox Jews cheat a little from time to time. Studies have been made in many communities and have come up with variable results. They show that anywhere from 25 to 60 percent of the Orthodox don't buy kosher meat regularly, that anywhere from 15 to 47 percent don't have two sets of dishes in the house.[1] All in all, though, my impression is that the instinct against eating *tref* runs very deep in the Orthodox Jew. I asked an Orthodox boy at Yale, brought up in a pious, comparatively poor Brooklyn family, whether he had ever succumbed to the temptation of finding out what bacon tasted like. He answered, "When I was a kid, a bunch of friends and I went to Manhattan once and tried some bacon. I didn't like it much, but I'm glad I did it. Now that I've tasted it, I can make an intelligent choice—I can reject it on the basis of experience."

The Reform Jew has emancipated himself from this instinct. The laws of *kashruth* are among those which have been declared unnecessary for him in this day and age. He enjoys his ham and eggs without a twinge of guilt. Curiously, though he feels no distaste for *tref* food, he sometimes feels a positive distaste for kosher food. "After a few days of eating kosher," one Reform rabbi said, "it's easy to understand why there is Reform Judaism."

Conservatism's approach to *kashruth* is, theoretically, the same as that of Orthodoxy. The laws are immutable; no sanction is given to the Conservative Jew to break them. But as usual in Conservatism, the rabbis lay down the laws and the laymen work out their own ways of handling them. The most common Conservative compromise is to eat kosher at home and *tref* outside. Many people follow this pattern religiously—if it is possible to use the word in this connection.

In matters of worship in the synagogue, the differences among the three divisions of Judaism are equally characteristic.

Strict Orthodoxy adheres to all the old forms of ritual. The service is conducted entirely in Hebrew. No instrumental music is allowed, and there are no female voices in the choir. The men worship with their heads covered; if they don't have a hat, the synagogue will supply them with the small skullcap known as a yarmulke. Around their necks they wear a white prayer shawl, the tallis; in the old-fashioned synagogues it can reach all the way down to the ankles, though in most modern synagogues the *tallis* sedately stops below the shoulders.

The service itself is largely led by the cantor, and his chanting and the audience's accompaniment, often rather loud, are an important feature. At a certain point in the service the scrolls of the Torah are removed from their ark and brought forward. The Torah is the most sacred object used in the service (though it has no miraculous properties, like a saint's relics), and the silk bag which contains it is often ornately decorated with gold and silver tassels. The Torah is opened, and members of the congregation are called up to read the daily sections from it—an honor which, in the *shtetl*, often rewarded superior learning and generosity. Near the end of the service the rabbi delivers his sermon in Hebrew, Yiddish, or English, depending on the age of the congregation. At certain services the *Kaddish*, the prayer for the dead, is then spoken by recent mourners in the congregation. Services more or less like this, of varying length and intensity, are held daily, on Friday night and Saturday morning of the Sabbath, and on most of the religious holidays.

To the Orthodox Jew the style and flavor of the service are matters of great importance. If he has been exposed to the Orthodox style long enough and early enough, it may remain in his blood for the rest of his life. I have talked to many lapsed Orthodox Jews, professed atheists today, who nevertheless feel uncomfortable and impatient in a Reform temple. "This isn't the kind of Judaism I'm used to," they say.

The most curious and controversial aspect of Orthodox worship is the rule that men and women must not sit together. In fact, the women must not even be visible to the men during the service. In the *shtibl*—the small old-fashioned East European synagogue that was once common on the Lower East Side —the women sit at the rear, separated by a full-length screen which has a couple of peepholes in it, so that a few of the lucky ones can see what's going on. In a modern edifice with a large auditorium, the women may sit in the balcony, their seats pulled back far enough from the railing so that they can't be glimpsed by the men below.

In the *shtetl* this separation of the sexes was merely one manifestation of the general feeling that women have a subordinate place in Judaism. Their place is essential, and in certain home ceremonies they must take the lead, but still it's subordinate. The modern Orthodox, however, can't bring himself to say this in so many words, and so he has come up with other justifications for separate seating. Rabbi Ephraim Sturm, the director of Young Israel, explained it to me this way: "Prayer means searching your soul. It's an intimate activity. I just might be able to do it next to my wife, but can I do it next to yours? That would be too distracting. Could I lie on the psychiatrist's couch and pour out my soul with another man's wife right there? Group therapy is no good for religion."

The Orthodox Jew's need to devise rationalizations like this suggests that he feels a certain uneasiness about separate seating. And the fact is that a great many Orthodox synagogues, particularly outside New York, don't have it. The rabbis want it, and do what they can to encourage it, but the resistance from laymen continues to be great.

In Reform temples (which are sometimes called synagogues, just as Conservative synagogues are sometimes called temples) women sit downstairs among the men, seeing and being seen, and presumably distracting everyone else's husband from his prayers. What does it matter, an Orthodox might say, since the kind of praying that goes on isn't worth paying attention to anyway? Actually the format of the service is not very different from Orthodoxy. But there is much less Hebrew; in some temples it is restricted to one particularly holy prayer and the *Kaddish;* in other temples the rabbi reads a good deal of Hebrew, but the congregation responds in English only. Instruments are permitted to accompany the singing, and the choir will include women's voices—sometimes gentile women's voices. Men don't have to wear hats or tallises while they pray, and the custom of calling them up to read from the Torah is sometimes allowed to lapse—or worse, it is polluted by the inclusion of women. It is the rabbi now who conducts the service, and the cantor is relegated to a strictly performing status. Daily services have been abandoned. Nevertheless, the bringing of the Torah from its ark and the reading from it are as much the heart and soul of the Reform service as they are of the Orthodox.

The Reform philosophy, with its emphasis on freedom and individual judgment, produces many variations from one temple to another. One rabbi wears a tallis and a yarmulke and looks just like an Orthodox; another rabbi wears a black suit and a white bow tie, the official uniform of the Protestant clergy. Some temples have confirmation ceremonies for the fifteen-year-olds of the Sunday School class, but absolutely refuse to perform the traditional ceremony of bar mitzvah, wherein a thirteen-year-old boy, standing before the congregation all alone, reads passages in Hebrew from the Torah and symbolically enters into his manhood. Other Reform temples —most of them nowadays—bar mitzvah their boys with all the trimmings. In the North so-called "Classical Reform" is regarded with suspicion or hostility, but down South it still has a holy aura in many places. A typical figure is the middle-aged southern Jewish lady who, when the rabbi says, "Let us pray," bows her head and assumes a devotional posture just like a worshiper in a Protestant church. Hebrew has an unpleasant sound to her, and she would walk out of temple if she heard the cantor chanting; yet her piety is intense, and she never misses a service.

One thing all Reform services have in common, however

—an overall atmosphere of decorum and dignity. There is nothing "foreign" about them. Indeed this was the original attraction of Reform to the more successful East European immigrants. The Orthodox synagogue seemed dirty, shabby, unruly, un-American. "It wasn't the sort of place," one of them has said, "that you wanted to bring your wife and kids to." And not just your wife and kids; many businessmen turned to Reform so that they could, without embarrassment, invite their gentile associates to their daughter's wedding.

Much of the Orthodox criticism of Reform has been directed against this "un-Jewish" atmosphere of decorum. And Reform itself is made uneasy by the charge. It has become much less classical in the last ten years. Gone are such anachronisms as the temple in San Francisco which required men to take off their hats, and if they refused, the usher would escort them out. No leader of the Reform movement laughs any more at the old joke about the temple which was so Reform that it closed for the Jewish holidays.

Among the Conservatives, synagogue worship is, of course, a compromise. Conservative Jews, most of whom made their money later than Reform Jews, were motivated by the same desire for decorum and dignity. But they were motivated also by their nostalgic attachment to the old rituals. The result is a service in which there is less Hebrew than the Orthodox but more than the Reform, in which men are frequently called to the Torah (and occasionally women), in which the cantor doesn't quite run things but serves as a kind of assistant stage manager, in which the mellow notes of an organ and the sounds of female voices may or may not blend with the choir's singing. Tallises and yarmulkes are required for the men in the congregation. Services are often, if not always, held every day, though the rabbi is just as likely as not to stay away from them.

Men and women, however, are not separated during services. The popularity of Conservative Judaism was fostered even more by this fact than by the urge to decorum. In America the immigrant woman discovered that she was equal to her husband, and this discovery made her reluctant to accept inequality in the synagogue. In many cases she was willing to hold on to every single one of the trappings of Orthodoxy— except this one. Where no accommodating Orthodox synagogue could be found, she usually steered her husband and family into Conservatism.

A major concession which Conservatism has made to women is the ceremony of bas mitzvah. It corresponds to bar mitzvah (all Conservative boys, of course, are bar mitzvahed), but it is performed by thirteen-year-old girls. The logic behind it is obscure. Are they supposed to be entering into womanhood, as their brothers do into manhood? In fact, it isn't a logical development at all, but a peculiarly Conservative adjustment between the Orthodox rejection of women and the Reform rejection of bar mitzvah. The ceremony has done well enough among the rank-and-file, but not spectacularly. One woman explained to me why her daughter isn't going to have a bas mitzvah: "For my son we'll give a big party on his bar mitzvah. For my daughter we'll give a big party on her wedding. Is it fair that she should get two parties?"

———•◦•———

Outside of the synagogue the *halakic* habits of the three divisions of Judaism vary just as greatly. For example, a blessing is supposed to be said after every meal. Conservative Jews often say it decorously, getting it over as quickly as possible. Reform Jews seldom say it, except at large public dinners. Orthodox Jews say a blessing all the time, in a manner that can give a small shock to somebody who isn't used to it. I attended an informal luncheon at Yeshiva University. At the table with me were a dozen distinguished scholars who engaged in an abstruse discussion of Jewish history and literature throughout the meal. Then, after the coffee, it was time to say the blessing, and in an instant they all turned into swaying, muttering, chanting East Europeans. On and on they went, each man bobbing his head, rolling his eyes, improvising in Hebrew on a theme of his own. There was no time limit. Several of them came to a stop, but the others didn't notice; their prayers weren't finished yet. Those who had stopped, however, turned to one another and resumed, with as much enthusiasm as before, the scholarly discussion they had just interrupted.

But these are modern Orthodox. The ceremonials of Hasidic Jews, the ultra-Orthodox, are much wilder and stranger. At a Hasidic wedding party the men and women sit at different tables. After the service the bride walks several times around the groom, with her face turned away from him. Then they are taken off to a room and allowed to spend one hour by themselves. Then they are brought back, and the dancing begins—

joyous unrestrained dancing, in which the sexes never mingle. The Orthodox Jew who described this ceremony to me was horrified by it. "There was that beautiful girl! And that groom —dirty, no tie, a beard already! And later on they shaved her head!"

A married woman is supposed to shave her head, according to the law, and then wear a wig (a *sheitel*) for the rest of her life. Few Orthodox women nowadays do it—and I can imagine what a Reform or Conservative woman would say if the suggestion were made to her. A married woman is also supposed to abstain from sexual relations for a week after menstruation, and not resume them again until she has been purified in the ritual bath, the *mikveh*, which is operated by the community. There are about 177 of these in the United States, and Charles Liebman thinks the number is rising—but I cannot believe the rise is substantial.[2] The observance is nonexistent among Reform and Conservative women, and my impression is that many Orthodox women find it distasteful.

The wearing of the yarmulke is another custom that is practiced in different ways by the three divisions. Reform Jews hardly practice it at all, unless they do so out of courtesy in the home of an Orthodox Jew. Even so, I have seen a Classical Reform rabbi politely refuse to put on a yarmulke when he sat down for dinner at an Orthodox table; his principles wouldn't allow him to. On the other hand, Orthodox Jewish men are supposed to wear their skullcaps not just while praying and eating, but at all times—even when they go to bed. Conservative Jews wear their yarmulkes in the synagogue, but seldom anywhere else.

The three branches of Judaism reveal their characteristic attitudes most clearly in the celebration of religious holidays. These are *mitzvahs* like everything else, and the Torah tells us in great detail how to observe them.

The holidays that are celebrated with least variation by the three groups are Rosh Hashanah (the New Year) and Yom Kippur, the Day of Atonement. They come about a week apart, and are the most solemn of the holidays. At this time of year the synagogues are full—often with Orthodox, Conservative, or Reform Jews who never set foot in one at any other time. On Yom Kippur the Jew must eat and drink nothing for twenty-four hours, from sundown to sundown. (If he is really conscientious he won't even brush his teeth, for fear that he might swallow some water.) This commandment to fast on Yom Kippur is recognized just as fully by Reform as by Orthodoxy and cannot believe the rise is substantial.[2] The observance is non-ally obey it.

The holiday that is celebrated with the greatest variation is the Sabbath. From sundown on Friday to sundown on Saturday the pious Jew stops working and spends his time in prayer and relaxation. He goes to synagogue Saturday morning if he's a purist, or Friday night if he's more "modern." But mostly he stays home with his family. His wife comes into her own on the Sabbath too; it is she who lights the candles and says the blessing in the Friday night ceremony which ushers in the holiday. To the true believer the Sabbath can be an emotional experience that becomes the cornerstone of his life. One young Orthodox father, a chemist for an oil company, said to me, "You can't imagine how good I feel when the Sabbath comes. It's a time when, no matter what's on my mind, I forget it all and enjoy my family. If every Jew knew what the Sabbath could offer him, we wouldn't have so many neuroses."

Nevertheless, for the conscientious Orthodox the Sabbath can create a host of problems. He's not supposed to do any work—but "work" is interpreted to mean an extraordinary number of apparently effortless human activities. He mustn't, for instance, turn on the lights or the gas, because to operate any kind of machine is work. (A current topic of discussion is whether the deaf can turn on hearing aids on the Sabbath.) He mustn't carry money. He mustn't engage in any commercial transactions, like buying a newspaper or a pack of cigarettes. He mustn't ride in any vehicle. Not only must he not do any of these things on the Sabbath, he must not ask any other Jew to do them for him. On the other hand, he can enjoy the benefits of gentile labor; the gentile, because he doesn't belong to the covenant, isn't endangering his immortal soul by breaking the law.

The Sabbath, in fact, provides more opportunities than half a dozen other holidays put together for the legalistic talents of the Orthodox Jew. He takes an intense intellectual satisfaction in calculating how certain everyday acts can be performed without breaking the Sabbath. He pins a handkerchief to his shirt; thus it becomes a part of his clothing, and he won't break the rule against carrying things. He puts an automatic timing device on his TV set, so he can watch the Saturday football game without actually operating the machine. The owners of Grossinger's, the famous kosher hotel in the Catskills, are not supposed to do business on the Sabbath; yet clearly it would be impossible to close down the hotel and send away the guests every weekend. So every Friday night before sundown Jennie Grossinger "sells" the hotel to one of her gentile employees for the sum of one dollar—and every Saturday night after sundown she buys it back again.

But if no legalistic loophole can be found, the Orthodox Jew is obliged to keep the Sabbath just the same, no matter how much inconvenience or disadvantage this entails. Charles Liebman estimates that fewer than 200,000—about 20 percent of all Orthodox Jews in America—actually have the patience or the piety to do this.[3] I am inclined to think that his estimate is high. There is an old joke which asks the question, "What is the difference between an Orthodox Jew and a Reform Jew?" The answer is, "About three blocks"—that being how far away from the synagogue the Orthodox Jew parks his car.

The real difference between the two divisions on the matter of Sabbath observance is that the Orthodox Jew worries about his lapses, while the Reform Jew doesn't. Though he still celebrates the Sabbath in temple—mostly at Friday night services—and still lights the candles at Friday dinner, he has completely abandoned all the traditions about not working, not riding, not carrying things. One Reform temple in the East holds its business meetings on Friday night after the Sabbath service—"so the annual meeting may be entirely free for social affairs."

Conservatism, like Orthodoxy, accepts the principle of not working on the Sabbath, but isn't nearly as far-ranging in its ideas of what work is. The movement has found it particularly impractical, with its large suburban membership, to prohibit riding in cars. So a few years ago the law committee of the JTS ruled that walking to synagogue on the Sabbath, though preferable in terms of *halakah*, is not essential. Long before this ruling, however, Conservative Jews worked out their bit of pragmatic *halakah;* most of them ride to synagogue on the Sabbath, but expect their rabbi to walk. If they pass him on the way, they aren't likely to offer him a lift. A pious man like that

—they wouldn't insult him! Or as one rabbi gently puts it, "They let me be pious, and I let them be free."

———— •·• ————

Each of the three movements in American Judaism represents a compromise, a fairly consistent approach toward the problem of obeying the law in the modern world. Yet it must be admitted that the vast majority of American Jews go even further. Whatever their affiliations might be, their actual religious practice is infused by a kind of muddled but determined individualism. Within those great official compromises of Orthodox, Reform, and Conservative, each individual works out his own peculiar little compromises, most of them totally illegitimate by any conceivable Talmudic standard.

Observe, for example, the strange and various ways in which holidays and special occasions are celebrated. Hanukkah, an unimportant holiday from the *halakic* standpoint, is popular among people who observe little else—because Jewish children are entitled to "their Christmas." On the High Holy Days thousands of people who neither fast nor go to synagogue nor repent a single sin nevertheless wouldn't dream of working, shopping, or taking in a movie. Jewish brides march down the aisle to the Wedding March from *Lohengrin,* though purists from all three establishments are constantly pointing out that Wagner was a notorious anti-Semite and suggesting substitutes from the works of Felix Mendelssohn; but after all, say the brides and their mothers, "everybody" in America gets married to *Lohengrin.* Grandma's funeral must be strictly Orthodox, except that her family won't leave out the flowers; law or no law, what's a funeral without flowers?

Equally strange and various—and irrelevant to the official differences among the three branches of Judaism—are the million and one peculiar compromises devised by individuals in following the dietary laws. One man, a Reform Jew, eats seafood but not pork at home, and pork but no seafood outside. One traveling salesman will eat anything in hotel dining rooms, but has scruples about ordering *tref* food from room service. A Conservative rabbi who teaches at Columbia University lunches regularly at the faculty club, and maintains his sense of dietary purity by always removing the frankfurters from the lentil soup. The president of an Orthodox synagogue takes his family out for lobster dinner every Sunday—"but I wouldn't do it on Saturday," he insists. And the oddest phenomenon of all is that many people who want to eat kosher food also want it to look as if it were *tref*. Thus Grossinger's will give you "bacon" and eggs for breakfast, the "bacon" being made out of strips of corn meal, and catering firms will serve "seafood" canapés with the halibut carefully prepared so that it looks like crabmeat.

This *halakic* smorgasbord seems bewildering until we grasp its underlying principle. Each individual's notion of what Judaism ought to be is determined by that familiar inner conflict which we find in other phases of his life—his drive to be an American versus his drive to keep some hold on the old traditions. And so, regardless of the official views of the three religious establishments, every man has his own approach. He decides for himself what he owes to America and what he owes to Torah—and because this decision, whatever it may be, doesn't really satisfy him, he keeps changing it. All the time, of course, he laughs at himself for his inconsistency. But he never quite settles the matter with either half of himself.

VII.

"Give Us the Child—"

One of the most important of the *mitzvahs* commands the Jew to educate his children in the law. All three branches of American Judaism attempt to perform this *mitzvah*. They all share the belief that the way to keep young American Jews from leaving the fold is to give them more and better religious education. They start disagreeing, however, on what kind of religious education will do the job best.

To the Orthodox, nothing will work except the day school, the yeshiva (not to be confused with Yeshiva, the university). Children who aren't kept in a "Jewish atmosphere" constantly, who are permitted to spend any large segment of their time at "gentile" schools, have little chance of surviving as Jews. They won't learn enough about Judaism, and the "contaminating influences" will have too much opportunity to work on them. Torah Umesorah, the National Society for Hebrew Day Schools, provides advice, information, and supervision for any school that requests them. According to its figures there are now 69,000 children in 274 Orthodox day schools on the elementary level and another 105 high schools—about half of them in New York City. The number has been increasing; in 1955 there were only forty-seven day schools, and in 1966 there were twenty-one more than in the previous year.

To send a child to such a school requires some sacrifice. The yearly tuition for the smallest, shabbiest yeshiva in a lower-middle-class neighborhood is not likely to be less than $300. It isn't unusual for $700 to be charged, and the Ramaz School, which serves wealthy Orthodox in Manhattan, charges $1,000. Yet most of these children come from nonobservant Orthodox families, and many don't even have Orthodox affiliations.

Parents are willing to make the sacrifice for a variety of reasons: they want the child to be a better Jew than they themselves are; they dislike the public schools; they don't want their little girl spending too much time with gentile boys; the local public school just became integrated. One thing seems clear—only a minority of the parents who send their child to an Orthodox day school know what he's getting there.

A liberal school like Ramaz has a very different orientation from a Hasidic school in Williamsburg, yet the underlying principle of the curriculum is the same for all of them. The day is divided between religious studies in the morning and secular studies in the afternoon. In one school I observed, a school that stands philosophically halfway between the left and right wing, classes run straight through from nine to five, with only half an hour for lunch. From five to six is gym period—for anyone who still has the energy. In addition, students on the high school level are encouraged to come to night sessions several times a week for more intensive religious study. School is open every day of the week except Saturday—and on Friday it closes early, so that students can get home for the Sabbath. But twenty-four hours a week of religious study, plus extra night sessions, still don't seem enough to the rabbis who run this school. Each student in the high school must pledge himself to continue his religious studies for one more year after graduation, before he goes on to college. This extra year, during which he will concentrate on nothing but the Torah and the Talmud, is considered necessary to arm him effectively against the perils that await him on the campus. "The more they know, the better," says the principal of the school. "Their very first lecture at college can be dangerous."

Both boys and girls go to this school. They occupy the same building, but never the same classrooms. At lunchtime they eat in separate cafeterias in the basement. The school library keeps to a rigid schedule—boys are allowed in at certain times only, girls at different times. In a more liberal yeshiva this separation wouldn't be so strictly maintained; on the other hand, a more right-wing yeshiva would be horrified at the idea of having the boys and girls under the same roof, even though they never see each other.

In most yeshivas "English" (a generic name for all secular studies) consists of the usual subjects. The religious curriculum involves a bit of Jewish history, a bit of Hebrew, some instruction in ritual, and a great deal of reading and discussion of the Talmud. The proportions will vary from school to school, but the backbone of the religious program at all yeshivas is the Talmud—in its two parts: the Mishna, and the Gemara, which is a collection of commentaries that later rabbis made on the Mishna. Though the student usually begins his Talmudic studies at the age of ten or eleven, he never gets through the whole book, not even by the time he graduates from high school—unless perhaps he belongs to the Satmar Hasidim, whose children begin their studies of the Talmud when they are three years old.

The subject matter of any particular Talmud class seldom has much connection with what the students are studying elsewhere or with what may be going on in the world at the time. It is determined by nothing except the page in Mishna or Gemara which the class happens to come to that day. A class of fourteen-year-olds might discuss the moral responsibility of a father who, while lawfully beating his son for disobedience, became overenthusiastic and accidentally killed the boy; a class for seniors might consider the various conditions under which a high priest of the temple is permitted to give sanctuary to a criminal. I sat in on one class where the youngest pupils in the school tried to establish why a certain minor biblical figure was justified in executing, without benefit of trial, a Jewish soldier who was about to marry a Midianite woman.

In reading from the Talmud the students and teachers use the traditional singsong voice. Discussions tend to be lively, energetic, and highly ingenious. The students are encouraged not only to talk, but to disagree with the teacher and with the Talmud itself. I heard one teacher snap at a boy angrily, "Don't be bashful already! Stop pussyfooting! Take a stand!" Despite this freedom and intensity, however, one little warning is continually being sounded by the teachers. "Make a strong case for your point of view," a teacher said to one of his brightest boys, "but don't make it too strong, because in the end, don't forget, we'll have to come out the way it says in the Mishna." This is the fundamental philosophy of Orthodox religious education.

The student is encouraged to develop his powers of reasoning, to let his mind range free; but he must also be made to understand that Torah is immutable and infallible; his mind can't ever range beyond that.

I wasn't surprised, then, to hear from the principal of a mildly right-wing school how it deals with children who have religious doubts. "We care very deeply for all our children," he said, and I could believe it, because this small round-faced man in his sixties was the picture of kindliness. "We observe every one of them carefully from the day they enter the school. Individual attention—that's essential to our success. The symptoms of doubt usually show up early in a child; we can usually catch it before it's too late. If the doubt continues, though, well, sometimes the child has to be dropped. We try to do it gently—we don't want to hurt his feelings—but it has to be done. Frankly, we can't afford the luxury of mavericks here."

This particular yeshiva is a successful one. The proof is that many of its youngest students are the children of parents who went there themselves. Even so, it faces problems that are common to all Orthodox day schools. The first problem is money. Costs are rising all the time, and its efforts to keep its tuition down grow more desperate every year. Money is a particularly nagging problem when it comes to finding qualified teachers. There aren't many men who know Talmud well enough to teach it. I was impressed by the quality of the teaching at this school—and amazed to hear that its top salary is $5,000 a year. Apparently it has been lucky. I have heard students from other yeshivas complain bitterly about the "idiots" who teach them—and especially about that great inherited burden of the day school movement, the old-fashioned Hebrew teacher, relic of an age when the most common method of getting Talmud into the heads of school children was to beat it in.

An even greater problem is what one rabbi calls "the cultural schizophrenia" of the yeshiva. There is constant debate as to which should get more attention, the secular or the religious curriculum. On this point disagreements often arise between the men who run the school and the parents who send their children there. Parents, no matter how devout, are generally concerned that the secular education should be a good one. They want their child to go to college, to become a doctor or a lawyer or a teacher. Within the yeshiva movement, however, there are many people who more or less consciously resent the fact that their school has to supply a secular education at all. They yearn for the days of the *shtetl* when *nothing* was taught except Mishna and Gemara, when a good Jewish boy's mind wasn't polluted with all these *tref* books and all this worldly information.

Those days are dead and gone, but the attitude remains and subtly infects the atmosphere of most yeshivas. It is the most constant cause of complaint by students who have attended them. "In my last year they kept pressuring me to go on to Yeshiva University instead of an Ivy League school. I should've been valedictorian of the class—I had the highest marks and all—but they picked this other guy because *he* was going on to Yeshiva." "This old Talmud teacher kept saying to us, 'Don't read philosophers. Philosophers are bad.' He kept telling us we shouldn't do our homework from the English classes."

In many yeshivas this attitude is stronger even than the traditional Jewish distaste for censorship. One principal explained to me the dangers involved in using the biology text which New York State required. "It's shot through with evolution," he said. "But we have no choice, or we'd lose our license. All we can do is order the books, then cut out the offensive pages."

The wonder is that so many yeshivas, despite their cultural schizophrenia, give their students such a good secular education. Half a dozen students from the Yeshiva of Brooklyn have applied to Yale every year for the last five years—and not one of them has been turned down. Neither Andover nor Exeter has as good a record as that.

The Conservative movement also believes in day schools, on the principle that the more education you give the Jewish child, the more chance he has to "survive." They are late in the field, however. So far there are only twenty-three Conservative day schools (they carefully don't call themselves yeshivas). They are very expensive. The Solomon Schechter School in Queens charges $695 for kindergarten tuition, and this rises by gradual stages to $1,000 in the ninth grade, which is as far as the school goes. The reason for these high costs is that Conservative parents refuse to skimp in any way on the secular curriculum. The Schechter School has first-rate laboratories, an excellent music and art program, tape recorders, and other modern devices for teaching languages, and teachers who are trained to handle everything from child psychology to the new math. That it's doing a good job is indicated by the number of applicants it has to turn down, most of them from families that are earning about $9,000 to $10,000 a year.

The parents who send their children to Conservative day schools, then, must want to do this badly. But of necessity there still aren't many of them. Most Conservative religious education in America is provided by the Talmud Torah, the synagogue-operated school that gives six hours of instruction every week, on two afternoons and on Sunday morning. It is a system that has its defenders, among both laymen and professionals. While admitting that the Talmud Torah can't give nearly as extensive a Jewish education as the day school can, they claim that it instills high motivation in its students. The child who, after a hard day in public or private school, gives up two hours of his afternoon to learn about his religion, is making a real sacrifice, and consequently he appreciates the importance of what he's doing. Furthermore, the Talmud Torah doesn't separate him from the world as the day school does; it doesn't make him "narrow."

At the Conservative day school the curriculum is divided, as at the yeshiva, between secular and religious. At the Talmud Torah, of course, all the classes are religious. But what passes for Talmud study in a Conservative school would fill a yeshiva boy with scorn. No attempt is made to go through the book from beginning to end. Those sections are read and discussed which seem "relevant," in the eyes of the school, to modern life and contemporary Judaism. And much more time is spent on Jewish history and literature, the works of non-Talmudic philosophers, and the great pride and joy (and, some think, the obsession) of Conservative education, Hebrew.

It came as a surprise to me that the Conservatives teach Hebrew much more effectively and thoroughly than the Orthodox. Partly this reflects the Conservative leaning toward the "peoplehood" aspects of Judaism, toward Israeli songs and folk dances rather than Talmudic *pilpul*. From his first day in the Talmud Torah, at the age of nine or ten, the Conservative child starts being drilled in Hebrew. By the time he's thirteen or fourteen he will be able to read the most difficult Hebrew literature. But with characteristic practicality, Conservative parents measure the real success of a school by its students' ability to speak the language. The child who has learned Hebrew in the Talmud Torah has something definite to show for his efforts, something that can be trotted out and displayed to the world. At the Passover seder he can ask the four questions without stumbling over the words. At his bar mitzvah he can read from the Torah with a speed and agility that will make his aunts and uncles sick from envy. And when his parents take him to Tel Aviv, he'll be able to order a dinner in any restaurant.

In recent years, however, the Conservative establishment has been making an effort to give its children more—not just facts and language, but a sense of values. The JTS has sponsored the Melton Research Project, whose aim is a complete overhauling of all Conservative religious textbooks. Bible stories would be taught in such a way as to make the student aware of the ethical problems they raise, to force him to think about them and apply them to his daily life and the world he lives in. A Melton Research text on Genesis has already appeared, and is being tested in a large number of Talmud Torahs around the country.

I sat in on a class of twelve-year-olds who were using this text, and listened to a discussion of the Creation. By dint of gentle prodding from the teacher—and from the questions embodied in the text—the boys and girls (no separation is made in Conservative schools) were soon hotly debating the question, "Did God create the world, and if so, what about Darwin's theory of evolution?"

Afterward I discussed this with the young rabbi who runs this Talmud Torah. I asked him if he weren't afraid that this method of teaching would encourage the children to doubt the existence of God and the truth of Judaism. He answered, "Why not? Let them doubt now, while they're still young enough to be open to the right answers, while they still aren't prejudiced. Sure, it's a risk, but their Judaism will be stronger later on. Besides, their doubts are intellectual. Underneath we're giving them something emotional that'll make them believe in Judaism whether they know it consciously or not. We're teaching them to think about the meaning of creation, to realize that this is a wonderful life which you mustn't take for granted. We're giving them respect for life—and that *has* to lead them to faith in God."

This is the ideal. Its implementation is frustrated by the one big problem that plagues Conservative religious education. Boys are bar mitzvahed at the age of thirteen. The tension and excitement of this event inevitably encourage the idea that it represents the summit of a child's achievement, the purpose of all his religious education. After bar mitzvah age most Conservative children stop going to religious school. This is disturbing to the rabbis, for, like their Orthodox brothers, they believe that the four years or so between bar mitzvah and college are the crucial ones. Many synagogues in the last few years have set up high schools, on a six-hour-a-week basis, to fill this crucial gap, and rabbis apply as much pressure as they can to keep the thirteen-year-olds from quitting. One rabbi, for example, much in demand for letters of recommendation to college admissions boards, refuses to write one for any boy or girl who hasn't attended his Hebrew high school.

Elegant blackmail of this kind—and, in most cases, somewhat more kosher methods—seem to pay off. In synagogues where the rabbi really tries, he usually succeeds in coaxing half to three-fourths of his young people into the high school.

Where high schools don't exist, the Conservative movement gives its young people an extra chance for "safety" with its network of summer camps around the country. At the Ramah camps—there are six of them—Conservative boys and girls live together for two months in a "totally Jewish atmosphere." They pray together, eat nothing but kosher food, study in the mornings, swim and play ball, strenuously engage in Israeli folk dancing, and work on local philanthropic projects. Everyone, even the strongest critics of Conservatism from within the movement, thinks highly of the Ramah camps. The campers are enthusiastic; there are far more applications than available places. As for their contribution to "survival," the JTS points out that most of the young men whom it trains for the rabbinate have spent at least one summer at Ramah during their teen-age years.

———— •◦• ————

Reform religious education has traditionally been the whipping boy, the stepchild, the pariah. Nobody has a good

word to say for it—often not even the Reform educators themselves.

Just as the Conservative movement believes in day schools
but is obliged to concentrate on afternoon schools, so the Reform movement believes in afternoon schools but is obliged to
concentrate on Sunday schools. All Reform temples operate a
religious school for two to three hours on Sunday mornings.
Many temples also provide religious instruction on two week-
day afternoons, but on close inspection these usually turn out
to be special tutorials for three or four advanced students with
a talent and enthusiasm for Hebrew.

The inadequate Reform Sunday School belongs to the
childhood memories of all those who have gone to one. They
all remember, with a kind of wry affection, the silly middle-
aged lady with frizzly hair who read them those inane, improb-
able Bible stories; the assembly period, during which they
threw paper airplanes at one another while the rabbi intoned
about Moses; the disorderly classes from which it was so easy
to play hookey; that excruciatingly boring textbook on Jewish
history which was issued every year—because moving to a
higher grade in Sunday School didn't mean for one moment
that the work got any harder or more challenging. Especially
inept, in my own Sunday School, were the weekly Hebrew
lessons. On the first day of Hebrew class we were taught one
prayer, the *Sh'mai Yisrael*, most sacred and frequently spoken
of all the prayers. When I collected my confirmation certificate
five years later, that was still the only Hebrew prayer I could
repeat. The rest had fled from my mind as surely as the meaning of those oddly-shaped Hebrew letters.

Even though the Union of American Hebrew Congregations is doing its best to raise the standards (among other
precautions, teachers must be licensed now), its director of
religious education confirmed my impression that Sunday
schools still have the same old problems—the lack of time, the
shortage of teachers, the indifference of parents (one mother,
when she saw her daughter doing her Sunday School homework, asked the girl if she wasn't feeling well). When he had
finished with the dreary list, his eyes lighted up, and he said,
"Now you should talk to the people in charge of our youth
movement! They're the ones who are *really* doing a job! After
Sunday School, after confirmation—that's when the kids *really*
start to learn about Judaism!"

The youth movement he referred to is the National Federation of Temple Youth—known to its members as NIFTY. There are four hundred and fifty NIFTY groups around the country, with twenty-five thousand members. The Reform movement takes them very seriously; the national officers of NIFTY have an equal place with their elders on the board of UAHC. NIFTY activities, which are arranged independently by each individual chapter, may involve anything from "creative worship" (the young people invent and perform their own services) to tutoring high school students from depressed areas, to joining a civil rights march on Washington, to taking a chartered tour to Israel. NIFTY is pervaded by a hearty "rah-rah" spirit which its professional staff deliberately encourages. At the end of a recent conclave in New York, a couple of dozen NIFTY members gathered on Fifth Avenue, in front of the UAHC offices, held hands in a friendship circle, and sang farewell songs. Obviously this sort of thing isn't for everybody —friendship circles and farewell songs are among the things that make many teen-agers happy to leave their teens—but NIFTY believes it works for most.

Still, I'm not sure that the Reform educators need to invest all their optimism in the youth movement. Some Sunday schools, though perhaps not many, are extraordinarily effective. I observed one of the best in the country—the school operated by the Free Synagogue in Manhattan. Its basic theory is that the purpose of a Sunday School is not to feed its students "baby Judaism," Bible stories told in a saccharine manner with a few names and dates thrown in. Nor is its purpose to pump them full of Hebrew: "I could train my parrot to speak Hebrew," says a leading Reform educator. "Would that make it a good Jewish parrot?" Its purpose is to give the students "a reason for continuing to be Jewish."

It does this by carrying the Conservative method even further, by involving the students from a very early age in criticizing and analyzing Judaism with absolute freedom. When they're small they learn the Bible stories, but they learn to ask why: "Why did Cain kill Abel? What does it have to do with me?" When they're older they move on to the ethical precepts of Judaism, to Jewish literature (from Job to Saul Bellow), to the atom bomb or the war in Vietnam, or anything else that captures their imagination.

And all the time the emphasis is on thinking for themselves. "Don't accept what we tell you. Don't even accept what the Bible tells you. Work it out on your own. Say what *you* think, not what someone else thinks." Recently a class of twelve-year-olds in this school wrote essays on the question "What is God?" They handed in a collection of sweet, exquisite, inspirational sentiments—and the teacher got very upset. They were telling him what they thought he wanted to hear; to him this meant he had fallen down on his job. He consulted with the principal, and a special effort was made to convince these twelve-year-olds to come out and say what they really believed.

The technique used in Free Synagogue classes is Socratic. The teacher seldom tells his pupils what attitude they should take on any subject. He asks them questions, gets them arguing among themselves, tries to draw the truth out of them without any hinting or coaxing. Often the truth that he draws out is not what he wanted to hear at all. "I'm not so sure any more that I believe in God," said one boy, after a discussion about faith and reason. He was disturbed; so are many of the students at the Free Synagogue. "You're the teacher," they often say. "You're supposed to tell us what's true." But the more troubled they get, the better the school believes it's doing its job.

It isn't a typical Reform Sunday School. It has the advantage of being much smaller than most, better able to establish an atmosphere of warmth and intimacy in which each child has a chance of thriving and finding himself. Such an atmosphere can never exist in a typical surburban Sunday School, where there are over a thousand students, and no teacher knows more than a few by name.

And even the Free Synagogue is sometimes open to the charge of overintellectualism which is most commonly brought against Reform education. "They're too clever," says one critic. "They're not teaching Judaism at all, they're just teaching *about* it. They don't make the kids feel anything. Let's face it, it's what you feel, not what you know, that stays with you."

These words bring us back to the crucial point of religious education in American Judaism. All three establishments are in the survival business. With all the talk about values, the ultimate purpose of their schools—Yeshiva, Talmud Torah, or Sunday School—is to keep young Jews in the fold. By their own admission, the only real test of a religious education is, "How long does it stay with you?"

Naturally there is much disagreement as to which of the three methods is demonstrating the most staying power, which branch of Judaism is holding on to its young people most successfully. Orthodox young people do seem to observe *halakah* more conscientiously, but there also seem to be fewer of them; maybe they represent the hard core who are pious by temperament, who would go on being pious regardless of their religious education. Conservative young people do emerge from Camp Ramah transfigured, full of enthusiasm for their Jewish tradition, speaking Hebrew almost like Israelis—but statistics indicate that plenty of them go right on speaking it to their gentile wives. Reform young people come out of their Sunday schools knowing less about Judaism than anyone else, but several studies suggest that synagogue attendance at Sabbath is higher among Reform Jews than among the other two divisions. With all this contradictory information, nobody really knows which educational philosophy is doing the best job.

The experts themselves can only cross their fingers and hope.

VIII.

Holier Than Thou

It takes a strange kind of person to be an Orthodox Jew. Orthodoxy, after all, demands obedience to the Jewish law even when reason, logic, and ordinary common sense are violated. Many Jews who are nominally Orthodox, perhaps even a majority of them, can't really submit to this demand. Just like Reform and Conservative Jews, they persist in believing that they have the right to judge for themselves. But some people —the "committed" Orthodox, as Charles Liebman calls them —do submit. These people are fundamentalists; and the fundamentalist, even the Jewish one, is different from the rest of us.

According to most psychiatrists, the difference lies in his highly developed sense of guilt. This is the motivating force in people who blindly and unquestioningly perform religious rituals; it is, I think, the key to the personality of the Orthodox Jew.

The theology itself seems to make this sense of guilt inevitable. If you believe that God has laid down over six hundred rules and regulations for you to obey, and that your credit in His eyes depends on how well you obey them, how can you help but feel guilty? Obviously you will never succeed in performing all or even most of the *mitzvahs*. No matter how many you do, there will always be one more that you *could* have done. And there is always one fellow Orthodox Jew, more devout than you, who has done it. The pressure he exerts on you by his mere existence is unbearable. You are forced to ask yourself, "If he could do that one extra *mitzvah*, why couldn't I?" And maybe this leads you to perform not one but two extra *mitzvahs* to put the other fellow at a disadvantage.

This kind of competitive piety can have comic results. At a Young Israel synagogue outside of Boston, the superpious old-timers always gathered for daily services at eight thirty in the morning. Then a younger group, with even greater pretensions to piety, joined the congregation and started holding services at eight in the morning. Naturally this made it necessary for the first group to get to synagogue at seven thirty—which forced the new group to get there at seven. Finally the rabbi bowed out of the race. "I'm an old man," he said, "and I need my sleep."

But the Orthodox Jew's sense of guilt has consequences that go far beyond his religious practice. It cuts through his whole life. It affects his tastes, his opinions, almost every aspect of his daily conduct. It does this primarily by instilling in him a feeling of separation from other people. The split personality which characterizes most Jews in America—their struggle to decide which world they want to live in—is much less marked in the committed Orthodox. He has settled the matter with himself. His sense of guilt makes him fear contamination from impure influences, and so he chooses to keep himself apart from the "outside" world—not only from the gentiles, but from other Jews who haven't made the same choice.

Not all committed Orthodox separate themselves in the same way, of course. Some, like the Hasidim, impose a rigid physical separation on themselves. They have their own independent rabbinic organizations, and won't belong to those of the other Orthodox. They cluster together in their own neighborhoods—in Brooklyn or Detroit or Spring Valley, New York—and seldom venture out, except to satisfy the demands of earning a living. Their lives revolve around their own community and its spiritual center, their rebbeh. They emphasize this separatism by the way they dress—in long black coats and large black hats—and by the beards which all Hasidic men grow as soon as they are able, and especially by the long curls, known as *paes*, which all Hasidic males, even small children, wear over their ears. It is not by accident or perversity that they maintain this strange appearance. They feel that the true believer will forget the primary importance of obeying the *mitzvahs* unless a wall is built around him. The Hasidim are very realistic; they know what an effective wall can be made out of black hats and earcurls.

Yet even among the Hasidim there are degrees of separatism. The Satmar Hasidim keep strictly to themselves, but the Lubavitcher Hasidim are missionaries—not to the gentiles, but to the Jews. They believe that every Jew, no matter how far gone in heresy, has the Divine spark in him; their duty is to fan that spark into a flame. And so they send representatives to college campuses and attempt to persuade young Jewish men to spend their vacations in Williamsburg, living the Hasidic life from the inside. These bearded, black-hatted traveling salesmen of the faith sometimes make contact with the campus Hillel Society or with one of the local Orthodox synagogues, but often they find recruits simply by stopping likely prospects on the street. And they have been remarkably successful; hundreds of college students accept their invitations every year. Most of these go out of curiosity. No figures are available as to how many of them stay.

It is because they feel so secure in their separatism that the Lubavitcher Hasidim are able to be missionaries. They are even able to make use of the scientific achievements of this materialistic modern world which they reject. The Lubavitcher Rebbeh has started a technical school in Williamsburg. Why shouldn't his disciples be able to operate a lathe or fix an electrical circuit as well as the unbelievers? And in Los Angeles, that haven of offbeat religious cults, the Lubavitcher Hasidim have a sound truck which drives through Jewish neighborhoods, urging the inhabitants to give up their lives of sin and return to the fold.

The modern Orthodox don't try to separate themselves from the world physically, as the Hasidim do. Some of them say they don't want to separate themselves at all. But in fact their ritual observance, if they are conscientious about it, has the effect of cutting them off from close personal contacts with the nonobservant. Without cheating, Orthodox high school students can't go to the Saturday ball game with the gang. They can't go out for a hamburger after the big dance—in fact, as we shall see, they can't go to the big dance. Orthodox college students, because of the time they must give to daily prayers and Sabbath observance, participate less in campus social life and extracurricular activities.

If this separatism bothered them, they could break out of it easily enough. The ones who don't are the ones who want it —to whom it appeals temperamentally. This was admitted to me, though not deliberately, by a distinguished Orthodox rabbi, a man active in many organizations, including some devoted to interdenominational relations. When I asked him if Orthodoxy doesn't encourage its adherents to separate themselves from the world, he said, "Absolutely not. Orthodoxy simply suggests that it's necessary to have one's roots and strike them deep. Once that's accomplished you can go out and meet the world." And then he undid the effect of those words by adding, "Besides, who says it's a good idea to know everyone and see everything? Sometimes it's possible to know and see *too* much. I never feel the lack of meeting Moslems!"

———————

This feeling of separation—euphemistically described as having one's roots or one's own frame of reference—leads to a special Orthodox morality. Ultimately because the moral value of every act is determined by *halakah,* by Jewish law, they develop a rather cavalier attitude toward "gentile" law. For example, a tiny minority of Hasidim engage in jewel smuggling. In the *shtetl* this was a traditional trade. Nobody looked upon it as a crime, because nobody recognized the existence of national borders; the only borders that mattered were those that divided the Jewish from the gentile world. That handful of Hasidim who still have this attitude in America are sometimes caught and convicted—and invariably complain, with righteous indignation, that they can't get kosher food in federal prison.

Most Orthodox disapprove of this sort of thing, of course, yet occasionally the same kind of morality breaks out among them. It was expressed by a gang of Orthodox boys, one of them a rabbinical student, who burglarized synagogues in Brooklyn last year. When they were caught, they made it clear that their feelings of guilt were minimal. After all, they had never picked on Orthodox synagogues.

On the other hand, the feeling of separation tends to make the Orthodox Jew more moral than the average person. He is anxious to obey the Ten Commandments, not only because *halakah* requires him to, but because he sees himself as a representative of a unique community and wants it to make the best possible impression on the outside world, and especially on non-Orthodox Jews. This is why there is no LSD problem at Yeshiva and no pregnancy problem at Stern College, its counterpart for women. And this is why there can't be a Columbia type of revolt on the Yeshiva campus. The school, as a symbol of Orthodoxy, exacts absolute loyalty from its students. The Yeshiva newspapers have never had faculty advisers; the editors censor themselves spontaneously. They wouldn't think of printing anything that could hurt the school.

This quality of loyalty and of dedication to an ideal belongs not only to Yeshiva students but to all the committed Orthodox. They do give the impression of being made of finer stuff than the rest of us—purer, less self-centered, more idealistic. It would be a mistake to explain this away as hypocrisy. To be a committed Orthodox Jew does require a strength and selflessness that few people ever demonstrate. Because I am shortly going to make some serious criticisms of the Orthodox, I would like to convey clearly now my admiration for the kind of people they are. The basic human material is excellent; what they do with it is disturbing.

When a Yeshiva boy wants to break loose and be "immoral," he doesn't steal a car, or start a fight in a night club, or seduce a girl. He does what one boy rather shyly confessed to doing—he sneaks down to an off-Broadway theater and sees Le Roi Jones' *The Toilet.*

As this confession implies, there is a special Orthodox attitude toward sex. *Halakah* is interpreted to mean that boys and girls must have no physical contact with each other until after marriage. The arranged marriage of the *shtetl*—where the bride and groom sometimes hadn't set eyes on each other until they met at the altar—hardly occurs any more, not even among the Hasidim. Dating is allowed, but its purpose, clearly understood by everyone, is to find a marriage partner. Kissing and necking are strictly forbidden. Even social dancing is forbidden. Sexual relations between an unmarried male and female are, of course, a serious sin.

The most extraordinary aspect of this is that the young

people themselves appear to accept these taboos. A Jewish college boy I know was highly skeptical of this, until he visited the dormitories of Stern College with an Orthodox friend who was engaged to one of the girls. Several other Orthodox boys were also visiting their girls. To his amazement, the couples sat around all night and discussed the Talmud. "Tell me," he says, "are they human?"

They're very human, and they have their inner conflicts. The dean of students at Yeshiva, in fact, considers this to be the most difficult conflict which the boys there have to face. They deal with it in different ways. One Orthodox boy admitted that he can't accept the prohibition against necking. "I don't even think it's possible," he said. "So I'm doing it, but all the time I know it's wrong." One Orthodox girl, engaged to a boy who must finish college before they can be married, allows him to kiss her good night, and feels very defensive about it. "At least I'm not like my non-Orthodox friends. I'm debating about a kiss, but they're debating about premarital relations."

Since temptation is a constant source of danger, it must clearly be reduced to a minimum. Not only must the boy avoid touching the girl, he must stay far away from embarrassing or suggestive influences while they're together. One boy has stopped taking his girl to the movies completely. "Even if I check up on the picture ahead of time, and it seems to be perfectly all right, how can I be sure about the previews?" And one girl admits to being a bit tired of seeing nothing but Walt Disney pictures on dates. She prefers going to the movies with other girls. Then she can see a picture like Antonioni's *Blow-up*, which she cheerfully confesses to having enjoyed thoroughly.

Despite inner conflicts and practical lapses, however, the young Orthodox appear to accept the *halakah* on sex. They even find some advantages in it. Says one girl, "No group of girls today is luckier than we are. When we go out with a boy, we don't have to worry about him making passes at us or stringing us along or anything like that. We know that if he keeps showing an interest it's because he's got marriage in mind."

Here is where the feeling of separation becomes crucial. The marriage that the Orthodox boy has in mind is marriage to an Orthodox girl. The girl he dates—since dating is nothing but a prelude to marriage—must be Orthodox. Going out with a gentile girl is, of course, impossible. If an Orthodox boy were to bring a gentile girl to a party given by his friends, he would be glared at in horror; as one boy put it, "He couldn't insult us more if he ate a ham sandwich in our presence." But even going out with a Jewish girl who isn't Orthodox is frowned upon. One boy from Albany, where the choice is more limited than in New York City, fell in love with a non-Orthodox girl. He tried hard to win her over to Orthodoxy, but when she refused, he ended their relationship. He suffered intensely and genuinely—"but what could I do?" he says. "I would've done anything for her, but I couldn't sacrifice my soul!"

When the Orthodox do get married, their marriages end in divorce much less often than those of other Jews—and this in spite of the fact that they tend (possibly because of the *halakic* prohibitions against premarital relations) to marry younger. A leading Orthodox authority on Talmudic marriage laws gives this explanation for the low incidence of divorce among the Orthodox: "Our women aren't allowed to be financially independent, like so many American women. The Orthodox husband wants his wife staying home with the kids. That's what's causing all the extramarital activity nowadays, these working wives who are close to other women's husbands all day long!"

Another reason for the low incidence of divorce among the Orthodox might be the tremendous difficulty of getting one. According to strict Judaic law, divorce is a religious ceremony. The couples must appear before a rabbi who specializes in such matters. A scribe with a quill pen writes out a document, when the husband orders him to do so; everyone signs it, a blessing is said, and the divorce is granted. The couple may have gotten a civil divorce earlier, but this has no validity in Orthodox eyes.

———————

Nowhere, in fact, is the separatism of the Orthodox more clear than in their attitude toward the civil government. On the one hand there is a strong "render unto Caesar" feeling—obey the law of the gentiles, do your duty as a citizen, don't stick your nose into matters that don't concern you. For this reason the Orthodox are less likely than other Jews to get involved in social action, to march in protest parades, to sign petitions and carry banners—unless the cause happens to be a specifically Jewish one, like anti-Semitism in the Soviet Union or the welfare of Israel. The Orthodox are also less likely to accept help from the government. The Hasidim, by far the poorest of American Jews, nevertheless stay off welfare. Recently, when there was an outbreak of muggings in a Hasidic neighborhood in New York, the residents formed their own vigilante committee rather than call in the police; the muggings have stopped.

On the other hand, the emotional attachment of the Orthodox is to their own world, the "real" Jewish world. They feel no hostility to America, but they feel no special identification with it either—or with any particular government, including the government of Israel. One Orthodox scholar said to me, "I don't feel any love for America. When I hear about the founding fathers, and the Fourth of July comes around, and they play 'The Star-Spangled Banner'—well, it honestly doesn't do a thing to me." The man who said this is not an old bearded rabbi with a Yiddish accent; he is young, American-born, college-educated, intellectual, and sophisticated.

As sophisticated, that is, as any Orthodox Jew can be. Despite Rabbi Jakobovits' ambition to make Orthodoxy elegant and fashionable, there is something fundamentally inelegant and unfashionable about truly pious Orthodox Jews. I think this is inherent in their dedication to *halakah,* and the feeling of separation it gives them. How worldly can you be if in your heart you've renounced the world? To be elegant and fashionable takes time and effort; you have to care about a great many things which an Orthodox Jew simply can't bring himself to care about. Girls at Stern College, though they dress nicely and make themselves attractive, obviously pay less attention to fashion fads than most girls. Mini-skirts are almost as rare among them as illegitimate babies—not because some of them haven't got the money to buy fashionable clothes, but because the social atmosphere of Orthodoxy discourages competition over such trifles.

There can be few segments of American society today where money gives a man less of an edge. At Yeshiva University piety (or the appearance of it) and Talmudic learning are the sole measures of social status. A professor of history there, not himself Orthodox, tells me that after twenty years he still can't tell the difference between the wealthy boys and the scholarship boys. And even outside the rarefied atmosphere of Yeshiva, Orthodoxy tends to be a great leveler. The president of the synagogue may impress a lot of people with his Rolls Royce, but if he rides to Sabbath services in it the pious will criticize him—and even his loyal adherents will keep quiet.

But the Orthodox, unless they happen to be Hasidim, do live in the world, and sometimes it's curious to see how they manage to square worldly values with Orthodox values. Most people are surprised to hear how many Orthodox intellectuals, especially scientists, there are these days. Our immediate instinct is to ask the question that one nonobservant Jew, a biochemist, asked of the Orthodox biochemist who worked in the same lab. "How can you, a scientist, believe in a revealed religion?" The answer he got was, "I believe in it as a Jew, not as a scientist." This ability to live in two compartments at once permitted a recent meeting of the Association of Orthodox Jewish Scientists to feature a panel discussion called Religious Ritual and Neurotic Compulsion. The subject was debated from many angles, but at no time apparently did any of the participants feel that it touched their own lives.

The point was further illustrated for me by an Orthodox chemist who is an expert on plastics. A rabbi asked him once if a certain new plastic could be considered *halakically* "neutral" —that is, would a dish made out of this plastic be sufficiently nonabsorbent so that you could eat meat from it, then wash it, then safely eat dairy food from it too? The young chemist said uneasily, "Are you asking me as a chemist or as a Jew?" As a chemist he knew that the fibers would indeed absorb microscopically small particles of food; but if he let himself know this as a Jew, he would have to advise the rabbi to condemn the new plastic. The rabbi understood what was going on in his mind and immediately dropped the subject.

Obviously this form of doublethink works better in certain intellectual areas than in others. Among Orthodox scientists there are few anthropologists or archaeologists; it isn't easy for a religious fundamentalist to come to terms with the evidence of man's history provided by these disciplines. And there are only one or two Orthodox artists or serious writers of fiction. The complicated Talmudic game of chess which the Orthodox delights in playing with life is totally alien to the artistic imagination. There is something literal and matter-of-fact about the fundamentalist mind. What the Bible says is true—it isn't symbolic, it isn't metaphorical, it isn't a "beautiful story." The artist is almost always a kind of mystic; the Orthodox Jew, almost never.

Furthermore, to the extent that works of art express ideas, they are likely to be un-Orthodox ideas. "We don't have anything to fear from science," says a young Orthodox rabbi. "But art, literature, the humanities—they can hurt us. With their emphasis nowadays on Freudianism, on the sexual revolution, on intellectual anarchy, they could set up a bloody conflict in a religious young man. So mostly he stays away from them."

Some of the right-wing Orthodox, as we have seen, are so frightened of this bloody conflict that they censor the books in their schools. But I wonder if their precautions are really necessary. In the Orthodox mind there seems to be a built-in computer which infallibly transforms or rejects all un-kosher ideas from the outside. At Yeshiva all the great literature of the world is taught freely, often by professors who aren't Orthodox or even Jewish. Yet somehow the pious student survives this reading, with his fundamentalism intact.

A professor of literature at Yeshiva gave me an insight into the operations of this computer by describing how his students react to, and even manage to enjoy, certain books and writers whose ideas ought to repel them:

> Walt Whitman's poetry: "Yes, he does go in for nature worship and pantheism and all, but that's just the materialism of the nineteenth century. He doesn't really *mean* to be idolatrous."

> Theodore Dreiser's *An American Tragedy:* "The tragedy is that Clyde never had any real religious training. If he had, he never would've got into trouble."

> Saul Bellow's *Herzog:* "He made a bad marriage, but he'll get over his problems all right. Look at all that Talmudic training he had. A Jewish boy with a good Orthodox education is bound to come through."

> The bawdy parts of *Tom Jones:* "It's a classic. It doesn't have anything to do with real life."

> The poetry of John Donne: "I'm crazy about it. That religious fervor—it's exactly the way *I* feel!"

All of Shakespeare's plays: "Well, Shakespeare is in a class by himself."

As these comments suggest, the man who separates himself from the world, emotionally and intellectually if not physically, runs the risk of separating himself from a sense of reality too. We are all self-deceivers, just as much as the Orthodox Jew, but he deceives himself more successfully than most of us; he has an organization and a tradition behind him.

Maybe he has to deceive himself if Orthodoxy is to survive. Maybe a diet of illusion is necessary to give the plant its toughness. One thing I feel certain about, no pressure from the outside—especially not the carping of unbelievers—will destroy Orthodoxy in the foreseeable future. Can it destroy itself from the inside? To answer that question we must return to the source of all Orthodox attitudes and behavior, that pervasive sense of guilt.

Sometimes this sense of guilt seems comic, as we have seen, but hidden inside it is a real danger. It prevents the committed Orthodox from ever having stable relations with his conscience. Every concession, every accommodation he makes to the modern world or the American way of life can be interpreted as a lapse from duty. He can conceal this from himself, but only if nobody points an accusing finger at him.

In the twenties and thirties there were no accusing fingers. This was when "modern" or "liberal" Orthodoxy established itself. It allowed its women to sit in synagogue with the men, it allowed its young people to dance with each other; but its sense of guilt could remain dormant, because, after all, it still obeyed the law more faithfully than anyone else around. What was a little social dancing compared to the enormities perpetrated by Conservatism and Reform? But then, in the second half of the forties, a host of accusing fingers suddenly appeared in America—and the vulnerability of the Orthodox conscience was ruthlessly exposed.

The accusers were the Hasidim, the thousands of ultra-Orthodox who had somehow managed to survive the Nazi holocaust in East Europe. When they first came to this country they were laughed at a little. It was assumed that they would, in the course of time, shave their earcurls and drop their quaint ways and put on gray flannel suits like any respectable American Jew. It hasn't worked out that way. They have been here twenty years, and seem to be passing on their traditions successfully to their children. More astonishing, they have acted like a huge magnet, pulling all the rest of Orthodoxy, including the liberals, in their direction.

Hindsight makes it easy to see that something like this was bound to happen. Everything about the Hasidim is peculiarly adapted to exert pressure on a guilty conscience. First, they appear to be far more pious than anyone else. While it is true that Hasidism today has little in common with the inspiring cult of joy that grew up two hundred years ago, it still has less of a "decadent" look than the brand of Orthodoxy which it found here. The Hasidim do more praying, obey more *mitz-vahs,* and make more sacrifices. Second, Hasidism is far more separatist than native American Orthodoxy. Its members have their roots elsewhere, in a *shtetl* that no longer exists; the claims of America produce no conflicts within them. Finally, and most important, they are the survivors, the visible living symbols of all those millions who were slaughtered in the concentration camps.

Their presence here has brought to life all the dormant guilt in the Orthodox Jew. As a result, a holier-than-thou psychology pervades American Orthodoxy today. Everybody accepts that the man to the right of him is "within the pale"; everybody is a little afraid that he himself might be "beyond the pale." As one observer sees it, "Every Orthodox Jew today spends most of his time looking nervously over his right shoulder."

The most extraordinary illustration of this is the contrast between the younger generation of Orthodoxy, now in their teens and twenties, and their parents. It is often said now that Orthodoxy has great appeal to the young; it has "more guts, more bite," than the other forms of Judaism. The sacrifices it demands make it particularly attractive to its young people. "The more you sacrifice," one of them told me, "the more glorious it seems to be a Jew." At the same time it is often said that Orthodoxy today is not increasing in numbers, but in strength; fewer commit themselves, but for those who do, the commitment goes deep. In other words, only a minority of young people become Orthodox, but they are the minority with an unusually strong sense of guilt. Orthodoxy gives them a better chance to punish themselves than any other form of religious commitment could.

Not all Orthodox young people submit to this self-flagellation as supinely as others. Among the students at Yeshiva—all committed Orthodox, or why would they be there?—I found a great range of feeling. One boy finds himself in a terrible inner bind; he believes in liberalism and individualism, yet Yeshiva emphasizes the obligation of the individual to submerge himself in the community and in the law. Then why doesn't this boy leave Yeshiva? Because he believes that the survival of the Jews requires him to stay; if he left, he would feel that he had betrayed the cause for which the six million martyrs gave their lives. Another boy has an easier job of it; his sense of guilt has led him to kill any spirit of individualism within him. He accepts absolutely that Torah is revealed by God; anything that challenges it automatically challenges truth. A third boy stands halfway between the first two. "If anything ever successfully contradicted our knowledge of the truth as gained from Torah," he says, "that certainly *would* be an argument that Torah isn't revealed. But nothing ever *has* contradicted it, and nothing ever will." This boy wears the most anxious expression of the three; he feels so guilty about his doubts that he can't quite admit to himself their existence—which of course makes him feel even guiltier.

Nothing reveals this pull to the right among Orthodox young people more dramatically than the new significance of the yarmulke. The notion that the head must be covered not only in synagogue, during prayers, and at meals but at all times is comparatively new. It belongs not to *halakah* itself but to that immense collection of customs which the Talmudic rabbis have recommended as a means of "insurance" against violating *halakah*. Cover your head at all times, and then if you unexpectedly have to make a blessing to God you won't be caught, even by accident, with your hat off. But for young Orthodox Jews today the yarmulke has become an aggressive symbol of their commitment, and even more of their willingness to display that commitment to the world. They wear it not only in their own Orthodox neighborhoods, not only in the precincts of their synagogue or yeshiva, but "downtown," on Times Square or Fifth Avenue, where it used to be considered "dangerous" to wear it.

This emphasis on the yarmulke proves, I think, what

shrewd psychologists these young Orthodox are. One of them, a rabbinical student, explained to me how he instills a commitment to Orthodoxy in the high school boys in his neighborhood, most of whom come from nonobservant Orthodox families. "The most important thing is to get them to wear that yarmulke," he said. "Tell them it's a symbol of their Judaism, tell them they're cowards if they don't wear it, ask them why they're ashamed to admit they're Jews. Once they're willing to put on that yarmulke and appear before the world in it—and appear before their own families in it—you can be pretty sure you've got them hooked. They may not know a thing about Judaism, they may not know what they're committing themselves to, but that yarmulke commits them."

As this young man's statement implies, the new militancy of the Orthodox is often the cause of family conflicts. The Orthodox parent, out of his own sense of guilt, sends his son to a yeshiva "so he can learn to be a better Jew than I am." To the parent's astonishment, this is precisely what happens. Everybody in Orthodoxy has his favorite story of the yeshiva boy who came home one day and announced, "I can't eat here any more. You're not kosher enough!" In these cases the parents sometimes capitulate and "start living Jewish lives"; more often there is a great deal of bitterness, exacerbated by everybody's guilty conscience.

What if the family absolutely refuses to make changes in its domestic arrangements? That rabbinical student who performs conversions with the yarmulke advises his young converts to handle the stubbornness of their parents in this manner: "Just refuse to eat until they obey the laws of *kashruth*. Believe me, they'll give in. Is a Jewish mother going to let her baby starve?"

———————•••———————

This new spirit in American Orthodoxy is being vividly demonstrated right now within the world of Yeshiva University. Here in an atmosphere of intense dedication to Judaism, all of these conflicts, between right wing and liberal, between young and old, act themselves out every day.

The theological seminary of Yeshiva—REITS—was established in 1886, and in 1928 a liberal arts college was added to the seminary. This was an unprecedented step, unique in American Judaism. It was compounded in 1945 by Yeshiva's expansion into a university, and in 1954 by the establishment of Stern College for Women. Today Yeshiva has sixty-five hundred students and a faculty of twenty-two hundred. It stands as the greatest single accomplishment of modern liberal Orthodoxy.

Its uniqueness lies in this: it applies the double curriculum of the yeshiva to higher education. There have always been seminaries for Jewish boys who wished to continue their Talmudic studies after high school age, but those seminaries have never felt the need to supply a secular education too. Only at Yeshiva can a student get the usual B.A. or B.S. degree (majoring in literature or history or biology just like any other college student) plus an advanced program of Judaic studies. The familiar division—Talmud in the morning, "English" in the afternoon—characterizes the curriculum at Yeshiva. And what it means is that everybody works twice as hard as most college students do. It isn't unusual for a Yeshiva student to study from nine in the morning until midnight, plus the time he must spend at his prayers. One reason why Yeshiva boys and Stern girls seldom date each other is that Yeshiva is located a hundred blocks away from Stern—and how often does a Yeshiva boy have time to make that long subway ride downtown?

It isn't only time that he sacrifices. All that poring over Mishna and Gemara—which, in most editions, have hideously small print—causes students at Yeshiva to have 20 percent poorer eyesight than students elsewhere. I have yet to meet a Yeshiva boy who doesn't wear glasses.

But in spite of this spirit of dedication and sacrifice, the atmosphere at Yeshiva has, until recently, been liberal. In its secular departments it has some of the best teachers in the country—not only because it pays good salaries, but because it has never hamstrung them with fundamentalist restrictions. In its religious departments there have always been some old-fashioned East European rabbis, with beards and prejudices, but their influence has been tempered by the generally tolerant atmosphere. A few years ago one of these old rabbis found a student reading a copy of *The Great Gatsby* inside his Gemara. It was a paperback edition, and on the cover was a picture of a nude female leg kicking over a champagne bottle. The horrified rabbi sent the boy to the dean, and later the English professor who had assigned the offending book was called to the dean's office too. Not to hear the riot act, however. What the dean said was, "If your boys insist on doing their English assignments in Talmud class, would you please tell them to put a plain brown wrapper on the books."

Officially this liberal spirit still exists at Yeshiva. Representatives of modern Orthodoxy on its religious faculty are always saying to their students, "It takes more courage to be flexible than to be rigid." But in fact everyone at Yeshiva, like everyone else in Orthodoxy today, is caught in the same pull to the right. The faculty, especially its younger members, includes people of right-wing beliefs who wouldn't have been considered thirty years ago. The old rabbi who says that the Ptolemaic system of astronomy must be true because one of the ancient Talmudic commentators said it was true would have been laughed at thirty years ago; today nobody dares criticize him too loudly.

This same fear of criticism from the right has affected Yeshiva's admissions policies. There are few dropouts among its students, but this is because Yeshiva takes great care to accept people who will unquestionably adapt to the system. There are occasional exceptions, but by and large, as one of its professors says, its admissions policy shows "too much conformity, isn't nearly adventurous enough." Like any right-wing yeshiva on the lower levels, it "can't afford the luxury of mavericks."

The pull to the right at Yeshiva showed itself clearly in one recent incident which has become famous in Orthodox circles. For many years Yeshiva College has held a reception in the fall, to which its boys were allowed to invite Stern girls. It took place in the college lounge, and has been described to me by a graduate as "a mild, drab affair, with nonalcoholic punch." No *tref* shenanigans like social dancing were allowed, of course. But a few years ago this "dean's reception" was suddenly denounced by right-wing faculty members, on the grounds that it was inappropriate for a school of religious education to serve as official sponsor of a mixed social event. Immediately there was a furor among the students. The issue was debated vehemently in the school newspapers. The administration was petitioned and counterpetitioned. The reception was canceled one year, and the next year a vote was taken of the whole student body. It resulted in an exact tie between pro- and anti-reception forces, and in the end a compromise was worked out. The reception has been abandoned for good, but in its place something very much like it has been established under a different name.

The reception means nothing in itself, of course. The significance of the incident is that it happened at all. A decade ago the right-wing rabbis wouldn't have felt themselves strong enough to raise objections, the administration wouldn't have taken such objections seriously, and the student body certainly wouldn't have divided fifty-fifty on the issue.

———◦•◦———

What's happening to Yeshiva is precisely what's happening to the whole modern Orthodox establishment. It is being besieged from the right, and its own sense of guilt prevents it from putting up more than a half-hearted struggle. Charles Liebman, one of the most intelligent and effective of the besiegers, dismisses all the ideals and accomplishments of modern Orthodoxy in one sentence—"It was never an ideology, only a compromise." He deals with one of its best-known leaders, the chief rabbi of an influential Orthodox synagogue, in this fashion: "Nobody takes Lookstein seriously any more. He commands a lot of money, so he can throw his weight around, but he's a joke among the youth. He just isn't observant enough."

In response to this kind of attack, the most eloquent spokesmen for modern Orthodoxy seem to be undermined by their own more or less unconscious acceptance of the charges against them. Rabbi Norman Lamm, in a speech expressing the view that Orthodoxy must not turn its back on the challenges of the modern world, feels called upon to qualify and modify and apologize at every turn. "Now please bear in mind and make no mistake about it—I absolutely do not, heaven forbid, speak of changing the *halakah* or any of its articles. I speak only of making them *relevant*. Relevance does not mean compromise or submission to the presuppositions of Western culture." [1] In an interview Rabbi Lamm elevates his fear of compromise and submission to the status of a positive virtue: "I must admit that there is a measure of personal timidity evident among the Orthodox, but such timidity is a natural and maybe even a healthy phenomenon. The dangers of cowardice are no greater than those of reckless courage." [2] Yet Rabbi Lamm is far more courageous than most of the modern Orthodox today.

Sometimes, it is true, the establishment of modern Orthodoxy acts as if it were going to take a stand against the pressure from the right. The Rabbinical Alliance and other right-wing groups have been agitating for several years to withdraw the Union of Orthodox Jewish Congregations from membership in the Synagogue Council. Because the Council contains representatives of Reform and Conservative Judaism, they say, any Orthodox group that belongs to it is implicitly admitting the legitimacy of those heretics. To the true Orthodox there *are* no divisions in Judaism; there is only Orthodoxy, and those who fall short of it. At the annual conventions of the UOJC the right-wing rabbis always propose its withdrawal from the Synagogue Council, and this proposal is always defeated by a large majority.

The UOJC is deeply committed, organizationally and financially, to the Synagogue Council, and cannot drop out without difficulty. The inroads of the right wing, therefore, must be measured in connection with issues that are less public. A few years ago, for instance, the modern Orthodox Rabbinical Council was on the verge of announcing a new interpretation of *halakah* which would allow people, under certain circumstances, to carry things on the Sabbath. Much discussion had gone on among leading Talmudic authorities, and it was felt that this dispensation was compatible with *halakah*. Then a handful of right-wing rabbis sent telegrams to the Rabbinical Council denouncing the proposed dispensation, and it was quietly dropped.

This, I think, is the weakness which could destroy Orthodoxy from the inside. Its overdeveloped sense of guilt could eventually undermine the very quality which gives it its greatest strength—its selfless adherence to principles, its integrity. Something of this sort could be seen happening recently to an organization which bears a curious resemblance to Orthodoxy —the American New Left. These young people are also fundamentalists, the political rather than the religious kind, and are also riddled with guilt. It led them, at their Chicago convention in 1967, to capitulate to a minority of Black Nationalists, to accept demands that they knew to be unreasonable, to subscribe to opinions that they didn't really believe. As a result of preferring the "dangers of cowardice" to those of "reckless courage," they have lowered their moral credit.

It would be a shame if the same thing happened to American Orthodoxy.

———•••———

In fairness to the Orthodox, they don't have a monopoly on the sense of guilt. Plenty of it can be found in the other two divisions of American Judaism. The destruction of East European Jewry and the presence in America of the ultra-Orthodox survivors have pulled Conservatism and Reform to the right too.

For example, the same conflicts which we have seen in Orthodox families are taking place in Conservative families. One large contributor to the JTS has recently bought two sets of dishes and set up a kosher kitchen, in response to pressure from his children. (The Reform equivalent of this occurred recently in a family I know; their daughter came home from her first day at Sunday School and said to her parents, "We can't have a Christmas tree any more.") And a Conservative girl I talked to, whose family has never kept the dietary laws, admitted that she feels guilty every time she eats a meat sandwich in front of her Orthodox friend in school.

The pull to the right shows itself also in the extreme touchiness of many Conservative leaders whenever the Orthodox attack them. The attacks have grown stronger, of course—especially from the modern Orthodox, who must lighten their burden of guilt by calling attention to those who are less pious than they are—but even so, the Conservative response is strangely belligerent. Rabbi Jacob Neusner, in the official magazine of the movement, declares that Orthodoxy is "heretical." [3] The only reason why Conservatives have never made this charge before, he explains, is that they have been too polite and too broad-minded to do so. But now that Orthodoxy has grown insulting, Conservatism will show that it can be just as insulting in return.

Underneath this militant posture, however, Rabbi Neusner appears to feel just a bit shaky about his own piety. He reveals this in another article in the same journal. "Like Reform Judaism," he writes, "we [Conservatives] affirm the need for reform, but we believe that adaptation of Jewish law to modern conditions should be based mostly on the principles of change inherent in the laws themselves." [4] The force of his affirmation is vitiated by that little hedging word "mostly." Conservatism either does or does not base its claims on "the principles of change inherent in the laws themselves." The rabbi believes this officially, I think, but isn't quite so sure about it deep down in his heart.

And the Reform establishment, once so confident in its opposition to Orthodoxy, has lost much of its cockiness too. The famous *"tref* banquet" of 1883—when the Reform establishment of Cincinnati invited the leading Orthodox rabbis to a big public dinner, and served them clams, shrimps, crabs, and frogs legs—couldn't happen today; Reform banquets today are mostly kosher. Bar mitzvah, once the anathema of all Reform temples, is now the rule rather than the exception. The rare Reform rabbi who still refuses to perform this ceremony feels beleaguered; suddenly *he* has become the defender of the pure faith against the infidels.

The sense of guilt accounts for all this as surely as it does among the Orthodox. For a long time Reform has put most of its emphasis on social action, on the ethical content of Judaism, and Conservatism has put most of its emphasis on "peoplehood," on the ethnic content of Judaism. Suddenly the Orthodox are demanding to know, "What have you done with the religious content of Judaism? Why have you left out God and Torah?" And Reform and Conservatism, despite a certain amount of official bluster, both feel a little guilty.

But even Jews who are committed to none of the religious establishments aren't immune from this virus. Even a "secular" Jew can feel a twinge of guilt in the presence of one of those powerful magnets from East Europe. Recently I was in the office of a Conservative rabbi, modern, well dressed, very much at home in the contemporary world. While we were talking, an old Hasidic rabbi came to see him on some kind of missionary business. He was a fat little man with a black beard and the usual outlandish costume. A comic figure. The modern rabbi stood up, shook his hand, and said amiably, "How do you do?" The Hasid looked him in the eye and answered, *"Shalom."* Though the ancient Hebrew greeting came out mildly enough, it was a reproach. What it clearly said was, "Look at you, with your expensive office and your fancy manners—what kind of a Jew are you, anyway?"

For a split second the modern rabbi lowered his eyes. And so did I.

IX.

Our Father, the Rabbi

Presiding over the whole glorious fantasia of American Judaism—with its separation into three parts, its underlying conflict that cuts right through the separation, its pride and its guilty conscience—is the rabbi. He is an extraordinary figure, and of course an ambivalent one.

The word rabbi means teacher, and by extension, scholar. Traditionally he is the man who knows more about Jewish law than anyone else in the community, and he imparts his knowledge on the highest levels of Talmudic study. But unlike the Catholic priest or the Protestant minister, he performs no sacramental function whatsoever. In no sense, not even symbolically, is he supposed to be an intermediary between God and his congregation. There is no blessing or prayer which he alone is permitted to say. Ten Jewish males over the age of thirteen make a *minyan,* and can conduct a service just as legitimately whether they have a rabbi or not. Many synagogues in small towns don't, in fact, have a regular rabbi, because they can't afford one or can't find one who suits them.

The rabbi's position would seem to be clear then, but the fact is that few synagogue-goers really understand it. Each individual, each congregation, has its own notion of what the rabbi is, and of how he ought to be treated. The effects of this confusion on the religious life of the American Jew are strange and significant.

It is impossible to say exactly how many rabbis there are in America today. About nine hundred and fifty Reform rabbis belong to the Central Conference. About the same number of Conservative Rabbis belong to the Rabbinical Assembly. Eight hundred and thirty Orthodox rabbis belong to the Rabbinical Council; but there are half a dozen other Orthodox rabbinical associations, representing all different complexions of Orthodox opinion. If all of them are to be believed, more American Jews are rabbis than doctors or lawyers.

Though most rabbis serve congregations and synagogues, many are teachers at the various seminaries and yeshivas; others hold chairs of Judaic studies at colleges or administer Hillel societies; others work for the American Jewish Congress, AJC, ADL, and B'nai B'rith. And among the largest employers of rabbis today are the rabbinical organizations themselves, and the United Synagogues, the UAHC, and the UOJC.

In addition, a man càn acquire a certain prestige in the Orthodox world from studying to be a rabbi even though he never serves as one; and so, about 40 percent of those who graduate and are ordained from Orthodox seminaries go into other businesses or professions. Levenstein's, the kosher catering firm in New York, has a rabbi on call to perform weddings in their "synagogue"; during the week he works as a broker on Wall Street. Finally, rabbis are performing all sorts of odd jobs on the periphery of the synagogue world—sixty-six of them, divided equally among the three branches of Judaism, are chaplains in the armed forces (three or four are now serving in Vietnam); others are attached to hospitals and mental institutions.

A generation ago the rabbinate attracted a different kind of person than it does today. In the twenties and thirties only about 50 percent of all rabbis were American-born, and most of those were Reform rabbis from German backgrounds. The young rabbi in those days was probably the son of East European immigrants. The chances were that he would be raising himself in the world. His parents would be poor people; in his new career he could expect in a short time to be making more money than his father. Today, however, the parents of the young rabbi are American-born. The rabbinate represents no particular improvement in his financial prospects; his father may well have a business for him to go into. Statistically the families of rabbinical students are a little bit below the Jewish average in terms of annual income, but not enough below it to make much difference.

The unctuously "spiritual," the elaborately oratorical, and the juicily professorial rabbi who never used a short word where three long ones could do the job—these are vanishing types. Rabbis today are almost indistinguishable from the lawyers, insurance salesmen, high school teachers, and garment manufacturers who belong to their congregations. One young Orthodox rabbi told me how glad he was that so many young people are embracing Orthodoxy: "We have to combat the old bad image of the foreigner with an accent and a long black beard." On the mantelpiece behind him, as he talked, was a faded framed photograph of an old man with a long black beard and a yarmulke—his grandfather, perhaps.

This young man was clean-shaven, but more and more often the young American rabbi will have a beard. (This is especially true of Hillel rabbis, possibly because of their contact with college youth.) By wearing that beard he seems to be making a comment, witty yet serious, on the union between modernity and ancient tradition which he conceives of himself as representing.

A large number of rabbis' sons become rabbis themselves. This seems to be a genuine tribute to Papa's way of life, because no career advantage can be gained from following in his footsteps. The rabbi's son seldom has any professional dealings with his father. He might become the assistant rabbi of his father's congregation, but this happens rarely; the emotional stresses and strains are too great. Most rabbis would agree with a certain distinguished one who said to me, "On my son's graduation from the seminary, I took him aside, shook his hand, and told him, 'I love you, my boy, but I never want you as my assistant!' "

Naturally rabbinical fathers feel a certain pride in their rabbinical sons. But there are few cases on record of the father encouraging the sons to go into the rabbinate. Quite the contrary, they often do their best to nudge the boy in some other direction. One rabbi, when his son called him up from college and said, "I've decided to go to the seminary, Dad," shouted at him over the phone, "Don't do it! Don't be a damned fool!" Then he stopped himself, remembering that his own father, also a rabbi, had said exactly the same words to him thirty years before.

There are no female rabbis. The Orthodox and Conservative rabbinical organizations won't accept them—though several women have studied at the JTS, without intending to be ordained. The Central Conference a few years ago did pass a ruling which permits women to enter the Reform rabbinate, but so far there have been no candidates.

Why does a young man from a middle-class background, often from a family not especially committed to Judaism, decide to become a rabbi? One thing seems clear—he doesn't feel a "call," a mystical sense that God is whispering in his ear, as clergymen are often supposed to feel. The rabbi, because he has no special spiritual function in Judaism, is not likely to be an unusually "spiritual" person. Strictly speaking, he could lose his faith and still go on performing his duties as a rabbi. A Hillel rabbi with whom I talked was trying to persuade a boy in the senior class to go into the rabbinate—a strange project, I thought, because the boy admitted to having grave doubts about the validity of Judaism. But this didn't bother the Hillel rabbi one bit. "The kid's got brains, personality, and guts," he said. "He'll make a great rabbi. They'll teach him to believe in God after he gets to the seminary."

Yet the young rabbi today seldom enters into his career cynically, for purely material reasons. If he did that, he would be a fool. He becomes a rabbi probably because he has an interest in Jewish learning and some sense of responsibility to the Jewish community. In short, he has ideals.

———•◦•———

At the very beginning of his career his dedication to these ideals must undergo a severe test. He must spend five years at a seminary which is much more demanding than the majority of graduate schools.

If he's Conservative he goes to the Jewish Theological Seminary in New York. If he's Reform he may go to the Hebrew Union College in Cincinnati, or to one of its smaller branches in New York and California. If he's Orthodox he may go to Yeshiva College or to one of the old-fashioned right-wing seminaries. JTS and HUC graduate about thirty rabbis every year. The Orthodox seminaries have more graduates, though fewer enter the active rabbinate.

The Conservative and Reform seminaries require a B.A. degree from every entering student. The Orthodox seminaries

are less particular: they will accept an advanced yeshiva education in place of the B.A. degree. The pressure is intense.
Students ordinarily have twenty hours of class each week, and
there is no stinting on the homework. In the summers and
during vacations they are encouraged to pursue their studies
independently, or to gain practical experience at Jewish camps
or yeshivas.

At all of the modern seminaries the curriculum is basically
the same: detailed examination of the Bible, the Talmud, and
other Jewish sources; Jewish history, philosophy, and philol-
ogy. Some training is given in the practical problems of the
rabbinate through courses in such subjects as pastoral psychology and social service, though the consensus seems to be that
these aspects of the rabbi's job are largely unteachable. In
addition, all the seminaries give their future rabbis some in-
service training, opportunities to gain practical experience on
the weekends with small congregations that don't have a regular rabbi. The idea, according to a member of the faculty at
JTS, is "to cushion the traumatic shock of that first sermon."
(But many rabbis say that the real trauma is the first funeral.)

In the course of their five years, students at the seminaries
face certain personal problems which in some ways are like the
problems of graduate students in other schools, but with a
special religious twist. Often, right in the middle of their training, they are beset by doubts about the truth of Judaism or
even the existence of God. This happens particularly to what
their teachers call "late bloomers," pious young men who have
somehow never gone through the usual siege of skepticism in
college. When the late bloomer catches the virus of doubt, the
disease is liable to be as virulent and painful in him as mumps
or measles in a grown man. Much tact is required from teachers
and fellow students, and usually he survives.

A more serious problem is the effect of those first in-service
congregations on many students. The young prospective rabbi
has probably been motivated by a sense of responsibility to the
Jewish community; he believes passionately in the survival of
the Jews, and wants to do his share to help. But after one or
two training congregations, he often finds himself completely
disillusioned with the Jewish community that he has dedicated
his life to. He sees indifference, hypocrisy, ignorance, and ve-
nality. He wonders if he really *does* want these people to survive. Often it takes a long time for him to get over this feeling

and develop a tolerance for human weaknesses and foibles. (Many rabbis never do. They go from pulpit to pulpit, sometimes rising very high in the Jewish community, but are gnawed at by bitterness all the time.)

But like all students everywhere, the seminarian's most traumatic moment comes when he finally graduates. Suddenly he realizes what a warm cocoon the seminary was. All that is over now; the harsh realities are lying in wait for him. The chances are he has gotten married during his time at the seminary—and so his spiritual fears are complicated by the usual worries about earning a living. A seminary graduating class contains many anxious faces.

Yet he has one great advantage over the seminary graduate of the previous generation. Because there is an acute shortage of rabbis today, he often has several offers to choose from. These offers are lined up for him by the placement office of his rabbinical organization. Thirty years ago no such offices existed, and an atmosphere of cutthroat competition prevailed. Certain rabbis with national reputations were so much in demand that wealthy congregations often pirated them from one another. The first placement office was instituted after the war by the Rabbinical Assembly—Conservatism, as we have seen, has always been able to impose better discipline on the troops —and the system was soon taken up by the Central Conference and, more informally, by the Rabbinical Council.

A congregation looking for a rabbi, and a rabbi looking for a congregation, must make contact through the placement office. Neither party is permitted to act independently; want ads are severely frowned upon. A congregation can put in a request for a particular rabbi, but the placement office has the final word as to whether or not the request will be granted. And it lays down some rigid rules: no new rabbi, for instance, may apply to a congregation with over a thousand families; that's a plum which belongs to a more experienced man. And no new rabbi may be considered by a congregation for which large numbers of older men are competing. Furthermore, all seminary graduates, before they can assume a pulpit, must hold themselves available for at least one year's service in the chaplaincy of the armed forces.

As soon as a rabbi, new or old, is being considered for a pulpit, the congregation's pulpit committee, a dozen to fifteen men and women, will ask to meet him. These interviews can be grueling. The placement offices try to make them as easy as possible; their printed instructions for the benefit of candidates are full of useful tips on how to handle a pulpit committee interview. Get to know a member of the committee ahead of time, if possible, so that you'll have a friend in the room. Try to remember each person's name; there's nothing a pulpit committeeman likes better than for the prospective rabbi to call him by name. Don't be in a hurry to bring up questions of salary, pensions, traveling expenses, and so on.

Sometimes the pulpit committee wants the rabbi's wife to be present at the interview. This often happens if the congregation has had an unpleasant experience with its previous *rebbitzin*. The placement office has a set of instructions to cover this contingency. The rabbi's wife is urged to get to the interview on time, to reply graciously to all questions, and above all to let her husband do most of the talking.

After the interview the pulpit committee makes its report to the congregation. The placement office suggests that this report should not settle the matter; the congregation should take a vote, and no rabbi should be offered a job unless a majority have agreed. "Otherwise everyone will be fighting with him," says one placement officer. "Most of the congregation will be sure he was put into his job over their heads, by a small clique. Let's face it, every Jew is in business for himself."

The newly graduated rabbi who has survived the ordeal of the pulpit committee must now decide among the various offers. Usually he must make this decision blind. Only small congregations in small communities are likely to be available to him. He knows and they know that he probably won't stay more than two or three years.

But once he has that first pulpit behind him, his future choices will probably be determined by practical considerations about his career. Most rabbis hope to land eventually in a large or medium-sized city. Their main reason is not that the congregations are larger and the salaries higher. As one placement officer says, "If high salaries were what mattered, they'd all be fighting to go to Texas." But they're not fighting to go to Texas, because what most of them want, even more than money, is a good religious school for their children, some decent cultural facilities, and—perhaps the most important factor —a chance to be with other rabbis. In the middle of Texas or

Iowa or North Dakota these advantages are not likely to be available.

But at any particular time there won't be too many pulpits that fill the bill. Competition is intense, then, for each really good opening. Luck and timing are just as important for getting ahead in the rabbinate as they are in any other profession. The man who hasn't found the right job within the first ten or fifteen years—not the big job, but at least the stepping stone— must reconcile himself to modest congregations and smaller salaries for the rest of his life.

Clearly, then, the system of placement offices has given the rabbinical organizations considerable power over the careers of individual rabbis. When the strategic opening appears, the Rabbinical Assembly and the Central Conference can use their influence to steer the pulpit committee toward this man and away from that one. They can never exercise absolute authority, but short of that, they can certainly make their opinions felt. Rabbi Arthur Hertzberg, in an article in *Midstream* in 1965, contended that the rabbis who get the good jobs today are the "organization men," the ones who obediently go along with the official views of the establishment.[1] The fury with which his article was greeted by the rabbinical establishment is a pretty good measure of its truth.

Whatever the rabbi's pulpit might be, however, his working conditions have improved immensely since the war. In the twenties a young rabbi in his first pulpit considered himself lucky if he was paid $3,000 a year. Today the starting salary for a Reform rabbi is $8,000 to $9,000 a year, plus medical benefits, and a pension plan (half of which is paid by his congregation). At the height of his career he can reasonably expect to earn about $25,000. Conservative rabbis make slightly less on the average, and Orthodox rabbis just a bit less than that—if you don't include special cases of poverty, like the Hasidim. The highest salary paid to any synagogue rabbi in the United States is a matter of disagreement. Some authorities say $40,000, others go as high as $60,000.

In the old days rabbis had verbal contracts with their congregations. Today the terms are put in writing. The contract is usually for one or two years, renewable by agreement of both parties, until the rabbi finally goes to his congregation and says, "I want a lifetime contract or I quit." What doesn't appear in the contract, however, are the unofficial fringe benefits—the house that may be given to the rabbi at reduced rents, the annual travel allowance so that he can go to his rabbinical convention, the new car, and the trip to Israel. "If a congregation likes you," one rabbi told me, "they'll treat you like a king."

In return for this royal treatment, the rabbi generally works harder than most professionals today. His duties include conducting services, preparing sermons, training children for bar mitzvah or confirmation, supervising the religious school, performing weddings and burials, visiting members of his synagogue in hospitals, doing interfaith work in the community. And what about his traditional role of teacher and scholar? Most rabbis simply give up on this. They just don't have the time to keep up with their Talmudic and historical reading. "I can't understand," one rabbi said to me, "why the rabbi's office is always called his study. Believe me, that's the last thing I ever get to do there!"

And so, after forty years or so of honorable service, the rabbi finally reaches the compulsory retirement age of sixty-five. Now he collects his pension, assumes the courtesy title of rabbi emeritus, and is permitted to occupy a chair on the podium, just behind his successor. Old rabbis, like many other old people, have trouble letting go of the past. Often they will try to take on little extra privileges—for instance, the privilege of saying the benediction at the end of the service. Not surprisingly, benedictions spoken by rabbis emeritus have a way of expanding into something very much like full-length sermons.

The placement offices do their best for retired rabbis. As much work as possible is found for them. They fill in for ailing rabbis, take over small congregations which can't afford to pay a full salary, even become chaplains on cruise ships or at resort hotels. The ones who stop working altogether seldom have a long retirement. Rabbis, like everyone else, do better when they're in harness.

———◦•◦———

Obviously a rabbi's success, not to mention his peace of mind, will depend to a large extent on his relationship with his congregation. This relationship is delicate and complex at best. Each congregation has its own idea of what its rabbi ought to be, and it isn't always the same as the rabbi's idea.

New congregations are the hardest of all to please. Because they haven't decided yet which faction will run things, a constant tug of war goes on, and the rabbi often finds himself in the middle. No matter what proposals he makes, one faction or another will pounce on them and use them as a pretext for a power struggle. There is a saying in the profession that every new congregation kills at least three rabbis before it settles on one.

Old, established congregations generally make much more clear-cut demands of the rabbi. These demands are often determined by where the synagogue happens to be located. Outside of the biggest cities, American life is divided along the lines of religious affiliation. This is the unofficial system that Will Herberg, in *Protestant, Catholic, Jew,* has called "pluralism." The Jew is accepted—but as a Jew. He belongs to "the third religion." But he needs a rabbi to legitimize his position, to provide him with credentials into the American way of life. The small-town congregation, therefore, wants its rabbi to be an "ambassador to the gentiles." Whatever his other qualifications, he must first of all be presentable, diplomatic, Americanized in speech and manner—capable of being the town's "representative Jew" in those crucial relations with the majority. In the South and the Midwest it is so important for the rabbi to be a member of the Rotary Club that his membership fee will often be included in the synagogue's annual budget.

In the suburbs and in large cities congregations make other demands on the rabbi. Because going to synagogue must have its entertainment value for them, they may ask him to be, if not a great speaker, at least capable of delivering a sermon that won't bore everyone to death. The orator who thunders at his flock in the manner of an Old Testament prophet wouldn't be tolerated today, however. Rabbis, particularly in New York where the *Times* gives them good coverage, still try to attract attention with their sermons, but in place of histrionics they put topicality. "The Susskind Syndrome," "Go-Go Judaism," "From Sinai to Saigon"—these are some of the titles of sermons given recently in New York synagogues, and duly advertised in the *Times.*

It doesn't hurt the rabbi either to start a little controversy. In 1919 Rabbi Stephen Wise delivered a sermon against the strike-breaking methods being used by U.S. Steel. A group of businessmen in his congregation tried to force his resignation,

but Wise held out against them and a majority of his congregants supported him. The precedent was set then—"I speak *to*
my congregation, not *for* it," one rabbi says—and most Jews
have accepted it ever since. The placement officer for JTS says
that he can't recall a single case in over fifteen hundred place-
ments of a rabbi who was asked to resign because he differed
with his congregation on ideological matters. One rabbi gave
sermon after sermon in favor of Medicare in front of a congregation full of prosperous medical men. The board of the
congregation adopted an anti-Medicare resolution—and at the
same meeting they offered the rabbi a lifetime contract.

More even than his ability to give a good sermon, many
congregations care about the rabbi's ability to run a good
religious school. He may not do much of the teaching, but the
selection of teachers, the planning of the curriculum, the whole
morale of the school, depend on him. It is the instinct for
survival, of course, which makes the parents feel so deeply
about this—and just a bit of buck-passing is mixed in with it.
Most rabbis would agree with the one who said to me, "We're
expected to inspire the kids with an undying love for Judaism
that the parents themselves don't have."

On a more down-to-earth level, many congregations expect the rabbi to be a public-relations man for the synagogue.
He is supposed to do a selling job, and his success, like the
success of all salesmen, is measured by the number of "orders"
he gets—that is, the number of new members he brings into
the congregation. This is especially true of the Conservative
rabbi in the suburbs. His synagogue is often called "the community center," and he is expected to be good at programing,
arranging extracurricular activities, enticing well-known speakers, thinking up gimmicks that will attract more people than
the gimmicks of the Conservative synagogue in the next
township.

This concept of the rabbi's function has created a new
type, the big-businessman rabbi, whose outlook and manner
are almost identical with those of the modern corporation executive. Under his aegis, synagogue life sometimes seems to be as
competitive as garment manufacturing. The pressure is especially intense in terms of building—what several rabbis have
called "the edifice complex." One rabbi reported the following
exchange between himself and a colleague, when they met on
the street. "How much did your new chapel cost?" "Four mil-

lion." "Well, I've got news for you—*ours* is costing five!"

In the end, then, a rabbi will be most effective when what his congregation expects from him coincides with what he expects from himself. Yet even this idyllic state of affairs won't necessarily bring an end to his problems. For even if he manages to satisfy every one of his congregation's conscious expectations, he must still satisfy their unconscious expectations, those intense unrecognized feelings which every congregation has about its rabbi. These tend to be the same everywhere, in big cities, suburbs, and small towns, and they are very difficult to deal with.

Most people have a double attitude about the rabbi. On the one hand, they never feel quite comfortable with him. They may allude scornfully to his worldly ways and human weaknesses; they may laugh at rabbi jokes, of which every Jew knows dozens; but this laughter is a symptom of their uneasy belief that the rabbi is a man of God and therefore a reproach to sinners. To some people this acts as a challenge, a goad. They feel an irresistible impulse to prove what a hypocrite the rabbi is. Someone always tries to get him drunk at a party. Certain women get a kick out of trying to seduce him.

Other people react in the opposite direction. Their embarrassment in the rabbi's presence leads them to treat him as if he were some fragile object whose pious sensibilities mustn't be jarred. "Damn!" somebody says, and then immediately afterward, "Oh, sorry, rabbi." This excessive delicacy is extended to rabbi's children too, and has given more than one of them a miserable childhood. A rabbi's son who became a rabbi himself told me he could never feel completely close to the other boys at his school. They always stopped telling dirty jokes when they saw him coming.

Under the circumstances it is easy to understand why rabbis like to live in large communities where there are plenty of other rabbis; why small-town rabbis look forward to their annual convention with as much eagerness as Elks or American Legionnaires; why rabbis' children feel a special kinship with other rabbis' children and even have a nickname for one another: "R.K."—Rabbi's Kid.

But along with this feeling of separation from the rabbi, many members of his congregation also have a strange feeling of closeness to him, almost of dependence on him. One rabbi says, "My congregation devotes half their dinner table conversation to cursing me out, but whenever I'm out of town and they have to make their own decisions, they feel a visceral fear."

The fear they feel is the child's fear when his father leaves him. Dozens of rabbis have used exactly this image to me: the rabbi is a father figure. "Congregations are like children," says one of them. "They crave attention, and they're hurt if you don't give it to them." "And they can get pretty jealous," says another rabbi, "if you pay too much attention to the other children." Another rabbi, with a large metropolitan congregation, says that people are constantly playing games with him, like going up to him after services and saying, "Who am I?" and feeling insulted if he doesn't know their names. And another rabbi reports a variation of the same game: "People tell me how hurt they are that I didn't call on them in the hospital. I point out to them that they never let me know they were in the hospital. They say, 'If I was important enough, you would've noticed that I was missing.'"

Because the rabbi is a father figure to many of his congregants, it often happens that those who had a bad relationship with their own fathers will project it onto the rabbi. Either they will vent on him all the bitterness and resentment which their own fathers made them feel, or they will shower on him all the love and adoration which their own fathers never let them feel. The result is that congregations tend to be divided into two warring factions, those who hate the rabbi like poison and those who love him just short of idolatry. There are exceptions, of course. Occasionally a rabbi is so distinguished or so "saintly" that nobody dares to attack him. And occasionally the pro-rabbi forces are so powerful that the opposition is driven underground. But in most cases the rabbi must resign himself to living in a permanent state of dissension.

Not even weakness can free him from this. There are rabbis who try to be diplomats, who make efforts to placate their opponents. This never works for long. The hostile elements in a congregation can't really be satisfied by a few crumbs from the rabbi's plate. Their identification with the father figure is too intense. They must compel the father to submit to them completely; they must gain more and more power until they have full control over him. Even when the rabbi is temperamentally inclined to let them, it doesn't help much, because he is obliged to shut out another group equally intent on controlling him. And so eventually the blandest, most compliant, most diplomatic rabbi finds himself with those two warring factions on his hands again.

———•—•———

The intense emotional involvement which a congregation has with its rabbi provides him, in the opinion of many observers, with a unique opportunity. They believe he should try to influence his congregants toward conduct and attitudes which he thinks are right, not simply direct their services, bar mitzvah their children, and hold their hands when they're sick. Since he *is* a father figure, let him be a strong decisive father who lays down the law to his children, not a flabby, permissive father who lets himself be a buddy to them. With a little more courage and imagination, the rabbi could change the whole quality of American Judaism.

The fact is, however, that most rabbis don't care to make the experiment. They play golf with their congregants, discuss the pro football scores, and are careful to do very little that might offend or upset anybody. They will give their congregations hell on Vietnam or civil rights—which permits everyone to smile indulgently and say, "Poor rabbi, he's such an idealist! What does he know when it comes to practical affairs?"—but they seldom have a word to say about the vulgarity of the latest bar mitzvah or the pillars of the temple who own property in the Negro slums. What primarily interests them is being on good terms with everybody, because this will affect the number of members in the congregation. They are very much afraid of frightening anybody away.

They can't be blamed too much for their fears. To some extent they are simply echoing the whole religious establishment today. The rabbinical and synagogual organizations are no more anxious to antagonize members in good standing than the rabbis themselves are. Affiliation is the name of the game. How can it be otherwise when you're in the survival business?

Yet occasionally a rabbi will have the strength of character to stick up for what he believes, risk his congregation's disapproval, and still hold onto his members—or at least gain as many new ones as he loses. A rabbi with real guts can carry a lot before him in the Jewish community. I have met several of this type. Here is how one of them, a Conservative rabbi, established a Talmud Torah in a synagogue that had been getting along with only a Sunday School for forty years:

His first move after he took over the pulpit was to announce that the Sunday School was finished. From now on any boy or girl who wanted a religious education would have to show up for six hours a week. A deputation of the five richest men in the congregation called on him the next day. "You don't mean *our* kids, do you, rabbi? What about my son's riding lessons? What about my daughter's music lessons?" The rabbi told them there would be no exceptions, and the amiable tone changed to a threatening one. "If you go on with this, rabbi, we'll withdraw our pledges for the building drive." The rabbi shrugged and said, "In that case, I think we'll all be better friends if you resign from the congregation. It'll be a blow if we have to do without the new building, but we'll manage somehow." The five men shuffled out, muttering, and the subject was never brought up again. Their children showed up for the Talmud Torah, and the synagogue got its new building.

In his controversial article Arthur Hertzberg suggested that the American rabbi could still show this kind of leadership, in spite of all the obstacles.[2] This was the real reason why it was received so indignantly by a majority of American rabbis. In their hearts, as a partly-Jewish politician once said, they know he's right. The ambivalence that the average congregation feels toward its rabbi—the guilt, the awe, the confusion over the exact nature of his role—gives him a powerful moral and emotional weapon. Most of the time, unfortunately for him, he's afraid to use it.

There *are* prophets among the Jews in America today, people who are telling us unpleasant truths for the good of our souls. But hardly any of them are rabbis.

X.

The Synagogue Machine

Today, when we speak of the synagogue, we mean much more than a large hall where people gather to pray. The synagogue in America is a complex machine performing dozens of different functions, some of which happen to be religious. It is as much a business organization, social center, and political arena as a house of worship. Consequently, the labels Orthodox, Reform, or Conservative have very little to do with synagogual life, except for the religious aspects of it—and even then, as we have seen, the distinctions often get blurred. The truth is that all synagogues in America, regardless of affiliation, have many things in common.

That Jews themselves recognize this is indicated by the large number who affiliate with more than one synagogue at the same time. Such people never hesitate to play hopscotch across all three branches of Judaism. And many people who belong to only one synagogue feel they're worshiping in the wrong camp. In AJC's Baltimore study of 1962, one-third of those with Orthodox affiliations considered themselves to be "really" Conservative, and one-tenth of those with Conservative or Reform affiliations also had their doubts.[1]

And yet it wouldn't be accurate to say that it doesn't matter what synagogue a man belongs to. It's true that all synagogues have much in common, but it's also true that all synagogues are different.

First, they look different. There is no standard style of synagogue architecture or interior decoration. They can look, as some Lower East Side Orthodox *shtibls* do, like shanties; or they can look, as Temple Emanu-el in New York does, like Radio City Music Hall. One synagogue down South has been described to me as "a gem of Protestant religious architecture." On the other hand, I have seen a synagogue in New Jersey so anxious to assert its Jewish character that it is shaped like a Biblical *hoopah*, an ancient marriage tent.

Synagogue architecture is often greatly influenced by local styles. Shaarey Zedek in Detroit is a huge ultramodern pyramid similar to other new buildings in the area. The Reform temple in a lower-middle-class section of Brooklyn looks like a 1930s WPA project, and was, in fact, put up at the same time as the neighborhood post office and subway station. In the suburban towns of California, where land is plentiful, synagogues are built horizontally, not vertically—a few ranch-style connected buildings, lots of landscaping, huge parking lots. The West Coast synagogue, like the supermarket complex which it resembles, couldn't survive without an adequate parking lot.

The styles of decoration inside synagogues have just as many variations. The lobby and auditorium of one synagogue in Westchester are so cozily wood-paneled that you might think you were in a respectable old English club. But another synagogue in Long Island is ornately overdecorated in bright gold and blue; in the words of a rabbi who spoke there, "It looks like a French passion parlor."

All synagogues are generously covered with plaques or bronze tablets that have the legend "in memory of" engraved on them. Similar legends are found on the backs of the seats in the sanctuary. If there are stained-glass windows, an "in memory" message will often be prominently worked into the pattern. These tributes to the dear departed have not, we may be sure, been put up by the congregation in spontaneous affection for its past members. They have been paid for by sizable contributions—to the Torah fund, the altar fund, the prayer book fund, the choir fund. Smaller "in memory" contributions, not substantial enough to warrant a bronze plaque, are acknowledged each week in the synagogue bulletin. This, in fact, is one important way in which the synagogue finances itself.

Another way is by charging annual dues—a fairly small fee, usually, even for an upper-class synagogue like Temple

Emanu-el. Unlike country clubs, the synagogue must be open to any Jew who wants to join; it would be bad for the image if it kept people out on financial grounds.

The synagogue charges no admissions fee to services, except on the High Holy Days, Yom Kippur and Rosh Hashanah, when everybody comes to worship. Then most synagogues require worshipers to buy tickets, and many sell reserved seats; the closer to the altar, the higher the price. At Temple Emanu-el in New York City the best seats go for about seven hundred dollars, but the demand still exceeds the supply. Your reserved seat at Emanu-el stays with you, if you want it, for your lifetime; you can improve your position only when somebody in front of you dies or moves out of the city. (The same system is used for subscriptions to the Metropolitan Opera.)

The most frequent forms of fund raising are the endless appeals which the rabbi makes from his pulpit, usually just before he launches into his sermon. "Passing the plate" is not a custom in the synagogue. Sometimes a plain white envelope is left on the worshiper's seat. Inside he finds a slip of paper with his name on it, and a list of suggested contributions, from twenty dollars up; he will put a check next to the amount he prefers, and slip the piece of paper back into its envelope. In old-fashioned Orthodox synagogues the method is often less decorous; the rabbi reads out the members' names, and each man is expected to call out how much he intends to give. If he doesn't happen to be in synagogue that day, the rabbi will often put him down for what everyone thinks he can afford.

The synagogue may also employ more frankly commercial methods for supporting itself. If it has a social hall it may rent it out during the week to wedding and bar mitzvah parties. One synagogue in the Riverdale section of New York defrays half its yearly expenses in this way; its social hall does such a thriving business that the leading kosher caterers in the neighborhood send bottles of scotch to the rabbi every Hanukkah.

And the synagogue that doesn't have a social hall surely has a gift shop. Located in the entrance lobby, staffed by volunteers from the sisterhood, it displays its wares in a glass case right near the front door. An informal inventory of one such glass case reveals much about American Jewish life. There, in no particular order, we see a Jewish cookbook, a desk-size menorah (a candlestick with seven branches), Israeli scarves, wrist charms in the shape of the Torah, hymnals, napkins with the Purim story illustrated on them, a "My Bar Mitzvah" photograph album, gold and silver plates ornately embossed with Jewish symbols, paperbacks of novels by I. B. Singer and Bernard Malamud, wine glasses, a Passover cup to hold salt water, a book for children on Jewish sports champions, small ceramic reproductions of Chagall's Jerusalem windows.

The money raised in these various ways is used to pay the mortgage on the synagogue building, buy materials like prayer books and yarmulkes and rabbinical robes, and pay the salaries of the *shamus* (the janitor), the religious school teachers, the choir and cantor, and the rabbi himself. In small congregations the rabbi will often double as cantor, and his wife will run the religious school.

Another common expense is the synagogue bulletin. It may be one smudged sheet, run off on the mimeograph machine in the basement, or it may be a slickly printed six-page brochure, but I have yet to discover a synagogue that does without one. Their contents are all pretty much the same. The latest synagogue function will be described in detail on the first page, including all the names of everyone who served on the committees "which made this highly successful affair possible." There will be news from the religious school (who's being bar mitzvahed, who won the first-grade Hebrew prize), and announcements of coming events, and time schedules for the next week's services. There will be a chatty little column devoted to "the women" and another devoted to "the men," in which everyone will invariably be referred to as Dot and Irv and Mike and Shirl. The rabbi will contribute a few paragraphs on the meaning of the next religious holiday, the importance of charity, or some topic of current interest. Finally, scattered among the news and the chitchat will be ads for the local kosher butcher, restaurant, and undertaker.[2]

As this survey of a typical bulletin suggests, the life of a synagogue lies not in its theological positions or its architectural beauty or its rabbi's influence in the national organizations. The synagogue is the congregation. Its personality is the congregation's personality.

The size of congregations can vary greatly. The bottom limit is ten men, a *minyan*. The largest congregation of all is Temple Emanu-el in New York, sometimes known as the Cathederal of American Judaism. Three thousand two hundred families belong to it. During the High Holy Days, when almost everyone shows up for services, it has to open three auditoriums in addition to its main sanctuary. An assistant rabbi leads the services in each auditorium, and the chief rabbi's sermon is pumped in by a loudspeaker system. Yet with all its fame and grandeur, Emanu-el is a synagogue without personality. The immense size of the congregation prevents it from generating any warm, unified feeling; the people who gather in Emanu-el for Yom Kippur seem to have about as much connection with one another as the people who gather in Madison Square Garden to see the ice show.

In all synagogues the affairs of the congregation—unless they are specifically religious, and under the jurisdiction of the rabbi—are carried on by a complex political structure. At the center of it is the board of trustees and its officers, including a president, a treasurer, a secretary, and chairmen of the committees which control such aspects of synagogue life as keeping the grounds in repair, looking for new members, selling plots in the cemetery (if the synagogue has its own cemetery), and maintaining relations with the community. Many synagogues today have a social action committee, which sponsors resolutions—and sometimes even action—on everything from civil rights marches to planned parenthood. In addition, most synagogues have a sisterhood and a men's club, which sponsor lecture programs and social activities; these groups also have their hierarchy of officers.

In many synagogues it's never very clear who really has the power. In large communities the *macher* (the big shot) of the synagogue may be the president of the congregation, and the power struggle may center around his election. Some presidents are conscientious, hard-working men whose only concern is to improve the synagogue. Other presidents, equally conscientious perhaps, may exact a higher price for their devotion. The president of one congregation in New York is well known in the world of theater; on Sabbath evenings, in the lobby of his synagogue, you can pick up printed flyers with his picture on them and photostats of the latest article about him from *The New York Times*.

In small communities the president carries less weight. Everybody knows everybody else; the synagogue is far from providing a man's only contact with his fellow Jews. And so his prestige among them depends much more on his business suc-

cess or his social position. In such communities the synagogue
jobs rotate, and when it's your turn to be president, you're
more likely to groan than cheer.

Still, among this complicated collection of officers and
subofficers there are always a few people who wield more
power than others. These tend to be the ones who either contribute the most money or work the hardest. They do not tend
to be the most pious, the most intensely dedicated to Torah. In
fact, attempts to impose piety as a standard of power are
invariably resisted by congregations. A few years ago the president of a synagogue in New Jersey tried to put through a rule
that all members of the board must attend services at least
once a month. He was a popular president whose congregation
had supported him in everything he wanted to do, but this
suggestion touched a raw nerve. An open board meeting was
held, people shouted at him as if he were their worst enemy,
and the rule was voted down by an overwhelming majority.

Old-timers say that the politics of synagogues used to be
more colorful and exciting than they are today. In the old days
one man could dominate a synagogue, and rule it for years as if
it were his personal domain. This was the way Louis Marshall
ruled Temple Emanu-el. In the words of the present rabbi, "If
he didn't see a quorum, there was no quorum." But synagogue
life is much more involved today, and no one man can possibly
keep his fingers on all the strings. And so, though the power
struggles continue, the power itself will rest—as it does in so
many American organizations today—with a committee.

————◆•◆————

It has been estimated that most synagogues devote more
time to social activities than they do to religious worship. This
fact is openly acknowledged by the typical suburban Conservative congregation which calls its synagogue the Jewish Center.

It is an inevitable development, because social pressure
has much to do with why people join synagogues in the first
place. In New York and a handful of other big cities this
pressure hardly applies, but Jews in small or even medium-
sized towns, and Jews in many suburbs, feel it keenly. What
happens is this: A group of Jews and a group of Christians
move into a suburb together. The local Episcopal church starts
giving dances and teas. Often the Jews are invited by their

Christian friends, but they feel uncomfortable. After all, it isn't
their church. Then the children of their Christian neighbors
start going to the church's Sunday School. "Why can't we go to
Sunday School too?" say the Jewish kids. Finally, in self-
defense, the Jews start a synagogue, and every Jewish family
which arrives after that is forced, by the same pressures, to join
it.

This explains why synagogue affiliation is only 50 percent
in New York and Los Angeles, but 100 percent in Muncie,
Indiana. It isn't a religious revival; it's simply Will Herberg's
"pluralism" in action. One man was asked why he was active on
the board of his synagogue, but hardly ever went to services.
"Listen," he said, "I don't need a synagogue to pray in." [3]

The variety of social activities which synagogues provide
is immense. They recognize the hard truth about this age of
competition: if you want to sell your product, you have to keep
up with the latest developments. For this reason no synagogue
is built now without a large social hall—larger, in some instances, than the sanctuary itself. One synagogue that I visited
makes no bones about which is more important. The first thing
you see when you go through the front entrance is a long bar,
then the archway leading to the social hall; the sanctuary is
reached by an obscure door on the side.

The main activity that takes place in the social hall is the
dinner dance, described by one rabbi as "the most common of
all synagogual tribal rites." Parties for all occasions, not just
weddings and bar mitzvahs, but anniversaries, birthdays, and
sweet sixteens, are held in the social hall. So is the annual
synagogue show, which seldom has a particularly sacramental
flavor. I visited a synagogue in Long Island that was advertising its "new musical hit," *Money and Sex!*

Amusement for young people is a vital part of every synagogue's social life. For the teen-agers there is probably a fully
equipped gym, a basketball court, a swimming pool. For the
toddlers there is a nursery school and a summer day camp. And
many synagogues have their own Boy Scout troops, with scout-
masters from among the members of the men's club. I attended
a bar mitzvah once at which the rabbi first declared that the
bar mitzvah boy was a man and then declared that he was an
Eagle Scout.

Finally, the synagogue caters to the wives and mothers
with duplicate bridge tournaments, a weight watchers' club,

lessons in gourmet cooking, and, of course, the weekly meetings of the sisterhood. These often have an educational slant to them. "This week," one temple bulletin announced, "we will have a fashion show and a skit entitled *Flora Dora Daze to the Mambo Craze*. This will be followed by the rabbi's talk, 'A Time for Torah.'"

———————

Amazingly enough, American synagogues still have time for a full schedule of religious activities. And yet, in the light of what we've observed, we can hardly help wondering how much real significance these activities have. If people join synagogues out of social pressure, if they spend most of their time playing bridge or jockeying for power, if they go to services as seldom as possible and fidget and yawn when they do—where does religion come in anyway? How religious are American Jews, the ones who affiliate as well as the ones who don't?

The answer depends, of course, on what you mean by religion. Do you mean belief in Judaism? Or do you mean, more generally, belief in God? It's possible to consider the American Jew from both these points of view.

Does he believe in Judaism?

If his belief is to be measured in terms of knowledge, he has very little belief. American Jews are notoriously ignorant about their own traditions. A few years ago the Hillel Society gave a questionnaire to college freshmen, and the results shocked everyone. For example, only 17 percent of these young people knew anything at all about Hanukkah; only 14 percent could name as many as three Hebrew prophets. Yet 85 percent had been to religious school. Obviously they didn't care enough about Judaism to pay attention in class.[4]

Is belief to be measured in terms of ritual observance, then? Well, we've seen the quality of ritual observance among American Jews.

And yet, with all the indifference and sloppiness and equivocation, certain things make us wonder. Very few Jews, no matter how nonobservant, are willing to get married without a religious ceremony. Very few Jews fail to have their sons circumcised. Very few Jews wouldn't give their close relations a religious funeral—and wouldn't want one for themselves. The funeral may violate *halakah* in a dozen ways, the circumcision may not be accompanied by a bris, the wedding may be

travesty of tradition. Nonetheless, in these three crucial moments of life, most Jews find themselves expressing some kind
of faith in Judaism.

Beyond this, the security which young people today feel
about being Jewish has led many of them to a genuine belief in
Judaism. Such young people may be in the minority, but they
are a proud minority, unashamed to express their religious
convictions publicly.

Nobody can be sure, however, whether or not they justify
us in concluding that belief in Judaism is on the increase.
Teen-agers, after all, often go through a religious phase, which
they snap out of after a few months at college. An AJC study [5]
showed that 96 percent of all teen-agers in Wilkes-Barre believed in the Judaic God; a study at Brandeis showed that only
6 percent of its students believed in the Judaic God. [6]

As for adults who talk about their renewed faith in Judaism, they are often, to say the least, suspect. "My kid got me
back to the synagogue," a father told me proudly. Later I
repeated his remark to his rabbi, who gave a weary sigh: "I
wish he'd tell me *which* synagogue, because it sure isn't this
one."

What about God, then? How many American Jews,
though they might have doubts about the forms of Judaism,
nevertheless believe in God? Again there seems to be evidence
on both sides of the question.

On the one hand, many studies indicate that Jews have
less belief in the existence of God than other Americans. According to a recent study, 87 percent of all Americans say they
believe in God, but only 70 percent of all Jews. [7] (The Catholics
do best along these lines; 92 percent of them claim to believe in
God.) Nobody who has lived among Jews is likely to doubt
these results—except to wonder, perhaps, if 70 percent isn't a
rather high figure. A Jewish student at Yale recently was on the
verge of converting to Christianity, to the horror and despair of
his parents. Finally he decided not to convert; instead he
became an observant synagogue-going Jew. "I'm glad you didn't
become a Christian," his father said to him, "but why do you
always have to take everything so seriously?" This feeling will
be understood and shared by a great many Jews.

In Judaism, in fact, even going to synagogue and praying
may not necessarily imply a belief in God. The daughter of one
man, intensely active in his congregation, died a few years ago.

This tragedy, he says, made him stop believing in God, but he's as active in the congregation as ever, attends Sabbath services, and still says *Kaddish* on the anniversary of her death.

This same paradoxical attitude underlies a current phenomenon which, I think, could have occurred only in Judaism. Agnosticism is the philosophy preached by Rabbi Sherwin Wine in his temple in Birmingham, Michigan. Rabbi Wine is a graduate of HUC and a member of the Central Conference, and technically his temple is affiliated with the Reform movement—but he is a constant source of embarrassment to them. He believes that the whole concept of God is outdated; Judaism can function perfectly well without it. He has edited God out of the prayer book entirely; he has reinterpreted and, when necessary, rewritten the Bible to bring it in line with modern skepticism and free it from "superstition." Nevertheless, he and his congregants, one hundred and forty-eight extremely respectable middle-class families, insist that what they believe is not Ethical Culture or Unitarianism, but Judaism. And they aren't shy about pointing out to the members of the Central Conference that the rate of intermarriage in the Birmingham congregation is much lower than the national rate.

And so it seems we must agree with Rabbi Richard Israel, who writes in *Commentary*'s symposium on Jewish belief, "[The current discussion on] the Death of God will cause Jews to ask, 'So what else is new?' . . . The Jewish funeral was a much more private affair. We buried him quietly and in the middle of the night." [8]

But then the evidence starts piling up on the other side. The *Commentary* symposium itself—the mere fact that a hundred pages of theological discussion could appear in a national magazine—suggests that many Jews, even intellectuals, aren't entirely convinced of God's nonexistence. At the UAHC convention in San Francisco in 1966 the best-attended event was a discussion by several rabbis of the question, "Why Believe in God?" Eighteen hundred people, mostly laymen, packed into the auditorium, and many had to be turned away.

And another suggestive fact: Among Jewish college students today the most popular writer does not appear to be one of the secular skeptics, Roth, Malamud, or Bellow, but Isaac Bashevis Singer, with his stories of mysticism and the supernatural in the *shtetl*. Singer himself believes that college students like his work because they are reacting against the materialism, the rationalism, the antimystical philosophy of their elders. The young Jew, whether he realizes it or not, seems to be making some kind of approach toward God.

Once again, who can be sure? Examine any individual case, and it will seem to prove both sides of the question at once. What do Jews who say they believe in God really mean by that? Are they experiencing a genuine sense of the Divine mystery, or a panicky reaction to the Hitler holocaust, the bomb, and the cold war? How many of these people are searching for what one rabbi calls "instant religion" as an anaesthetic for their anxieties? Along with the increase in synagogue attendance and home prayer in the last ten years, there has been an increase in the use of drugs. Is religion a respectable man's LSD—or is LSD a dropout's religion?

These questions can be asked not just about Jews but about everybody in the Western world today. Christianity is going through its own ambiguous crisis. People seem to be turning away from it and at the same time taking a greater interest in it than they have since the end of the Renaissance. There seem to be more Christian mystics and anti-Christian dissidents than ever before.

But the ambiguity is greater for the Jew, though the crisis may be no more painful. The Christian can abandon his religion if he wants to; his problem is deciding whether or not he wants to. But the Jew, even if he wants to, finds it almost impossible to abandon his religion. For Judaism is more than a religion. Rip it out, stamp on it, bury all traces of it—and you'll still be left with that something more.

This may be why there are so many Jewish atheists. It's easy for a Jew to throw away his faith, because he knows that the gesture won't leave him empty-handed. "Who needs praying?" he says to himself, perhaps without even realizing that he's saying it. "There are so many other ways to be a Jew."

Part Three

Joining

XI.

Pledge of Allegiance

Americans, by and large, maintain a strict separation between their religious lives and their secular lives. They may live in both worlds, but not at the same time. The American Jew tries to do this too, but his tradition is against him. Somehow it isn't enough for him simply to divide his life between the world of the synagogue and the world of America. He has had to create a third world, a kind of halfway domain in which, without actually being religious, he manages to be very Jewish.

This domain is cut up into many subdomains, worlds within worlds, some of which are powerful and highly organized. The most important of these is the world of philanthropy —or, as it has been called by friends and enemies, the Charity Establishment. It derives its strength and influence from the curious fact that most middle-class American Jews, regardless of their other affiliations, feel a need to identify with the Jewish community by giving away money.

In doing so, these people, though they may never set foot in a synagogue, are performing a *mitzvah. Zedakeh*, the spirit of charity, is as much a part of the law as *kashruth*. God has commanded His people to help the poor and unfortunate. Unfortunately God's instructions on this point, as on so many others, are ambiguous. Does He mean all of the poor and unfortunate, or just those who happen to be Jewish? When the angels of the Lord, disguised as poor travelers, came to Abraham's house, he fed them though he had no idea who they were or what people they belonged to. Later, however, the Bible says that "Abraham taught the children of Israel they are dependent upon the other for survival . . . that each man must live for the other." Does "each man" mean each Jew or each human being? The Talmudic rabbis give different interpretations at different times. The question, as we shall see, is still being debated. And what feelings are we supposed to have when we give charity? Torah and Talmud are ambiguous about this too. At certain times they seem to require that we give in a spirit of loving-kindness, of genuine compassion for those we help. But at other times they suggest that actions, not feelings, are what count; as long as you do your duty by the poor and unfortunate, it isn't necessary that you love them.

One thing does seem to be clear—to Jews charity has little mysticism connected with it, as it does to Christians. It's literally a down-to-earth thing. We believe that our chief concern must be life on this earth; we are committed to the idea that it can be improved, here and now, materially. My obligation is to do what I can to alleviate your suffering while you're alive, not to brush you off with ephemeral hopes of an eternal reward. And I expect you to feel the same obligation to me. Charity is given to people not because they deserve it, but because they have a right to it.

In the *shtetl* this principle—that no man, regardless of his weaknesses or poor character, must be allowed to sink so low as to shame the community—led to the formation of dozens of associations and organizations designed to help the needy. There were associations to give loans, to educate orphans, to bury the dead, to provide dowries for poverty-stricken girls. And this tradition was followed even by the first Jews in America. In applying for permission to enter the Dutch colony in the seventeenth century, the Jews promised to "look after our poor and to bury our dead." They have been keeping that promise ever since. During the Depression, though Jews were as hard hit as everybody else, an unusually small percentage of them were on relief; in many communities there were none at all.

The American Jew's methods for taking care of his own have changed through the years. In the nineteenth century the German Jews engaged in social work, often on a person-to-person basis. Each small community handled its own problems and had very little involvement with other communities. But by the turn of the century, with the tremendous influx of immigrants from East Europe, it became clear to the Germans that this method wouldn't work any longer. There were too many people and too many problems. A rich man might be approached twenty times a week by *schleppers,* an unkind name for solicitors who came to the door collecting money for their own special causes. Appalled by the waste and inefficiency of these haphazard handouts, the wealthy Germans devised the federation system. All contributions and all applications for help would be made to one large umbrella organization. Much faster and better help for the poor, much less bother for the rich. And so in 1895 the first of these great umbrella organizations was established in Boston, and the system was soon taken up by big cities all over the country and by non-Jewish philanthropies too.

The Germans were primarily interested in local needs. The East Europeans, however, were just as interested in the needs of Jews in Europe, first because many of them still had families there, and then because the *shtetl* tradition emphasized the peoplehood aspects of Judaism as much as the religious aspects. To cope with the needs of their fellow Jews overseas, the East Europeans had to establish their own philanthropic institutions. During World War I they began in a small way, and with some German money as well. The Joint Distribution Committee (JDC) was formed to help Jews in Europe who had been uprooted by the war. It was supposed to disband after the Armistice, but found a reason to continue when a series of pogroms broke out in Poland in 1925.

The Hitler holocaust led to the creation of other organizations. In 1934 a coordinating committee was formed in greater New York to take care of refugees from Germany, and in 1939 it was expanded into the National Refugee Service. Also in 1939 the United Jewish Appeal (UJA) was founded. Originally it was a temporary organization created by contractual arrangement between JDC and another East European group, the United Palestine Appeal. Today it has grown up; it has been supporting its parents for years.

What's more, it has made an alliance, sometimes uneasy but firmly based on mutual interests, with its chief rival. The refugees who came to America were obviously of concern to local federations as well as UJA. Hitler, as we have seen, shocked many German Jews into a sense of peoplehood. And once the war was over, the new state of Israel was a cause that most Jews felt they could support. UJA and local federations in most cities began to combine their annual fund-raising campaigns. Together they became—without quite intending to at the start—a collective voice for the Jewish community. In short, the Charity Establishment.

The gross national product for Jewish philanthropy is over $680 million a year. Since 1939, when UJA was founded, the growth in federated fund raising has been spectacular. It began with a total of $27 million. Then, between 1945 and 1946, it doubled itself, and by 1948 it reached $200 million. That was the peak; it represents the American Jewish response to the survivors of the Nazi slaughter, to the problem of bringing them back to life and finding them somewhere to live. Between 1949 and 1955 there was a decline in Jewish giving—at its lowest the total was $107 million. Since 1956 it has been rising steadily again. In 1965 it was $142 million.

Between 1939 and 1966, the total amount of money produced by federated fund raising among American Jews was over $3 billion.

Individual cities around the country vary widely in their philanthropic records. New York, for instance, though it contains nearly half the Jews in America, is a comparatively poor giver. Its Federation and its UJA together—it is the only city in America where they still conduct separate campaigns—raised about $50 million in 1965, a little more than one-third of the national total. Cleveland, on the other hand, with eighty-five thousand Jews—about one-thirtieth of the Jewish population of New York—raised $6.4 million, the highest amount per capita of any Jewish community in the United States. Similarly, Atlanta's local federation raised $945,000, while Camden, New Jersey, with the same Jewish population as Atlanta, raised only $345,000. One explanation for these differences is the giving habits of the non-Jewish community. Atlanta gentiles are more charitable than Camden gentiles, and this tendency is reflected by the Jews.

Nevertheless, Jewish fund raising is invariably ahead of gentile fund raising. A typical example is Detroit. Its all-faith appeal raises about $25 million a year; Detroit's Allied Jewish Campaign raised about $5 million in 1965, yet the Jews of

Detroit account for only 4 percent of its total population. Furthermore, in evaluating these comparative figures, we must remember that the Jews of Detroit and everywhere else don't contribute only to their own federations; they are also among the most generous contributors to the local Community Chest or United Fund. It has been estimated that Jews give about one-fourth of their annual charitable contributions to non-Jewish organizations.

The figures I've given so far have referred only to federated campaigns. To complete the picture we must understand that many Jewish organizations don't belong to local federations; yet they raise money too, and a lot of it. Synagogues, for instance, account for about 15 percent of all Jewish giving. The City of Hope Hospital in California and the National Jewish Hospital in Denver raise about $10 million a year independently. The Albert Einstein Medical School in New York raises $7.5 million a year. The B'nai B'rith Youth Service Appeal raises close to $3 million. Brandeis University, completely unconnected with any local federation, brings in $15 million a year. All in all, over $74.5 million are raised every year by independent campaigns.

Much of all this comes from people who make small contributions which represent 2 to 4 percent of their income. But the lion's share, well over 80 percent of all the money raised, comes from people who make very large contributions, amounting to 10 percent or more of their income. We can get a vivid sense of what these people do with their money by looking at the obituary pages of *The New York Times*. Whenever a prominent figure in Jewish philanthropy dies, the right-hand column of the obituary page will be full of tributes to him, paid for by the various organizations he has helped.

Yet American Jews don't seem to be so sure of one another's philanthropic achievements. In a study made in Newark a few years ago, members of the Jewish community were asked to guess how charitable other Jews were and to make comparisons with themselves. There wasn't a single respondent who didn't consider himself more generous than his friends, his neighbors, his business associates, and the members of his own family.

The distribution of all this federated money is a complicated process. The local federation gives allocations to national organizations, like ADL, AJC, the American Jewish Congress.

It may even give some money to religious organizations, like the Hebrew Union College and the Jewish Theological Seminary. Much of the rest will go to a wide variety of local needs, ranging from old-age homes to YMHA's. And, of course, hospitals. In New York City hospitals are the single most popular form of Jewish charity; New York Federation gives 35 percent of its money to medical care. In Chicago and other big cities hospitals are slightly less popular than YMHA's and other youth activities.

Finally, the biggest single recipient of federated money is UJA. Each local federation decides how much it will give to UJA. Nationally this averages out to around 54.4 percent. UJA itself then distributes this money among its several member agencies, by a complicated mathematical formula that strongly resembles the sort of thing unions and industries are always coming up with after long hard negotiations.

The various agencies—hospitals, old-age homes, and so on —which benefit from federated drives usually have certain obligations in return. They must show their records and put federation people on their boards. They must obey the First Commandment: Thou shalt not raise money independently. Discipline is pretty good, on the whole. Occasionally an agency will promote a few contributions under the table, but it seldom dares to carry on any large drives without federation approval.

Technically this is also true of UJA. It isn't supposed to carry on any separate drives either. But in most communities it maintains its own chapters, with its own group of professionals and its own reservoir of volunteers and sympathizers. If we didn't know better, we would think it was breaking the First Commandment. The truth is, the local UJA office exists as a kind of pressure group, whose main function is to influence the local federation in its decision as to what UJA's cut should be.

In theory, a federation drive is run by local volunteers. The chairman of the drive and his multitude of cochairmen will be prominent businessmen and professional men from the Jewish community. In practice, fund raising is a highly specialized activity that requires professional experts. These are supplied by an organization which, in most communities, calls itself the Community Relations Council. This council not only provides assistance to the nonprofessional volunteers in raising the money, but exercises considerable influence over how the money is to be spent. "Officially," one professional said to me, "the board member, the big giver, by his closeness to the situation knows where the money is needed and makes the right decisions without any prompting. Actually, any professional can pull the wool over the eyes of any amateur. Most of them are sheep, and we can make them agree to anything."

Twenty-three of these local councils, located in the twenty-three largest cities, belong to a national body, the Council of Jewish Federation and Welfare Funds, whose central offices occupy one floor of a building in New York. The CJFWF is a loose body whose members have complete autonomy. It serves primarily as a means for the professionals around the country to discuss their common problems.

This, then, is the elaborate nationwide structure of the Charity Establishment. Cynics often say that the expense of maintaining it swallows up a large percentage of the funds collected. Actually, the operating costs of Jewish philanthropy are extraordinarily low. National UJA uses about 4 percent of its fund for expenses—and this includes the $70,000 a year it is rumored to pay to its executive director, Rabbi Herbert Friedman. (He earns every penny of it; he is one of the great public-relations men of our time.) Local federations, by and large, also use about 4 percent of their funds for expenses. The fact is that Jewish charities cost far less to administrate than non-Jewish charities.

Simple arithmetic explains why. For the same investment, they raise more money.

◆●◆

Why is Jewish philanthropy so spectacularly successful? To answer this we must examine some of the reasons why people contribute. Their public reasons are one thing—compassion for the poor, Jewish survival, the obligations of wealth, etc. But their private reasons are often something else.

The most important of these is fear of community pressure. Philanthropy is more than a means of acquiring prestige in the Jewish community; it is essential for any acceptance at all. In most Jewish country clubs the man who wishes to become a member must satisfy the admissions committee that he contributes sufficiently to charity; and they can check his claims, because at least one member of the club's board will usually be an officer of the local federation. The new lawyer in town who wishes to establish a practice among the Jewish businessmen had better show up at federation affairs. There are even certain cooperative buildings in New York, owned mostly by Jews, which won't let a man buy an apartment unless his charitable contributions pass muster.

Objections are often raised to the "ruthlessness" of this kind of pressure, but the fund raisers and the pillars of the community feel no qualms about it. "It makes perfect sense," one man said to me. "When you join a club, you're saying you want to join the community. Well, the club charges an initiation fee—and so does the community. Your contribution to UJA, that's your community initiation fee. If somebody doesn't want to pay, okay, that's up to him. But if the bastard won't conform to our values, who wants him? Why should we take him into our golf club if he won't join our Jewish club?

Community pressure can be exerted in many other ways. Some federations publish a book at the end of each campaign, in which the names of all contributors and the amounts of their contributions are listed. In Cleveland this book is mailed free of charge to every affiliated member of the Jewish community. "For a week," says a Cleveland resident, "it's the most exciting reading in town." It isn't surprising that Cleveland has the best money-giving Jewish community in America. Newark's federation also publishes such a book, but technically it is distributed only to paid employees of the Community Relations Council. In fact, everybody gets to see it sooner or later. "It's a very big black-market item," says a Newark resident.

But the most common method of applying community pressure to the individual donor is the fund-raising dinner. The campaign—that great annual orgy of Jewish identification—consists primarily in a series of such dinners, carefully graded according to the financial status of the guests. The opening dinner—the "big" dinner—will be held in the best hotel in town, will feature a speaker of national importance (often a political figure), and will be open only to the select few who are willing to pledge, say, $5,000 or more to the campaign. The second dinner, for the benefit of those who contribute $1,000 to $4,999, will be held in a slightly less prestigious hotel, with a slightly less distinguished speaker. And so on down to the $100 to $200 category, which may get nothing but a luncheon. (The man who gives less than $100 has to eat at home.)

At all these dinners, however, the same thing goes on. Pledges are made by a system known as card calling invented in the early thirties by Joseph Willen, the recently retired executive director of New York Federation. After the food and the speeches, the name of each guest is read out from a stack of cards, and he is required to stand up and announce how much he intends to give—and to hand in his signed pledge then and there. Sometimes the names are called alphabetically, but more often the biggest givers are called first; experience shows that this tends to prod the smaller givers into raising their donations.

An exquisite refinement on this system is comparative card calling. Not only is the man's name called out, but also the amount of money he contributed the previous year; thus, everybody can tell instantly whether or not he's living up to his capacity. Many organizations shy away from comparative card calling; even in a good cause it seems a bit too rough.

Obviously the effect of card calling depends on who's at the dinner and who calls the cards. In small towns and many suburbs the federation has a quasi-governmental function; your chances of getting favors or rewards from the power structure hinge on your standing with the local federation. Every adult member of the Jewish community will be at the fund-raising dinner, and the card caller will probably be the most prominent Jew in town. In large cities federations subdivide themselves into special-interest groups and exert pressure by that means. UJA and Federation in New York, for instance, have chapters in each industry and profession. At a fund-raising dinner you will meet all your peers and competitors in the business world.

A kind of card calling, on a very high level, was practiced a few years ago by Max Fisher of Detroit, the former national campaign chairman for UJA. Mr. Fisher had just been appointed campaign chairman for Detroit's Allied Jewish Appeal, and a gentile friend of his, who was the new campaign chairman for the Community Chest, came to him for advice. "How do you Jews manage to raise so much money?" he asked. Mr. Fisher invited him to sit in on the first meeting of the board for the new Jewish campaign.

A dozen men attended this meeting, all of them wealthy and prominent. Mr. Fisher opened the proceedings by telling them that they themselves, in the past, had always made inadequate contributions to the campaign. How could they expect other Jews to be generous if they didn't lead the way? "I'm naming no names," he said, "but I'm going to start the ball rolling with a pledge of thirty thousand dollars." He then asked the man on his right for his pledge. In a tentative voice this man pledged $3,000. Mr. Fisher sighed. The man said, "Isn't that enough, Max?" Mr. Fisher shook his head wearily. The man said, "How much do you think I should give?" Mr. Fisher said, "In view of your circumstances, Sam, I think you could afford thirty-five thousand." Sam gulped a little, but he came across with his pledge. When Mr. Fisher continued around the room to the other board members, none of them wasted his time with inadequate pledges. By the end of the meeting the board itself had pledged half of the total campaign goal.

Afterward Mr. Fisher went up to his gentile friend and said quietly, "That's how we do it."

Card calling comes in for constant abuse, of course, but the fund raisers simply shrug. They point out that it brings in over 60 percent of all the money raised, and has an incalculable influence on the other 40 percent. They easily dismiss people who disapprove of card calling. "They just don't want to put their money where their mouth is," says one fund raiser.

Furthermore, most American Jews don't really object to this method. Public pledging has become a way of life to them. It has become almost a conditioned reflex. A few years ago the American Women's Gymnastic Team gave a demonstration for the guests at Grossinger's, before flying to the Olympics. When the demonstration was over, the Grossinger's master of ceremonies announced that one of the girls, a pretty fifteen-year-old, didn't have the money for her plane fare to Europe, and suggested that the guests take up a collection for her. The words were hardly out of his mouth when a little bald-headed man in the back row shot his arm in the air and shouted out, "I pledge the first hundred!"

Community pressure being such a strong motive for philanthropy among American Jews, it would seem that no other motives are required. But in fact other motives do operate in many people.

Vanity is certainly a big one. The man who gives money, whether or not he was pressured into it, seldom hesitates to proclaim his generosity to the world. Maimonides wrote that the holiest kind of giving is anonymous giving, and his words are quoted every year in the Yom Kippur services. But such holiness is rare. Less than 1 percent of all contributors to Jewish charity are anonymous.

Donors not only like to have their names known, but immortalized. To satisfy this desire many organizations have adopted the practice of naming things after people. Hospitals give contributors' names to everything from new wings to new oxygen tents. Brandeis University has a Jewish name attached to nearly every building on campus. The Israelis refer to the United States as Plaquistan. The American Jewish Committee feels itself to be at a great disadvantage in this respect; it doesn't put up buildings or buy oxygen tents. Its public-relations staff are constantly thinking up new ideas for things to name after people. A few years ago AJC seriously contemplated giving names to the desks in its offices.

Do Jewish philanthropists want things named after them any more than non-Jewish philanthropists? It isn't easy to be sure about this. Fund raisers point out that charity has traditionally been a form of conspicuous consumption in America. Every college names buildings after their donors, and the names are very seldom Jewish. We have Carnegie Tech, the Mellon Institute, and any number of Rockefeller items. Yet the impression persists that this is a particularly widespread habit among Jews. I wonder if this impression isn't the price Jews pay for being so extraordinarily charitable. They seem to get more publicity because they make more gifts which entitle them to publicity. The Jew with $1 million is more likely to give away $50,000 than the gentile with $1 million.

Philanthropy can feed a man's vanity in other ways. Whether they know it or not, many people give money for the sake of the fuss that will be made over them, the flattery that will be lavished on them. Agency boards, by and large, owe their existence to this motive. The professionals who run agencies like to say that their board is essential to them, that the agency couldn't exist without "liaison between us and the community." But social snobbery is played on whenever possible. Many agencies let it be known that "not everybody is asked to join our board." In New York, Jewish hospitals which were built by German money before 1900 have the reputation of allowing nobody on their boards except people of the highest social status. It becomes less and less true every year, even of the sacrosanct Mt. Sinai Hospital board, but the reputation is useful; it helps to attract the people that agencies really want, rich people with rich friends.

UJA, without much social prestige, has its own tricks for tickling the vanity of big givers. One of the most effective is its Overseas Study Mission. Men who give more than $10,000 are gathered in a group and sent to Israel, "to see the wonderful work that UJA is doing." They make these trips at their own expense, but UJA arranges for them to get the red-carpet treatment when they get there. To many men—and especially to their wives—$10,000 is a small price to pay for shaking hands with Mrs. Abba Eban.

The card-calling dinner itself obviously appeals to vanity as well as fear. People who make good pledges get paid in the long run through the esteem of the community; but many of them also make sure to exact payment in the short run. There are always people who have to accompany their pledges with a few remarks. Sometimes the remarks are brief, and designed to show the company how cheerfully and offhandedly the speaker is able to give away money. "I pledge an extra five hundred because Bernie Nussbaum up on the dais there is such a great rabbi!" Sometimes, especially if the speaker is elderly, the remarks stretch out into a long speech on how necessary it is to have UJA.

People who donate their work to organizations are just as anxious to be compensated with attention as people who donate their money. The chairman at all Jewish communal affairs will invariably read the names of "the committee." These acknowledgments can go on as long as the main speech, especially if each person is asked to stand up and accept his little measure of applause. Yet no chairman would think of omitting this part of the ritual. I attended a function a few years ago where the chairman interrupted himself in the middle of introducing the main speaker—a highly distinguished diplomat —so that he could call out, "Wait a second, our old friend Jake Birnbaum just stepped in! Stand up, Jake, and take a bow for the great job you did on the mailing committee!" Jake took his bow, the guests applauded, then the chairman cleared his throat, looked solemn, and said, "Now, as I was saying, we are deeply honored to have with us tonight a man who—"

The vanity of charity givers has one more curious aspect. The man who gives money wants a fuss to be made over him, but he doesn't want to believe that the fuss is being made because of the money he's giving. He wants to be loved for himself alone, and the fund raisers try hard to satisfy this need. They have invented, for the purpose, a series of euphemisms to replace all distasteful references to money. One of the most popular is "education." Representatives of Hadassah, UJA, New York Federation, and the Jewish Theological Seminary all described their fund-raising activities to me as "a tool for education." Another euphemism, awesomely effective, was coined by a leading philanthropist in a major address. He informed the assembled group of wealthy men that they were not engaged in money raising but rather in "person-to-person responsibility." [1]

———— •●• ————

There are many other factors besides community pressure and social prestige which goad American Jews into supporting their charities. Feelings of guilt undoubtedly play a large part, though it is impossible to measure them. Sheer habit is a factor that is often underestimated. "I'm always willing to spend ten dollars to get one dollar," says Joseph Willen, on the theory that once a man gets into the habit of giving he'll go on doing it, and increasing his gifts, in spite of himself. Another factor is the federal tax deduction for charitable contributions. And a great deal of fund raising is done on a simple *quid pro quo* basis: you give $10,000 to my charity and I'll give $10,000 to yours.

No doubt there are still other factors, too obscure or personal or reprehensible for us to guess. But in this welter of venal, selfish, petty motives, what has become of the motive that ought to outshine them all? What has become of *Zedakeh?* Does any American Jew give charity out of a spirit of compassion and loving-kindness?

The answer is, I think, that most of them do—even the people in whom the other motives are working furiously. Community pressure may prod many people cruelly, but would they choose to join this community if they didn't accept its values to some extent? The country club which requires its members to give to charity is, after all, expressing a view of life very different from the country club which requires its members to own a yacht or have their names in the social register. The man who demands public acclaim for his philanthropy will often perform the same deeds without it, rather than not perform them at all. The assistant director of one federation tells about a perennial campaign chairman who was such a publicity hound that he became a joke in the community. People used to say to him, "How come you're not in the paper today, Al?" Eventually, to protect the federation's good name, he had to be retired from his job. Today he's in charge of the building fund for the old-age home; he gets no publicity at all, and he works just as hard and gives just as much as he ever did.

Furthermore, charity is still part of the Jew's fundamental instinct. His indoctrination begins in childhood. Each of us who was brought up in a Jewish family remembers being told, whenever we left food on our plate, that we ought to think of the poor starving people in Europe or China or the slums. At one time or another, of course, the question popped into all our heads, "What good will it do the poor starving people if I finish my leftovers?" Nevertheless, though the logic was faulty, the lesson undoubtedly sank in: when people are poor, you try to do something for them.

And every Jewish religious school, no matter how far to the left or the right, pounds in the same lesson. At a Hasidic yeshiva the children are urged to contribute their Hanukkah money to P'Eylim, an organization that works among Jews in North Africa; at a Reform Sunday school they are urged to contribute part of their allowances to the UNESCO Children's Fund. The cause may be different, but the principle is the same.

We see the principle operating among Jewish young people for whom community pressure and status seeking are equally unimportant. All the youth groups, Orthodox, Reform, and Conservative, get their members involved in service and welfare projects; so do the secular youth groups of B'nai B'rith and Hillel. The children of Jewish War Veterans get together on Saturdays to pack food parcels for soldiers in Vietnam. The boys and girls at Camp Ramah are obliged to take on service projects in the local community—and they accept some tough ones, like working with mentally retarded or palsied children.

A twenty-one-year-old, the son of wealthy parents, explained to me why he was working for New York Federation's New Leadership Division: "It suddenly hit me that it's about time I started doing something for somebody. I mean, my parents have always taken good care of me. Well, now I figure I have a responsibility to others. Not that I don't feel good when I'm doing this kind of work—and I have to admit it, I enjoy the challenge, trying to manipulate other people, and all that. So I suppose my motives are selfish really." It seems to me that this boy's sense of responsibility (as well as his uncertainty about his own motives) is very Jewish, and very much a part of most American Jews.

There are plenty of deadbeats, of course, the people who protest most vehemently, "I give anonymously!" But on the whole even the nongivers in the Jewish community turn out to have the same traditional instincts. Doctors, for instance, are notoriously poor givers. The story is told that the chairman of a big UJA dinner collapsed with a heart attack, and when someone called out, "Is there a doctor in the house?" nobody answered. But doctors justify their bad giving habits by saying that the kind of work they do, the kind of free service they provide in clinics, makes them genuine philanthropists every day of their lives. This may be a weak rationalization, but the fact that they use it rather than some other suggests that they accept the fundamental obligation of *Zedakeh*.

The same principle applies to other bad givers in the Jewish community. Rabbis are very hard to get money out of, probably because they think of themselves as already sacrificing a great deal to their fellow Jews. Hebrew teachers (those who have something to give) are bad givers. College professors are bad givers, especially those who work hardest for civil rights and other idealistic causes. And there is a strong body of opinion which says that professional fund raisers are the worst givers of all—though this opinion isn't shared by the professional fund raisers.

The entire machinery of the Charity Establishment, then, operates not to create in Jews impulses that they don't have, but "to nudge the inevitable," as one fund raiser says. Yet I think we must ask whether, along with all the good it does, the Charity Establishment isn't doing a lot of harm too. Its nudging techniques are frighteningly efficient, but nobody gives much thought to the effect they have on a great many young American Jews. A majority perhaps aren't bothered by them—these are the conventional good-hearted people who will eventually take their place in the establishment just as their fathers and grandfathers did. But there is a sizable minority, and it includes many of the most intelligent and idealistic, who react to the whole system with horror and disgust, who observe the annual card-calling rites and decide that Jewish life in America is nothing but blackmail and vulgarity.

The professionals have no trouble dismissing these dissenters. "They'll grow up and get over their rebellion. It happened to our generation, and it'll happen to this one too." Maybe so. Today's rebels do have a way of turning into tomorrow's conformists. But there will always be some who can't quite get over the distaste, even when they get over the rebellion, and these will be led to satisfy their charitable instincts elsewhere.

There are indications that something of the sort is happening already. At the 1966 convention of the CJFWF several papers commented on the small number of people on federation boards who are in their thirties. Many suggestions were made on how to get the young interested in Jewish philanthropy, but none of the papers, I think, were quite willing to face up to the whole truth. As long as Jewish philanthropy is adjusted to only one standard—raising the largest possible amounts of money—it will have no real place for those elements in the community which don't have much money, for the young people, the intellectuals, the activists, the very religious. As long as it offers its ultimate respect only to those who can give a lot, it will alienate those who can't. The Charity Establishment must face up to this difficulty, must treat it not as a problem in technique, but as a serious crisis in values, or else, in a generation or two, it will be in real trouble.

I'm not hopeful. Like so many great institutions, the Charity Establishment has become a victim of its own machinery. It is caught in the "moving-up" syndrome; it has to raise more money this year than last year. Each local federation must set a higher goal for its new campaign than it did for its previous campaign, and must meet that goal—because it has persuaded itself that this is the only justification of its existence. The entire Charity Establishment, from the smallest of small-town federations to the mighty UJA itself, is falling upward as swiftly and inexorably as a man who jumps off a skyscraper is falling downward.

XII.

A Country of Their Own

Nobody can deny the intensity of the American Jew's feelings about the state of Israel. Polls taken in 1967 during the six-day war showed that 99 percent of all American Jews supported Israel wholeheartedly against the Arab nations. Hardly any Jew who lived through those days didn't feel a weight of anxiety on his spirits—and a wild elation when the weight was finally lifted. Yet few could say exactly why the survival of Israel meant so much to them, why they were gripped by panic and horror at the possibility that Nasser might keep his promise and "drive the people of Israel into the sea." The explanation, I think, is one that no American Jew quite likes to recognize.

Israel owes its existence to a biblical idea. If Judaism is more than a religion, and Jews are not only coreligionists but a people, it follows that they must have a land. This is the land that God promised to Abraham, into which Moses led the descendants of Abraham after forty years of wandering through the desert, the Promised Land, the land of Zion. Twice in their history after that, the Jews were driven from this land by invaders, the last time by the Romans in the early years of the Christian era. Since then, according to the Talmud, the Jews have been living in exile, the Diaspora. But some day the Aliyah, the ingathering of the exiles, will take place, and the people and their Promised Land will be one again. This is the hope which sustained pious Jews in their *shtetls* and ghettos for almost two thousand years, and which is expressed in many prayers and blessings. At the end of the seder service on Passover, the holiday which celebrates the deliverance from Egyptian bondage, everyone says the words "next year in Jerusalem."

Zionism—the political embodiment of the biblical dream —was invented by the Viennese journalist Theodore Herzl in the late nineteenth century. It took hold among a vigorous minority of Jews in Europe, especially in East Europe where the blessings of acceptance and assimilation were unknown. A few pioneers, when they left the *shtetl,* went to Palestine to start kibbutzim, but a great many more of the East Europeans brought their Zionism with them to America.

From the moment Herzl began to preach his doctrine, differences arose among the Zionists themselves. Though the idea got its justification from Torah and Talmud, only one segment of the Zionists, and not the largest segment by any means, was religious. Many were radicals, even atheists, who gave socialistic shapes to the organizations they founded. They didn't believe in God, yet devoted their lives to fulfilling God's prophecy. Among the "secular" Zionists who came to America, there were all shadings, ranging from the extreme radicalism of the Hashomer Hatzair (the Young Guards) to the moderate social democracy of the Hobonim. And among the religious Zionists there were shadings too, with different groups representing different degrees of Orthodox commitment. During the twenties and thirties many different Zionist organizations existed in America; some were rivals, some were enemies, yet they all more or less cooperated with one another, sustained by the great hope which they shared.

Like many idealists, they could be tough, sometimes even ruthless. A friend of mine, now in his forties, belonged to Hashomer Hatzair from the time he was twelve years old. He came from a middle-sized Midwestern city, and his Jewish contacts were limited; outside of his family, his fellow members of the Young Guards soon became his whole world. When he went to college he developed a taste for literature and the humanities, and decided at the end of his freshman year to major in English. His chapter of Hashomer Hatzair held a solemn conclave and informed him that the kibbutz which eventually awaited them all in the homeland would have no use for students of English literature. He was ordered to major in veterinary medicine instead. He obeyed and stuck it out for a year, hating every moment, feeling that he was twisting his whole nature out of shape. At the end of the year he returned to his fellow Zionists and asked permission to switch back to English. He was told by these young people, most of whom had been his closest friends since the age of twelve, that he would have to follow orders or be expelled from the organization. He left Hashomer Hatzair, and Zionism too, but it was a long time before he could get over the feeling of dislocation, of utter loneliness, which this break produced in him.

Fanaticism of this sort was characteristic of many of these small Zionist groups, for each of them was, in effect, a transplant from East Europe; they carried on old-country methods as well as ideals. It was inevitable, then, that a different brand of Zionism, a distinctly American brand, should also appear. Henrietta Szold, from a wealthy German Jewish family in Baltimore, visited Palestine in 1912 and was converted to Zionism despite its unpopularity in her social circles. When she got back to America, she called a meeting of twelve ladies in New York's Temple Emanu-el—most of them from her economic and social background—and founded the extraordinary organization known as Hadassah. It became the woman's branch of the Zionist Organization of America.

Technically both groups were dedicated to the same ideal as all other Zionist groups—ending the Diaspora, returning the exiles to Palestine. But the style of ZOA and Hadassah was American rather than East European; their language was English, not Yiddish, and their emphasis was on philanthropic aid to the Palestine settlers.

As Zionism grew stronger in America, the reaction against it grew stronger too. From the beginning most of the German Jews were opposed to it. They were doing very nicely in America, and didn't take kindly to the suggestion that where they really belonged was a benighted stretch of desert in the Middle East. Zionism to them was just another example of the bad taste and primitive notions of the "Russians." But it wasn't long before this primitive notion began to seem less nonsensical and distasteful than downright dangerous. What these obstreperous Zionists seemed to be saying was that a Jew in America owed his first allegiance to some foreign country. The louder and longer they went on saying this, the more chance there was that somebody besides their fellow Jews would hear them. In the minds of the German Jews—and of East European Jews who had moved uptown and joined Reform temples and were emulating the ways of the "yahudas"—the horrid old question was raised, What will the goyim think?

An intense and sometimes virulent feeling of anti-Zionism sprang up. On an organizational level it showed itself in those two bulwarks of German influence, the American Jewish Committee and the Central Conference of Rabbis. Much of this antagonism was crystallized in 1939 with the founding of UJA. Though it was never specifically Zionist—it operated in the name of humanitarianism, not political ideology—UJA nevertheless aroused anti-Zionist feelings simply by sending money to the Jews in Palestine. It provided many anti-Zionists with a positive method of expressing their views—they would simply refuse to give money to UJA. As the years went by and more and more local federations combined their campaigns with local UJA campaigns, the die-hard anti-Zionists stopped giving to federations and turned to other charities, often non-Jewish ones.

The Hitler era gave the strongest impulse to American Zionism. Many Jews who were indifferent or even somewhat hostile to the Zionist ideal could understand the practical value of Palestine as a refuge for those who managed to escape from Hitler. Because no other agencies were available to help these refugees except the Zionist agencies around the world, many Americans found themselves in the position of supporting Zionism without actually believing in it. Others, a minority but a powerful one, rejected even this much cooperation. They claimed to feel as much sympathy for the refugees as anyone else did, but refused to allow their sympathies to trap them into giving any support, even indirect support, to the idea that Palestine had some kind of *special* claim on Jews. They were logical, but most of their fellow Jews found their logic repellent and castigated them as stubborn, hard-hearted old millionaires who would gladly see thousands of people die rather than admit a mistake. Clearly a showdown was coming, not between Zionists and anti-Zionists, but between the two factions among the non-Zionists.

The year of the showdown was 1942. A number of wealthy men in AJC, led by Lessing Rosenwald of Philadelphia, attempted to force the group into an open repudiation of all

Zionist connections. The majority in AJC, just as German and substantial as the minority, held out against the pressure; they believed that AJC could cooperate with Zionists without being controlled by them. The explosion resulted in the withdrawal of the Rosenwald faction from AJC and the establishment of the American Council for Judaism, an unequivocally anti-Zionist organization. At the same time as the laymen were splitting with AJC, many anti-Zionist Reform rabbis were having the same struggle with the Central Conference. These men became the spiritual backbone of the American Council for Judaism, gave it a legitimacy which even the old German money couldn't give it.

The lines were drawn now, and any number of minor explosions occurred in the following years. In 1943, for example, the New York Board of Rabbis—a group that is open to all the ordained rabbis in the New York area, whatever branch of Judaism they belong to—was about to elect Rabbi Hyman Schachtel as its president, an honorary title which rotated automatically from year to year. Rabbi Schachtel, however, was challenged by the great Rabbi Stephen Wise on the grounds that he was a member of the American Council for Judaism. A bitter fight took place, and when Schachtel lost, he resigned from the Board; eleven other rabbis, some of them among the best-known names in Reform Judaism, resigned along with him.

Yet it wasn't long before the American Council for Judaism and the anti-Zionist cause started losing rabbinical support. The end of the war, the full revelation of the concentration camp horrors, the growing influx of survivors to Palestine, had a powerful effect on many rabbis. As agitation for the establishment of the state of Israel grew, the American Council for Judaism issued stronger and stronger statements in opposition, and more and more of the rabbis among its members felt uneasy. It was one thing to say that American Jews owed no allegiance to a Jewish state; it was quite another thing to say that such a state should not be permitted to come into existence, that hundreds of thousands of refugees should be left high and dry.

Furthermore, in an excess of zeal the American Council for Judaism made a public-relations mistake which it still has cause to regret. Through its publications and its lecturers it allowed itself to imply that American Jews who weren't totally opposed to Zionism were guilty of the crime of "dual loyalty," that is, disloyalty to America. It made this charge openly only against the most extreme Zionists, but thousands of American Jews who supported UJA and felt sympathetic to the idea of a Jewish state took the charge as directed at them. No insult could have wounded them more deeply. After all, weren't they —or at least their parents—good Americans before they even got off the boat?

And then in May 1948 the whole situation turned topsy-turvy; Israel declared itself to be an independent state, and the following morning President Truman announced that the United States was recognizing it.

In the twenty years that have passed, the conflict between Zionism and anti-Zionism which once divided American Jewry has become not only unimportant, but irrelevant. It still rages on in a small minority of people, but it has moved off to the sidelines somewhere. Many American Jews aren't even aware of its existence. Ask most laymen under thirty-five what the American Council for Judaism is, and they will answer, "Oh, it's one of those defense agencies, isn't it?"

This is not to suggest that American Jews no longer have strong feelings about Israel, or that those feelings no longer contain an element of conflict and contradiction. But today the conflict isn't between two clear-cut points of view in the Jewish community, but something much more subtle which is going on inside each individual Jew.

On the surface, what's going on has no tension or ambiguity in it at all. Now that Israel is an established fact, most American Jews have accepted it and feel good about it; and this is just as true of Reform Jews as of any others. The degree of their good feelings can be measured by the amount of money they give to Israel.[1] In addition to the huge amounts of money that come through UJA, Hadassah raises close to $10 million a year, the National Council of Jewish Women raises $600,000, ORT raises $1.5 million, the Orthodox Pioneer Women raise another $1 million, nearly $5 million are given directly to Israel's three institutes of higher learning, the Jewish National Fund gets a little less than $2.8 million, and the labor organization Histadrut gets about $1.5 million from the American Labor Zionists. Besides these openly philanthropic

causes, the state of Israel sells $76 million in bonds to American
Jews and raises even more in bank loans which are guaranteed
by Jewish communities, using their future charitable funds as
collateral.

At the same time, very few American Jews would think of
heeding the Zionist call and settling in Israel. Every study of
the subject since 1948 comes to this conclusion. In the Riverton
study, 94 percent of the parents and 87 percent of the children
felt affirmatively about Israel, but less than 4 percent wanted
to live there.[2] And so, the American Jew's feeling for Israel is
often said to be the same as the American Irishman's feeling for
the Irish Free State—sentimental, nostalgic, even a bit belligerent, but in no sense conflicting with his love for America.

The sentimental side of the feeling can be seen in some of
the superficial influences that Israel has had on American Jewish mores. The new fashionableness of Hebrew, especially
among Conservatives, is an example; it is taught, and accepted
by parents and children (though perhaps not officially by the
rabbis), as a modern language rather than a religious one, a
language that can be used not so much for biblical research as
for shopping in Tel Aviv. Synagogues around the country have
become Israel-minded: they raise money for Israel; they say
prayers for Israel on the Sabbath; they display Israeli flags and
play Israeli melodies; they teach Israeli folk songs and dances
in their religious schools; they sell Israeli popular art, like dolls,
prayer shawls, and reproductions of those ubiquitous Chagall
windows, in their gift shops.

Israel has also become a major political issue among American Jews. Most of them don't know what the Diaspora is and
aren't aware of being in it, yet they would almost automatically
vote against any politician, Jew or gentile, who they felt was
anti-Israel. A few years ago a New York City congressional
candidate named William Haddad lost an election in a Jewish
neighborhood because the rumor was spread that he was an
Arab. Despite his constant public insistence that he was a Jew,
he became known as El Haddad among the voters; rather than
take a chance, they voted for the other fellow. No wonder that
both major parties are careful to include pro-Israel planks in
their platforms, and that politicians of all faiths are anxious to
appear at pro-Israel rallies or UJA dinners.

American Jewish tourism to Israel is still another manifestation of the love affair. In 1965 Israel received eighty thou-

sand American Jewish tourists, many of whom had been there
before. People have a way of going again and again; one rabbi
tells me that members of his congregation apologize to him if
they're planning to go to Europe without also going to Israel.
Tourists not only go to Israel individually, but in group packages. This has become a popular way for Jewish organizations
to reward devotion and service among their members. UJA's
"missions" to Israel are miracles of stage management. A UJA
group will get to Naples just in time to see a boat full of
refugees leaving for Haifa. A few days later they will get to
Haifa, where they will see that same boat full of refugees
pulling in. Thus, they are given a warm, satisfying sense of
having watched the complete process for which their money is
paying. The fact that the boat was held up an extra day on the
Mediterranean in order to make the timing come out right
need not be called to their attention.

But the unfortunate truth is that Israelis, by and large,
don't much like American tourists, especially the rich ones.[3]
Too many Americans have a feeling that their money has
bought them a slice of the country. They poke into private
places on the kibbutzim; they demand special service at hotels;
they complain loudly about the food, the heat, and the inconvenience of being unable to get a cab on Saturdays. And the
Israelis, being a blunt people, and definitely not a nation of
hotel keepers, often let these tourists know exactly how they
feel. Yet in spite of this, the same American Jew who has
traveled through Israel in a constant state of irritation will tell
all his friends back home what a wonderful country Israel
is—and will usually return for more irritation.

In this chorus of adulation, there are just a few dissenting
croaks. The American Council for Judaism still exists, though
within a year after Israel was established it lost 80 percent of
its members. A few determined old German millionaires keep
it going, and it maintains something of its old belligerent tone
in its pamphlets, but according to one of its paid employees,
"Sometimes the atmosphere of discouragement around here is
so thick you could cut it with a knife."

Other dissenting voices can be heard from an entirely
different direction, from the extreme right wing of Orthodoxy.
These people, though they believe more strongly than anyone
that Israel is the sacred land, have no respect whatever for the
Israeli government. They believe that this government, by dis-

tributing power among worldly elements as well as Orthodox elements, has betrayed the biblical prophecy; the Zionists are as much invading aliens in the land of Israel as the ancient Babylonians and Romans were. Thus, the principal of one right-wing yeshiva told me, "There are very few kosher history books about the Jews. Most of them smack of Zionism. The one that most Orthodox schools are using, for instance—it's a masterpiece of hidden Zionism!"

It is this same spirit which causes right-wing rabbinical groups to make loud protests every time the state of Israel does anything which offends their religious sensibilities. Recently they have been crying out against Israeli laws on autopsy, which they feel conflict with *halakah*. Often they go so far as to send pickets to the Israeli consulate in New York. A few years ago Orthodox pickets with beards and yarmulkes marched in front of the embassy in a parallel line with pickets from Arab student societies.

Yet even the bitterest of these Orthodox dissenters clearly have a strong strain of love in their hatred. A rabbi I talked to sat next to such a dissenter on the plane flying to Israel. All during the trip this old man inveighed against Israel, with curses and criticisms that might have lifted the spirits of the American Council for Judaism. When the plane landed in Tel Aviv, and the old man stepped to the ground, tears suddenly came to his eyes. "It's still home," he said.

———◆◆———

American immigrant groups traditionally achieve acceptance by having a "country of their own" whose existence somehow validates theirs. This sociological fact is usually cited by those who believe that the American Jew's feeling for Israel is the same as the American Irishman's feeling for the Free State or the American Italian's feeling for his native Sicily. Until recently, they say, the Jews were the only immigrant group who had no such "homeland," and this was a crucial cause of anti-Semitism and of the Jewish sense of insecurity in America. The moment Israel was established, the moment the American Jew had a "country" like everyone else, his position among the gentiles and his own self-confidence started to improve.

Undoubtedly there is a great deal of truth to this theory, but the same people who express it tend to weaken it by adding a second explanation. For centuries, they say, anti-Semites have declared that all Jews are cowards, that no Jew has the guts to fight. The Jew today can invoke Israel to convince the world that this stereotype is false. This is why even the most unwarlike American Jews delight in stories about the impact of Israel's military powess on anti-Semites—about the Congressman from Louisiana, for instance, who got off the plane drunk and referred to the Israeli soldiers as "sheenies," and was hustled right back on the plane at gunpoint and sent home. And this is why the majority of American Jews, who couldn't care less about Israel's religious associations, are thrilled by its economic success, its technology, its extraordinary ability to turn deserts into factories and cities. Once again it is Israel's power, its guts, which impress American Jews. The implied, and sometimes spoken, conclusion is, "That'll show the gentiles what kind of stuff we're made of!"

This curious feeling has very little in common, I think, with anything that the Irishman feels for the Free State or the Italian for Sicily. No Sicilian ever loved his country for its military power; no Irishman in his right mind ever praised the Free State for its tremendous economic expansion. What they feel for the old country is all nostalgia, but the American Jew's feeling for Israel has something else in it. He loves Israel because deep inside he is afraid that he doesn't love being Jewish. He sees Israel as a vicarious extension of himself. By identifying with those bronzed invincible heroes, he somehow takes on some of the bravery, some of the strength, that he feels he could never possess unaided. He isn't only trying to persuade the world that Jews aren't cowards; he's also trying to persuade himself.

There is a strong strain of magic in this—the superstitious magic of primitive people who believe that by drinking the tiger's blood or wearing his skin they can assume the characteristics of the tiger. It isn't a matter of logic, or even of facts. A number of years ago, in a debate with Rabbi Elmer Berger of the American Council for Judaism, Congressman Emanuel Celler of New York declared, "Israel has proved that Jews can fight." Berger wanted to know why on earth that proof hadn't been supplied by the thousands of American Jews who fought and died in World War II. The logic and the facts were on Berger's side, but the magic was on Celler's. The native who drinks the tiger's blood *does* gain courage and strength—and this sort of thing has happened many times to American Jews as a direct result of the establishing of Israel.

Revealing evidence of this superstitious feeling is provided by the Jewish community's reaction to the American Council for Judaism. This totally ineffectual organization has been reduced in recent years to a few thousand members, has no more pulpit rabbis on its rolls, controls not a single one of the congregations which were officially affiliated with it twenty years ago. It has stopped accusing Israel sympathizers of dual loyalty; its activities today consist of a few pamphlets about "the Zionist conspiracy" and occasional sulky releases to *The New York Times* about the "pro-Israel hysteria" of American Jews. One would think that the establishment would have given a pitying sigh and forgiven the poor old Council a long time ago.

But in fact the establishment's attitude could be no more violent if the Council were a powerful adjunct of the Arab League, with millions of dollars behind it and a dozen Senators in its pocket. The New York Board of Rabbis recently published a twenty-page booklet entirely devoted to refuting the pernicious lies of the Council.[4] AJC then used its immense public-relations machinery to distribute this booklet, plus a few diatribes of its own, to its members. When establishment people are asked about the Council and its recently retired director, Rabbi Elmer Berger, the responses range from immoderate to downright hysterical. Council members are referred to as anti-Semites, self-hating Jews, betrayers of their people. Rabbi Berger, a tall, weary-looking man—weary, I suspect, from the frustration of his pointless crusade—is described as a psychopath, a paranoiac, a schizophrenic. "He's *persona non grata* among American rabbis," says one of his colleagues. "He *has* to stay with the Council, because nobody else would hire him."

To account for this virulence on the part of people who pride themselves on their broad-mindedness and their belief in free speech, the Council's "unprincipled methods" are usually mentioned; but the real reason, I think, is the Council's anti-Zionist position. The fact that so many American Jews overreact to that position suggests to me how close they are to accepting the anti-Semite's view of them. Israel, with its bold and positive stance, makes them feel less uneasy about their own cowardliness, their shameful yearning not to be Jewish.

Anyone who attacks Israel, therefore, is attacking their inner defenses, the self-deception which keeps them going. Naturally they hate him.

————————•◦•————————

It might be assumed that very little of this applies to the younger generation of American Jews. They feel so much more at home in our society than their parents do; they have so much less to fear. We should hardly expect them to have any great emotional involvement with Israel.

Before the end of May 1967 there were many indications that this was the case. College activist groups with a high proportion of Jewish members were not simply indifferent to Israel but positively hostile. They took the official view of the New Left, that Israel is a bourgeois capitalist tool and Nasser represents the yearning of oppressed minorities for independence. The student newspapers of CCNY refused for a long time to print notices of Hillel events that involved Israeli speakers or themes—yet the editorial boards of these newspapers were almost entirely Jewish. (There is a certain Alice-in-Wonderland quality about the strange alliance of American Jews who oppose Israel: German millionaires who vote Republican, Leftist youths, and Hasidic rabbis. It's a temptation to say, "Only in American Jewry!")

Even among the nonradical majority of young Jews, however, Israel hardly seemed to be a burning issue. AJC's study of the Jewish teen-agers of Wilkes-Barre revealed that most of them were anxious to get more education in Judaism and Jewish life, but very low on the list of suggested subjects was Israel.[5]

None of the experts I talked to expressed any doubts about these findings. Rabbi Herbert Friedman of UJA said, "You can't expect young people to care about Israel the way we do. For them it's not something that had to be fought for, it's not an exciting new experiment. As far as they're concerned, it might have been going on over a thousand years."

And then came the six-day war of 1967, and not the least amazing phenomenon was the reaction of many young American Jews. Hillel directors on college campuses were besieged by students who wanted to go to Israel and take civilian jobs to replace men at the front. By the day the war broke out, ten thousand applications had been filed with the Israeli embassy.[6]

Every office of the Jewish Agency in America was swamped by young people volunteering for the Israeli army. According to observers, only about one-third of these young people had strong religious or Zionist backgrounds. The rest were evenly divided between those who came from ordinary, affiliated, but not intensely committed families and those who were deeply involved in civil rights and anti-Vietnam causes. The extreme radical groups of the New Left came out officially in favor of the Arabs, but it is generally conceded that there was much opposition from Jews in those groups. "Jewish kids in the Movement," one of them told me, "have a double standard on Israel. A non-Jewish leftist is much more likely to condemn Israel than a Jewish leftist."

These facts have been greeted with understandable satisfaction by the Jewish establishment. Rabbi Arthur Hertzberg expressed the official view—for one of the few times in his life —in a short article in *Commentary*.[7] He speculated that Jewish religious education may be doing a much better job at reinforcing identification among the young than it's been credited with doing.

To disagree with Rabbi Hertzberg is always perilous. Nevertheless, I think my own speculation is at least equally unsupported by conclusive evidence as his. I believe that these young people have their own fears about being Jewish in America. It seems likely to me that they, as much as their parents, need an unambiguously righteous and idealistic war in order to give them the illusion of overcoming those fears. If this is the explanation, then the response of young people to the six-day war is no special cause for rejoicing. After all, how often can the establishment hope to provide them with such a dramatic method of affirming their identity?

——————— ·•· ———————

Sometimes the footnotes to history are more dramatic or more moving than the main story.

In the struggle to win over American Jews to the idea of a Jewish state, the Zionists were in the vanguard; their influence was probably crucial. Once the battle was won, the new state established, the flow of money to UJA unimpeded, the American Zionists became a footnote.

They don't think of themselves in this way, of course. Certain outward appearances suggest that they still have

strength and influence. The Jewish Agency, the official arm of
World Zionism, maintains a building on Park Avenue in New
York. The Herzl Foundation, Zionism's cultural branch, publishes *Midstream,* a monthly magazine of Jewish affairs which is
the only serious rival in the field to *Commentary;* it would be
more serious if its emphasis were less on Israel. The Herzl
Foundation also sponsors regular series of lectures and concerts, publishes books on Israeli themes, sends material and
speakers all over the country. In these same New York offices of
the Jewish Agency are coordinators for almost all the Zionist
groups in America; youth groups and adult groups of all shadings find a meeting place here.

Individual Zionist groups are as numerous as ever, and still
run the gamut from superreligious to supersecular. They all
have their regular meetings, their bulletins, their schools, their
national conventions, their youth divisions and summer camps,
and of course, their banquets. Some of them even carry enough
weight to attract important political speakers. When B'Nai
Zion, an American Zionist fraternal organization, held its fifty-
eighth annual dinner, the guest of honor was Senator Robert
Kennedy; he made a pro-Israel speech, and the band played
Danny Boy along with the Israeli horas.

We need only look a little more closely at this picture,
however, to detect signs of trouble. The statistics suggest something of what's happening. In 1948, before Israel was established, the Zionist Organization of America had over 280,000
members; this number represented a steady, spectacular increase all through the previous decade. After Israel was established, the ZOA lost three-fourths of its membership; it claims
to have built itself up to 100,000 today, but few objective
observers are willing to accept this claim. Decreasing membership creates a steady, grinding fund-raising problem for ZOA.
Nor can it get money from UJA or most local federations, who
are anxious to support Israel but only on a "non-Zionist" basis.
"We sweat blood for every cent," says its president, Jacques
Torczyner.

These facts and figures will come as no surprise to anybody who has attended a few lectures at the Herzl Foundation.
The building is modern and air conditioned, the lecture rooms
are large, the speakers are often well-known authorities in their
fields; the World Zionist Organization, as distinguished from
its many American branches, has plenty of money for this sort

of thing. But a Herzl Foundation program rarely attracts as many as a hundred people, most of them elderly gentlemen who speak with foreign accents and exchange Yiddish greetings and jokes.

The youth groups, despite the appearance of bustling activity, aren't really much better off. Abraham Schenker, the Jewish Agency's youth coordinator, estimates that about 35,000 young people are scattered among the dozen or so Zionist youth groups around the country. Their weakness has a depressing psychological effect on many of these young people. They are tormented by the questions, "What's wrong with me? Am I really so far out?" And many of them are led by this torment to concerns that seem more immediate than Zionism —to civil rights, Vietnam, the American scene. This is less true of the young people who belong to the religious Zionists; their feelings about Israel are reinforced by their Orthodox commitment. According to Harold Isaacs in *The New Yorker,* most of the American Jews who actually settle in Israel come from an Orthodox background.[8] Yet even among these young people there are signs of demoralization.

The decrease in numbers isn't the chief cause of this demoralization. Far more important is a self-contradiction deep in the American Zionist's soul. The roots of American Zionism were in the East European ghetto; its shining goal was the pioneering life in the Jewish state. America, for those early Zionists, was simply a way station. Because of its atmosphere of political freedom, it was a good place to stay—until Israel was ready. What none of these people expected was that they and their children would grow to feel an attachment to America that had nothing to do with the Zionist dream. Yet this is precisely what happened. The great majority of American Zionists, even while vigorously pursuing their Zionist activities, were putting down roots in the way station. Few of them realized what was happening to them. They didn't have to. They could earn their living and bring up their children in America, and they could work hard, with no inner conflict, for a glorious ideal that seemed to be way out of reach.

Then the state of Israel was established. Aliyah was possible now; a Jew could stop living in the Diaspora; all he had to do was leave America and go to Israel. Now, for the first time, the American Zionist discovered the cleavage within himself. All his life he had fought to establish a homeland for his people. Now the homeland was a reality—and he didn't really want to go there. He wanted to be a Zionist, but he wanted to be an American too.

This mixed feeling has had fascinating effects on the American Zionist movement and on individual Zionists. First of all, there are those who actually do heed the call and go to Israel. They are only a handful; though every Zionist youth group in America is geared to the idea that its members will eventually end up on kibbutzim, hardly any of them make it. And the ones who do, as Harold Isaacs has shown, still don't escape from the self-contradiction; many of them can never quite bring themselves, even after years in Israel, to give up their American citizenship.[9]

The ones who stay in America have had to devise a rationalization for this choice, a way of squaring their attachment to America with their belief in aliyah. They rationalize as follows: Yes, eventually all Jews must go to Israel; the ultimate goal of Zionism cannot be denied or compromised. However, very few Jews in America today are willing to recognize that goal. As long as millions of them prefer to remain in America, there must be ardent Zionists among them, trying to persuade them to change their minds, keeping the centrality of Israel before them at all times, and on a more mundane level raising money to sustain those who *have* heeded the call. "I'll go to Israel some day, don't worry about that," said a young Zionist to me. "As soon as I'm not needed here any more." By means of this rationalization, many American Zionists have been able to tell themselves that their presence in America is not a form of backsliding but a further sacrifice to the cause.

This rationalization rests, however, on one important assumption. The average American Jew says to the Zionist, "Why should I go to Israel when I am able to make a perfectly happy and valid life for myself right here?" The Zionist has only one answer to this: he must assume that the rest of us are deluding ourselves. No happy, valid life is possible for us in America or anywhere else in the Diaspora. To sustain this conviction the Zionist is committed more than anyone else to the belief that a violent resurgence of anti-Semitism is imminent. For many American Jews, as we have seen, this is a nightmare that comes out of their inferiority complex. To the Zionists, however, this nightmare is a matter of policy.

Where the American Council for Judaism refuses to see any indications of anti-Semitism on the American scene, the Zionist refuses to see anything else. The more signs there are of increasing amity, the more certain he is that an explosion will take place. Friendly overtures from the gentile world are somehow more sinister than unfriendly ones. I asked a Zionist leader about the growing acceptance of American Jews in business, the arts, the academic world. Did he find nothing encouraging in all this? His answer was to smile condescendingly at my naïveté. "What's going on in America today," he said, "is the same thing that went on in Germany in the twenties. There too the Jews distinguished themselves in business, the arts, the academic world—and look what happened to them!"

The American Zionist's uneasy position is further exacerbated by Israel herself. There is a feeling among many Israelis that the Zionist has become a superfluous breed. Ben-Gurion, a great man but not much of a diplomat, has never hesitated to express this feeling. At regular intervals, until his retirement from politics, he infuriated American Zionists with provocative statements. "As far as I'm concerned," he said at a dinner in 1951, "a Zionist is a person who settles in Israel."

Though many Zionists I've talked to deny this, and eloquently defend the current rationalizations, my impression is that few of them have entirely succeeded in convincing themselves. There is a large residue of guilt inside them. It shows itself in many ways, often in a kind of desperate anti-Americanism, in sweeping condemnations of this country and of themselves as part of it. This idea was best expressed by Charles Liebman, the Orthodox sociologist: "I keep telling myself that I can't go to Israel until I find a satisfactory job there. But I feel guilty about this. The truth is, I've got too much of the American Protestant ethic in me."

Guilt may account for the anti-Americanism of many Zionists, but something deeper accounts for their anti-Israel feelings, for the strange impression that so many give of being disillusioned with Israel herself. A leading American Zionist, in a book review in *The New York Times*, described the unsettling feeling he had when he first visited Israel after the establishment of the new state. Against his own sense of logic, he somehow expected to find Isaiah walking the streets of Jerusalem; instead he saw that the latest Lana Turner movie was playing. The "discontinuity between dream and reality" troubled him deeply.[10]

For many Zionists, perhaps for most of them, that's exactly what Zionism has always been—a dream. It was, as one of them has written, "a sentiment, not a doctrine. It turned the disadvantages of being a Jew into a positive transcendant philosophy." To such men there can be no true Zionism without the idea of exile. This is a mystical concept, a privilege and an obigation imposed by God, and the force of this is felt even by those Zionists who think that they don't believe in God. If exile ends, the mystery ends. If you're living on hope, what do you do when the hope becomes certainty? What else have you got to live for?

It isn't fair, then, to dismiss the American Zionist as a weak hypocrite who can't tear himself away from the fleshpots. His dilemma is far more significant and more agonizing. He must live with the loneliness of the dreamer who sees his dream turned into reality—and corrupted in the process, as all realized dreams must be. He has seen the glorious ideal which he called Zionism turned into practical Zionism, political Zionism, public-relations Zionism. His fellow Jews in America can't understand him; his fellow Jews in Israel have contempt for him. He is one of the genuine tragic figures of our time.

XIII.

Locals and Cosmopolitans

On the surface Jewish communal life is a depressingly serious business. There doesn't seem to be a single Jewish organization which isn't serving some noble, high-minded cause. Is it impossible for Jews to seek a kind of official identification which is neither religious, nor philanthropic, nor Zionist, but purely and simply social?

This dreary state of affairs is more apparent than real. The American Jew has as frivolous a social life as anyone else, but when he joins a "Jewish" organization he expects it to justify its existence through a purpose more important than mere sociableness. At the same time, who says its activities always have to take place on that lofty level? As long as the overall purpose of the organization is serious, the meetings themselves can be as social as you please.

More American Jews belong to organizations that satisfy this double standard than to any other kind, with the possible exception of religious institutions. (And even these, as we have seen, satisfy the double standard in their own way.) In the *shtetl* they were unnecessary, because communal life and social life were all mixed up together; the *shtetl* itself was the Hadassah or the B'nai B'rith. When the immigrants came to the Lower East Side they tried to recreate some of the old social conditions in the new soil. They formed *landsmanschaften*, clubs made up of people who came from the same *shtetl* in the old country. Homesickness and a yearning to be among their own were the secret emotional springs of these clubs, but official reasons, compatible with the old ways, had to be found for them. Many of them were burial or insurance societies; members paid a weekly pittance and were guaranteed a plot in the cemetery or the services of a doctor if they got sick. Meetings were held every week or two, ostensibly to discuss how the money should be handled and what help could be given to a distressed member. But after the meeting, the tables would be set up, and everybody would play pinochle.

Some of the old burial societies still exist. Many more transformed themselves in the early years of this century into business and professional associations or Workmen's Circle groups, and in that form they continue to this day. No full-scale study has been made, but it was estimated fifteen years ago that two thousand of these groups could be found in the New York area.[1] They included the Jewelers Benevolent Association, the Theatrical Square Club, the East Side Mineral Water Dealers. The second generation of American Jews formed their own societies whose nature was determined much more by social and economic factors. Yet they retain the same outward seriousness of purpose that characterized the *landsmanschaften*.

The sociologist Daniel Elazar divides Jewish organizations into two types, local and cosmopolitan. The first are only concerned with parochial activities and have few connections with the outside world. The second are associated with large national organizations and officially contribute to national programs. He applies this same division to individual members. In each chapter of even the most cosmopolitan organizations there are plenty of people who have joined for local reasons, who are temperamentally more drawn to the coffee klatsches and the bridge games than to the fund-raising campaigns or the discussions of civil rights. This mixture of locals and cosmopolitans within each chapter is what gives an organization much of its character.

———◆◆———

Hadassah is the supreme example. Officially it exists to promote the cosmopolitan cause of Zionism. Its leaders make sure that it exerts a great deal of influence in the Zionist movement and on the American scene. Hadassah representatives appear at high-level policy meetings of national Jewish organizations, they testify before congressional committees, they fly to Israel and confer with cabinet ministers—and everyone agrees that they are fantastically well informed, intelligent, and effective in imposing their point of view. The few I've met are also just a bit frightening—bright, exquisitely dressed little ladies, with charming smiles and computer minds, and a trick of somehow turning an interviewer into the subject of an inquisition. If I were in charge of the commissary department for the Hadassah Hospital in Jerusalem, I wouldn't want to be short too many bagels when the lady from America comes around.

Yet Hadassah is different from all other Zionist groups in one respect. While others have been steadily losing members in the last twenty years, Hadassah has been just as steadily gaining members. In 1948, 250,000 women belonged to it; 318,000 women belong to it today. It has 1,300 chapters in all fifty states, and though it takes no money from UJA and hardly any from local federations, it still succeeds in collecting over $10 million a year. The secret of its success is that, on the rank-and-file level, Hadassah stopped being a Zionist organization a long time ago.

Its members are middle-class women, mostly conservative, from East European backgrounds. Their husbands tend to earn between ten and twenty thousand dollars a year—hardly up in the heights with the powers of the Charity Establishment, yet comfortably above the average national income. These ladies are sympathetic to Israel, of course, but in exactly the same way as most American Jews. They like the country but they wouldn't want to live there—and, unlike genuine Zionists, they don't feel the least bit torn about this. They belong to Hadassah because its Zionist program—its discussion groups, Israeli lecturers, money raising for the Hadassah Hospital—provides a serious background for its buffet luncheons, dances, card parties, bingo games, and bowling tournaments.

All of this was clearly illustrated to an Israeli friend of mine, a mother and a doctor, who addressed a meeting of a chapter in Princeton, New Jersey. She talked earnestly about the place of the pioneering woman in Israel today. During her talk she mentioned in passing that most Israeli women go through childbirth without anaesthesia and that she herself had done so. When she finished talking and called for questions, none of the women, who were mostly in their thirties, had anything to ask about the pioneering woman. They wanted to know how it felt to go through childbirth without anaesthesia.

———•◆•———

The male equivalent of Hadassah on the American scene is not its official mate, the Zionist Organization of America, but that great middle-class umbrella, B'nai B'rith. (It has its ladies' auxiliary, but this is far less important.) It was established in 1843 by German Jews; its original name was German, but it quickly switched to its present Hebrew name, which means "sons of the covenant." Today it has over 350,000 members in America, and lodges all over the world.

From the beginning B'nai B'rith had a double purpose. As the oldest service organization in America, it was devoted to helping humanity and Jews in distress. At the same time its purpose was to provide all American Jews with a club in which they could feel relaxed and comfortable among their own kind. For this reason it sets up absolutely no qualifications for membership, financial, social, or ideological. It acts on the assumption that all Jews are members of B'nai B'rith, only some of them haven't bothered to pay their dues yet.

In 1876 the New York lodge of B'nai B'rith celebrated its twenty-fifth anniversary in a manner which emphasized its dual purpose. A description of the gala dinner appears in the lodge's records.[2] We are told that "seven musicians of Silberberg's splendid orchestra were in attendance to discourse music, and at half past eight o'clock the doors to the banquet hall were opened, and the guests entered, while the music played a fine march." Later on, it appears, the Orphan Asylum Band played "that beautiful piece, 'Hail to the Chief,' " and "fireworks burned and general enjoyment prevailed." Nevertheless, before the general enjoyment could prevail, certain serious matters had to be disposed of. The records tell us that the guests of honor, earlier that day, were taken by carriage around the city to inspect the various charitable institutions supported by B'nai B'rith—including the Jewish orphanage, where the children were "all in their schoolroom arrayed in holiday attire."

The same duality characterizes B'nai B'rith today. The activities it sponsors are among the most important in the

Jewish community: ADL, the Hillel Society, adult study programs, retreats, the B'nai B'rith Youth Organization (BBYO) which had 1,650 chapters and 45,000 members in 1965, making it the largest Jewish youth organization in the world. The national leadership of B'nai B'rith in charge of administering these programs is probably the best in the country—dedicated, energetic, and imaginative. But few of these leaders bother to attend the meetings of individual B'nai B'rith lodges. The program at a typical meeting is much less likely to be a serious discussion of anti-Semitism than a bagel-and-lox breakfast or an analysis of the stock market. And BBYO activities aren't so different from those of the adults.

B'nai B'rith comes in for a lot of criticism and a lot of condescension—and much of it is justified. Its basic premise, that all differences among its members must be smoothed away or ignored, tends to discourage either the very rich or the very poor from joining. This premise also tends to discourage anyone who isn't a synagogue member; five or six men in a lodge may not be affiliated, but they will be looked upon with suspicion by the others. Above all, it discourages controversy of most kinds; people who believe strongly in any point of view that isn't commonly accepted had better stay away from B'nai B'rith. Except in small towns, where it may absorb the life of the whole Jewish community, it just isn't very high on the social or intellectual pecking order. Intellectuals and ideologues refer to it contemptuously as B'nai Babbitt. "Who needs them?" one Jewish leader said to me. "All they do is have parties and go bowling."

I wonder, though, if the B'nai B'rith membership can be dismissed quite that easily. The average B'nai B'rith lodge member is well aware of the accomplishments of his organization, and feels a loyalty and pride on account of them which is not unimpressive. Each lodge tends to have its favorite B'nai B'rith cause and works hard to raise money for it. The average member may feel like bowling or playing cards most of the time—"After all, I've had a tough day, I have to relax at night!" —but his emotional involvement in B'nai B'rith would be far less intense if it were simply a bowling team or a card club.

No doubt about it—if there were no B'nai B'rith, the middle-class American Jew would have to invent one.

For each of these great middle-class organizations there is an upper-class and a lower-class equivalent. Orthodox ladies on the lower economic levels can belong to the Pioneer Women or Mizrachi, among others. Both of these, like Hadassah, preach Zionism and practice benevolence and sociability. Reform ladies on the upper economic levels can belong to the National Council of Jewish Women. It has a higher percentage of college graduates than any other Jewish women's organization; its members have a higher percentage of Reform affiliation, and their husbands make more money. Its individual chapters engage in local community service projects. It pioneered in the formation of Golden Age clubs for elderly people; its ladies do much work with hospitals and with the blind and handicapped; in many areas they are active in civil rights. They also have luncheons, parties, dances—and are often sustained, in my observation, by the pleasant awareness that, socially speaking, they are at the top of the heap.

But what's so Jewish about them, except that they happen to be Jews? This is a question that continually teases the NCJW's national leaders. They constantly make efforts to get the chapters involved in projects of specifically Jewish concern—studies in Jewish education, for instance—but the ladies are usually more interested in other things. They want to identify with the Jewish community—otherwise why join the NCJW at all?—but somehow they want to do it in a way that isn't too Jewish.

If the NCJW can be described as the upper-class equivalent of Hadassah, then the Jewish War Veterans is the lower-class equivalent of B'nai B'rith. It claims to have close to 100,000 members, most of them in big cities in the East, most of them active in it alone and hardly interested in any other Jewish organization. Many are in small business or trades. Most are Orthodox, though not deeply so. Only 10 percent of its members have graduated from college, and 40 percent have incomes under ten thousand dollars a year. Its dues are very low—it costs ten dollars to belong to a JWV post, and there is always a loud protest when attempts are made to raise this. It has no money for big recruiting campaigns; its members simply go door to door, looking for prospects.

Of course JWV has a serious official purpose. It refers to itself as "the militant arm of American Jewry" and devotes itself to the fight against anti-Semitism and to the rights of

veterans and servicemen. It maintains thirteen service offices
around the country to help veterans, Jewish and non-Jewish, in
dealings with the government, and employs lawyers to take
their cases into court, if necessary. It sends packages to Jewish
servicemen overseas, gives scholarships to the children of its
members, and speaks out loudly on national issues. But, like all
other Jewish organizations, it provides its rank-and-file with
social satisfaction in the name of a good cause. Its posts are
constantly holding dinners or military balls with colors flying.

JWV's special blend of fun and earnestness was sampled
by a young college professor who worked with refugees in
Europe after the war and was asked to address a JWV post in
Brooklyn on "The Refugee Problem." He arrived early and
found himself in an old brownstone building whose inside
walls had been knocked down, turning it into one huge room,
much like an armory. He saw that tables were set up, obviously
for card playing. As he waited, men drifted in, one or two or
three at a time, greeted one another, sat down at the tables, and
immediately started playing poker or pinochle or gin rummy.
Finally there were fifty or sixty men in the room, the smoke
was thick, there was a lot of noise. The chairman arrived and
knocked on his desk for a long time, calling out, "Fellows, can I
have your attention? We've got something special on tonight,
besides the cards!" At last there was silence, more or less, and
the young professor began his speech. Nobody exactly interrupted him while he talked, but he was aware all the time of a
low undertone of murmuring voices and shuffling cards. Once
an argument broke out at one of the tables. The professor cut
fifteen minutes out of his speech and left quietly.

I asked him why he thought they had invited him in the
first place. "I guess they felt they had to have something a little
serious," he said.

The upper class organization for men is the American
Jewish Committee. Until recently it was so upper class that it
had no local chapters at all; its membership was restricted to a
few hundred men, representing the wealthiest elements in the
German Jewish community. But after the war it began to
realize the value of having some kind of mass base for its
activities. Today it has 20,000 members, and in most communities they will be the wealthy pillars of the Reform temple. Or
they may not belong to a temple at all; they may belong
instead to the cream of the Charity Establishment.

Again there is a split between AJC's official purpose and its social purpose. Its national programs are intensely liberal and are carried on by a staff of impressive experts. Anti-Semitism, Israel, civil rights, interfaith problems—whatever the subject, you may be sure that AJC employs one of the leading authorities in the field. Rabbi Marc Tanenbaum, in charge of interfaith activities for AJC, sometimes seems to be the *only* expert in the field. And Milton Himmelfarb, AJC's resident philosopher and social scientist, knows more about Jewish life in America, I suspect, than the entire staff of half a dozen Jewish organizations put together. AJC also publishes *Commentary* and sponsors surveys constantly, as we know. Its members, by and large, approve of its policies and support them with large donations.

But why do they belong to the organization? The social motive is strong. AJC has the reputation of being the elite organization, and this is what attracts much of its support. Many of AJC's older members do come from the German Jewish aristocracy and help to preserve the old-time anti-Zionist upper-class aura; but the majority of its members today are as East European as most of the people in B'nai B'rith. "Just between us," says one board member of AJC, "when we get together at meetings, every one of us could speak fluent Yiddish if he wanted to." It's the aristocratic image rather than the aristocratic reality which persists in AJC today. "They've lowered their stakes," says one observer. "Once they took only millionaires. Today they take Menasha Skulnick millionaires."

AJC's great rival, the American Jewish Congress, brings us back to the middle class again. It has about 30,000 members, and thinks of itself as a political action organization, not a "mass" organization. Its militant liberalism appeals to many of the old Zionists, the secular Yiddishist Jews, the socialists who have gone up in the world. Jewish identification for these people once meant the active espousal of a radical theology. Today they are comfortable businessmen and professionals, often members of Conservative synagogues, just as middle class as anybody in B'nai B'rith; but they want the sense of holding onto the old ideologies in a way which is Jewish, respectable, and not too overtly antisocial. So up and down the Grand Concourse of the Bronx and along both coasts of Long Island the Congress ladies and gentlemen have their own luncheons and coffee klatsches, inveigh against those "AJC millionaires" as they used to do in the good old days of Stephen Wise, contribute to the support of an admirable program under the guidance of some first-rate legal minds—and feel that they're being totally idealistic, not the least bit social.

———————

Neither Congress, with its diluted radicalism, nor B'nai B'rith, with its middle-class blandness, nor any of the other organizations we've examined, seems to be attracting young people once they graduate from college. The tendency among these young Jews, even those who belong to synagogues, is to refer scornfully to "the Hadassah banquet kind of life." The greatest effort to attract the young, outside of the religious establishment, is being made by the most ambiguous organization on the scene today, a fantastic mass of contradictions which only the American Jewish community could have produced.

The Jewish Community Center movement is comparatively new, but YMHA's have been around for a much longer time. The first ones sprang up in the middle of the nineteenth century, in response to the needs of Jews in small communities who didn't want to affiliate with synagogues. In an atmosphere which was partly social and partly cultural, young Jewish men could relax, read a book, and meet Jewish girls.

These early Y's were small and independent—either self-supporting or supported by local philanthropists. The settlement houses which appeared in big-city ghettos at the turn of the century were actually developments of the Y idea, but with a new emphasis—on Americanizing the foreigners, yet somehow permitting them to retain their Jewish heritage. So the Educational Alliance provided courses in Greek culture during the week, and opened its doors to famous Orthodox preachers on the Sabbath.

The Jewish Welfare Board was formed in 1917 to provide service clubs for Jewish soldiers, but when the war ended it had an unspent million dollars on its hands. It used the money to organize the Y's into one unified movement. They did well throughout the twenties, but the Depression struck them a bad blow. Though the people who used them were East Europeans, their financial support came from Germans; the president of the local Y would almost always be a German, though he never showed up except for board meetings and certainly never allowed his own children to go there. Now that many of these German fortunes were hard hit by the stock market crash, the Y's had no mass financial source to draw from. Many of them closed up; others were saved by the WPA, by federal projects in art, music, theater, and social service; but inevitably much of their Jewish content became Americanized and much of their Jewish character was diluted.

The war saved the Y's from falling completely under government influence. They revived in the early forties, and in 1945 they had 400,000 paid members. By this time they had changed their name. It was Mordecai Kaplan who suggested that they call themselves Jewish Community Centers, to emphasize their cultural rather than religious approach to Judaism.

Today there are three hundred Jewish Community Centers around the country, and they have 750,000 paid members; an equal number of people use their facilities without paying for them. They operate on an annual budget of $32.5 million, which they get from three sources: local federations, membership dues, and the Jewish Welfare Board. Dues vary from one center to another—in poorer neighborhoods they can be as low as ten dollars a year, in affluent neighborhoods as high as three hundred dollars a year. Detroit has one of these rich men's centers; it provides swimming pools, saunas, tennis courts, as well as the usual gym and basketball court. Miami has several super-Y's. This tells us a lot about Miami, and something about the JCC's generally—which serve, in many communities, as country clubs for those Jews who can't afford country clubs.

There are all kinds of Y's. The variety can be bewildering. In Long Island they offer nursery schools, bridge instruction, and courses in the newest dance steps. In Arizona and New Mexico they offer lessons in Spanish and Indian basket weaving. In Williamsburg there is a Y for the Hasidim which strictly separates the sexes. The Ninety-second Street Y in Manhattan, the oldest continuing Y in America, gives concerts of medieval music and far-out poetry readings that make it one of the city's avant-garde cultural centers. Yet each Y is not simply a unique and separate unit, reflecting the community around it and the tastes of its directors. There is a unifying principle to the movement.

This principle has been expressed by one of the JCC leaders in this way: "The JCC movement is an instrumentality that contemporary Jewish civilization has thrown up to salvage the past and be prepared for the future." In other words, like every other institution in American Jewish life, the Y's are in the survival business.

In attempting to fulfill this function, they are caught in a self-contradiction that grows more perplexing the more they try to wriggle out of it. On the one hand, the Y's are committed to the task of bringing into the Jewish community those people, especially young people, who might not become involved in any other way. If the synagogue doesn't attract them, maybe the Y can. Dedicated JCC leaders describe this task in terms just as idealistic as those used by religious or Zionist leaders. "How else are we to attract the assimilated Jews?" one of them said to me. "The ones who don't feel the pull of the religion or the idea of the Jewish state—are we just to write them off? Don't forget, assimilated Jews have made some of the greatest contributions to our history. Theodore Herzl was an assimilated Jew; for that matter, so was Moses." And then, in a voice of great conviction, he said, "The Y movement is the growing force in Jewish American life! It's the synagogue of the twenty-first century!"

The difficulty, however, is finding the right bait for these young Jews who are interested neither in Torah nor in Zion. Inevitably the Y tries to pull them in with the kind of activities that all people are interested in—handball, photography, theater, a chance to meet the opposite sex. Perfectly fine, but as a Connecticut teen-ager said to me, "The JCC in this town is a joke. All you do there is play volleyball with Jewish kids instead of gentile kids. As if there was such a thing as Jewish volleyball!"

This line of attack against the Y's was launched in 1947 by the historian Oscar Janowsky. Under the auspices of the Jewish Welfare Board he made a thorough study of the whole movement, and issued the *Janowsky Report*, which has become a Bible to some JCC leaders and a Book of the Devil to others. In his report Janowsky concluded, "Jewish agencies, however denominated, must be Jewish in content, or they have no reason for existence." Most Y directors have made sincere efforts to implement Janowsky's suggestions, but the practical problems are staggering. The type of young person the Y's are trying to attract, the type which isn't attracted to other institutions, probably won't respond very eagerly to the appeal of conversational Hebrew or Jewish Music Month. Most Y's there-fore have had to continue and expand their usual nonsectarian programs: handball and Bach still get more of the budget than the Old Testament prophets.

The dilemma has two more horns which are even more treacherous. The JCC movement is committed to the American ideal of democracy; it believes this to be contained in the traditions of Judaism, and so each Y must serve not only Jews but the neighborhood in general. Even in the early days this was the movement's official policy—many Italian and Irish immigrants made use of the old Educational Alliance—but today this ideal has become a headache. Neighborhoods are changing, becoming mixed, losing Jews entirely. Most of the people who use the facilities of the Educational Alliance today are Negro and Puerto Rican. And many suburban and small town Y's are patronized by as many gentiles as Jews. The Y used to be a place where your son could go to meet Jewish girls; now you never know *what* kind of girl he's going to meet there. "We're all worried about intermarriage," says one Long Island mother, "and what's the JCC doing? Running a bureau for in-terdating!"

JCC leaders take this kind of attack seriously, yet most are reluctant to give up the traditional policy of open membership. The reason is partly economic—the more members they have, the more solvent they are. But the reason is also idealistic. The JCC movement is in earnest about its democracy. It doesn't approve of what many of its leaders call "the pluralistic break-down in American society." It wants Jews and gentiles to mingle freely, and believes this will be a good thing for Ameri-can Jewish culture in the long run.

And so, at bottom, the JCC's are no different from all the other organizations I've been describing. Despite their critics, they see themselves as purveying much more than Jewish vol-leyball. They have a serious purpose. They stand for some-thing.

XIV.

The Power Struggle

The hue and cry against the JCC movement is no isolated phenomenon. It is one symptom of the great struggle which is going on within Jewish organizational life today—the struggle for power between the religious and the secular establishments.

This struggle is quite different from the one that split American Jewry a generation ago. When the East European immigrants challenged the German settlers, it was essentially a case of have-nots versus haves. The old-timers had the money, power, and social prestige; the newcomers wanted it. There was no clash of ideologies; both sides accepted the same standards and wanted the same things out of life. The struggle today is concerned, to some extent, with who shall control the purse strings, but it has its ideological aspect too. Two very different views of life are in conflict, and the victory of one over the other will have grave consequences for anyone who wants to identify with the Jewish community.

The religious establishment bases its attack on an argument which at first sight seems to be untinged by any self-seeking motives or any animus against other groups. All Jews are worried (so the argument runs) about the growing tendency of young people to drift away from Judaism, either through intermarriage or plain indifference. Whatever their disagreements, they are all united in their desire to halt this attrition.

Well, experience shows that the key to the problem is education. The more religious education a young Jew gets, the more likely he is to remain in the fold. But to improve and expand Jewish education—to establish more Talmud Torahs and day schools, raise teachers' salaries, buy books, and make all this available at minimum cost to everyone who wants it—will take a great deal of money. Who is to pay for it all? Obviously it must be the Jewish community as a whole—that is, the federations.

And so the religious establishment launches its offensive with the apparently innocent, straightforward request of more money for Jewish education. The federations are sympathetic to this request, but they are obliged to point out certain practical difficulties. New York Federation, for example, has an annual budget of about $24 million. The head of the Jewish Education Committee of New York estimates that it would require $10 to $12 million to do a really good job of improving Jewish education in the area. And that might be an unrealistic estimate, because if good Jewish day schools were established at low tuitions, throughout the city, who knows how many parents would decide to send their children there? Where is the money to come from then?

In answering this question the religious establishment reveals that its argument has been loaded with dynamite all along. The money must come, of course, from those other projects which the federations are supporting—from all those institutions and agencies which at present are getting such large amounts even though they make no real contribution to the survival of Judaism. Nobody in the religious establishment has gone so far yet as to suggest that UJA must get less money —the Israel nerve is still too sensitive to be touched—but every other activity in American Jewish life, if it happens to get money from federations, is now under attack.

We have seen the nature of the attack against the JCC's. Usually it is carried on in abstract language and strictly in terms of "survival," but sometimes in the heat of battle the more concrete motives show through. Several Conservative rabbis have said to me bitterly, "Why should their centers get support? We have our own centers! The competition is hurting us!"

The attack is equally vigorous against the defense agencies: ADL, AJC, and Congress. Their work is referred to scornfully as "peripheral." After all, the real danger to the American Jewish community is attrition, not anti-Semitism. And by what right do defense agencies push into the area of interfaith dialogues, to the point where they practically monopolize it? Surely that's the prerogative of the synagogues, if anything is! And why does the Community Relations Council of Metropolitan Boston, for instance, give $250,000 a year to the defense agencies and only $300 to the Synagogue Council? [1]

Finally the attack is turned against a victim who would certainly have been immune a generation ago—the local agencies of philanthropy, the ones who appear to be carrying out the demands of *Zedakah* most directly. What do we need Family Counseling Services for? Most of the people who come to them aren't Jewish. So-called Jewish hospitals are no better. Seventy percent of the people who use them are non-Jews, and most of the doctors, especially the Jewish ones, are anti-Semitic. As one rabbi said to me, "Let's face it, hospitals can't save Jews for Judaism." Nor can old-age homes. There are more of them in the Jewish community than ever, and they are run better than ever, but this doesn't prevent many rabbis from asking whether federations have a right to "cater to nothing but a vestigial group of elderly Jews."

All of this is being said in the name of Jewish education; yet there is one clear indication that power is the real issue. In the last ten years federations *have* increased their allotments to education. [2] Close to $6 million were given last year, an increase of 58 percent over 1955. To the schools who got this money it represented about one-fourth of their income; the rest came from tuition and individual contributions. Furthermore, all the big federations have been making plans for further expansion of this aid, and especially at the high school level, where everybody agrees the need is greatest. But the point is that the federations want to support communal schools—a few large religious schools, centrally located and open to children from all over the community—rather than synagogual schools, of which there might be dozens, open only to families who belong to the individual synagogue. The CJFWF argues that no small synagogue school can possibly afford the facilities and the teaching staff of a communal school; furthermore, high academic standards can't possibly be imposed on a large number of schools scattered all over the city.

In response to this the religious establishment raises the

cry of academic freedom. If the federations give the money, they will demand that the schools be run their way. The implication is that federation leaders, being practically atheists themselves, will use the communal schools to sneak their godless ideas into the heads of Jewish youth.

The CJFWF has a whole barrage of answers to this. The same fear was expressed, it says, by hospitals and other institutions in the early days of the federated system, yet they continue to exercise complete control over their own policies. Furthermore, communal schools would be divided according to the three different branches of Judaism, and the standards for each section would be set not by the federations but by the three branches themselves; in a Conservative communal school, for instance, the curriculum would have to be approved by the Jewish Theological Seminary, and the federation inspections would be made by Conservative rabbis. Finally, in those cities where the system already exists—Detroit and Philadelphia are two of them—it seems to be working well, and nobody complains about federation authoritarianism.

These answers make little impression on the religious establishment. Their real objection is not to communal schools, but to communal schools under federation control. In fact, the JTS and the Rabbinical Council have urged their rabbis to support communal schools on the high school level. Why is it all right for high school students to be put in the hands of the atheists? Because in most communities the synagogues don't yet have high schools of their own. The communal school is bad, it seems, only when it's competition.

———————

Who's winning this war? So far the secular establishment has the advantage. Federations still have the money, after all, and on the American Jewish scene, as on the American scene generally, money talks. Furthermore, the religious establishment is hampered by its own internal dissension, by that nervous "looking over the right shoulder" which we discussed earlier.

On the other hand, the religious establishment has one weapon whose effectiveness is still incalculable. American pluralism—the system by which each man justifies his existence through his affiliation with a church—has given a tremendous amount of symbolic power to the rabbi. As an individual he means nothing, but as a representative of the establishment he carries much weight. The rabbinical organizations, especially the Conservative Rabbinical Assembly, are just beginning to understand this situation. More and more in recent years they have been urging their rabbis to throw their weight on the side of religious power and against federation power. No fund-raising campaign in all but the largest cities can get off the ground if the local rabbis refuse to give it their blessing. No defense agency can gain support for its policies if the rabbis denounce it from the pulpit and talk against it among wealthy members of their congregations. The men who give to federations are also members of congregations: their rabbis could use these men as levers to pry more money and influence out of the federations.

In many places this has already been done. A few years ago the United Synagogues of New England felt that it was underrepresented on the Boston Community Relations Council. So it joined forces with the Union of American Hebrew Congregations, and then individual members of congregations who also happened to be big federation donors were urged by their rabbis to write letters of complaint. In most cases the rabbis dictated the letters and the rich men signed them. Within a short time the United Synagogues and the UAHC had four more delegates on the Boston Community Relations Council.[3]

When it comes to giving up money or power, the secular establishment will, of course, fight to the last ditch; but that doesn't mean that its fear of losing rabbinical support isn't intense. It has shown this clearly by capitulating on a point which is essentially symbolic, but significant just the same. For many years the religious establishment used to grumble at the blithe way in which the secular establishment ignored the demands of *halakah*. Today it has very little to grumble about. Few federations—except in small towns where the practical obstacles are insurmountable—would serve anything but kosher food at an official function. New York UJA, which holds hundreds of dinners every year, uses kosher caterers for all of them. The National Council of Jewish Women has started closing its thrift shops on Saturday, their biggest money-making day, even though *halakah*, strictly interpreted, would allow the shops to stay open with gentile employees. Community Relations Councils feel obliged to wrestle with problems that they wouldn't have discussed seriously ten years ago: one CRC for example, is currently debating whether emotionally disturbed children from pious homes should, no matter how badly they need treatment, be sent to institutions that don't serve kosher food.

This kind of capitulation is taking place only because the secular powers are already a little afraid of rabbinical opposition. What else would prompt a crowd of wealthy Reform Jews, gathered together in a posh banquet room, to give up their beloved shrimp cocktail?

Nobody can predict who will win this war. But one thing is certain—if the religious establishment gains control, there will be sweeping changes in American Judaism. In their bid for power, the rabbis are making a drastic demand of every American Jew: they are telling him that if he wishes to identify with the Jewish community, he must belong to the synagogue. Affiliation, they are saying, is the only acceptable form of identification. In a paper for the Rabbinical Assembly a few years ago, Rabbi Jacob Neusner made this demand explicit; he suggested that the Conservative movement condemn all organizations "designed to perpetuate the Jewish group on any other than a religious foundation." [4] And in 1965 the United Synagogues of New England hammered in the point by choosing as the theme of their annual convention, "The Centrality of the Synagogue in American Jewish Life"—and featuring a keynote speech which was nothing but an attack on the federations and the defense agencies.

In a way the rabbis can't be blamed for making this demand. They feel, with some justification, that the secular establishment has left them out in the cold for too many years. But in pushing for their revenge, they are taking a great risk. Many American Jews who are active in the Jewish community but not very interested in the synagogue are liable to be driven away completely. If there were no more JCC's, no more defense agencies, no more B'nai B'rith, no more fund raising except under synagogue auspices, where would secular Jews find an outlet for their loyalties? The Jewish community would be more religious—officially, at least—but it would also be a lot smaller.

The religious establishment, it seems to me, is trying to go

against the Jewish nature. By equating Judaism with the synagogue and nothing else, it is trying to define the indefinable, to
draw clear unambiguous boundaries around something which
is essentially elusive and mysterious. If the attempt fails, it will
be because the average Jew instinctively knows what he is
better than his rabbis do.

Recently the Kashruth Supervisors Union picketed a New
York Federation banquet because the food wasn't kosher. A
reporter from the *Herald-Tribune* stopped one of the guests in
front of the hotel and asked him what he thought about the
picketing. He gave a shrug and said "So?"

That little word may tell us more about American Jewish
life than any number of speeches before the Rabbinical Assembly or the CJFWF. For the truth is that the average American
Jew is detached from these great organizational struggles and
spends very little time thinking about survival and identity and
all those other awesome abstractions. Memberships and affiliations, whether secular or religious, are far less central to him
than his business, his political opinions, his ideas of right and
wrong, his family. Not that being a Jew is unimportant to him.
It's extremely important, more so than he himself may realize,
but it has its deepest influence on these unofficial, unorganized
—sometimes disorganized—aspects of his life.

Here, more than anywhere else, he can't escape from the
split personality. The paradoxes which characterize the American Jew when he's praying and when he's joining become even
more fantastic when he's just living.

Part Four

Living

XV.

The Best Merchandise

It is sometimes said that Jews are smarter than other people. To the Jew this compliment usually has anti-Semitic overtones. He suspects that the man who tells him how smart he is really means to accuse him of taking an unfair advantage. And this suspicion is often justified. Bigots through the ages have used the "superior intelligence" of the Jews as an excuse for persecution.

For this reason the Jew almost invariably finds a way of denying the accusation. We aren't smarter, he says, but in order to overcome discrimination we're forced to study harder. For thousands of years, he says, we were prohibited from owning land, and so there was nothing we could do but work with our brains. It's a self-fulfilling prophecy, he says; so many people keep *saying* Jews are smarter that eventually, whether or not it's true, everyone comes to believe it.

These explanations are plausible enough, yet the truth is seldom far beneath the surface. Sooner or later most Jews will confess—diffidently, apologetically, defensively—that they *do* think Jews are smarter than other people. An individual Jew, even when he knows that he himself isn't very smart, will take pride in asserting that other Jews are.

This pride has deep roots in Jewish tradition. Whether or not Jews are smarter, they are certainly more intently dedicated to education than almost any other ethnic group. The

Talmud says that the Jews are "the people of the book," and in the *shtetl* this conviction permeated the whole way of life. The boy who showed talent in his Talmudic studies was encouraged to devote the rest of his life to them. The community, poor as it was, paid for his board and lodging so that he could spend his days in the synagogue, poring over his books. Even men whose scholarly aptitude was no more than ordinary often gave up much of their free time to studying.

The immigrants on the Lower East Side, as we have seen, continued this tradition, even under the most adverse circumstances. A thousand people every day used to crowd into the reading room of the Educational Alliance. A famous photograph of the early 1900s shows Jewish children lined up all around the block, waiting for the public library to open its doors. At the turn of the century William Dean Howells wrote, "The literary taste of the Russian Jews on the East Side is superior to that of the average native American free-library public." [1]

As the children of the immigrants reached college age, the great channel for their educational passion became the City College of New York, CCNY. Tuition was free, and if you could pass the entrance exam you didn't need a high school diploma. And so, all through the twenties and thirties, it was the place where young Jews who couldn't afford private college got their educations. Many of the best-known figures in American Jewry came out of CCNY in those years. The rabbinate, the civil service, the teaching profession, the social welfare field—all of these were fed by Jewish graduates of CCNY.

Professor Paul Weiss of Yale, the maverick of American philosophy, describes what it was like at CCNY in those days.

> Eighty percent of the students were Jewish, from poor Orthodox families. We were noisy, talkative, anxious to learn, full of excitement. We devoured all the books that were assigned to us, and then grabbed for more. And we never stopped discussing, debating—let's face it, yelling about what we were learning. What a racket there was in the lunchroom! We were just as obstreperous and undisciplined as the kids at Berkeley today, but we weren't at odds with the administration, we were much too busy soaking up knowledge. Plenty of us went for days without shaving, because we begrudged every minute away from

our books. Our gentile professors used to say to us, "How
are you ever going to get jobs, if you don't shave?" And we
used to answer them, "Don't worry, when the time comes
to go looking for jobs, *then* we'll shave."

Later, when Paul Weiss became the first CCNY graduate
to be accepted by the philosophy department of the Harvard
graduate school, he brought his CCNY manner with him and
proceeded to disconcert everybody. In his very first class the
professor said, "Are there any questions?" and young Weiss
immediately raised his hand. Nobody had ever done such a
thing before; it simply wasn't "gentlemanly." But no Jewish boy
from the Lower East Side would ever have preferred being gentlemanly to finding out something he wanted to know.

There is something irrational about this Jewish belief in
education—as befits an idea that comes from a mystical source.
In his heart the Jew believes in the power of education to
accomplish almost anything, to perform miracles. He believes,
for instance, that education can cure anti-Semitism. Dozens of
studies, including the recent *Jews in the Mind of America,*
have shown that college graduates are just as likely to be
anti-Semitic as any other group of people. Nazi Germany was a
particularly nasty example of this; it was a middle-class, highly
educated country, yet Hitler received early support from doctors, lawyers, and other professional men. Nevertheless, when a
swastika was painted on a synagogue in Cleveland recently,
the rabbi said, "We must educate these people to the enormity
of their act. They wouldn't do it if it weren't for their
ignorance." [2]

Still, it must be admitted that the Jewish devotion to
education *has* achieved some miraculous results here in America. The statistics prove it conclusively. In 1963 AJC made a
study which showed that 75 percent of all American Jews of
college age were actually going to college. [3] At the same time, in
questioning Jewish teen-agers in their last year of high school
in Wilkes-Barre, AJC found that a little less than 100 percent of
them plan to go to college. [4] They won't all make it, of course;
but other studies show that among non-Jewish teen-agers only
30 percent expressed the same ambition.

There are no overall figures for the whole country, but
every local sampling suggests that Jewish young people do
remarkably well at school. At Yale every active member of the

Hillel Society was on the dean's list last year. For the last dozen years or so at least one out of the five top-ranking members of the Yale graduating class has been a Hillel officer. Two Hillel officers last year were Junior Phi Beta Kappa. Of the fifty college scholarships which New York State recently awarded to high school seniors from the New York City area, thirty of them were won by Jews. San Francisco's Lowell High School, a high-achievement school that can be entered only by competitive examination, has a far larger percentage of Jews than their percentage in the whole community. The dropout rate in Jewish schools, and among Jewish students in predominantly non-Jewish schools, is far lower than the national rate.

When Jews graduate from school they move into the "intellectual" professions at a higher rate than non-Jews do. We have seen already how many Jewish university professors there are in America today. In every department, as soon as the old restrictions were lifted and professional standards were applied, Jews began to get positions. The same thing is true of the law. Since the Ivy League law schools lifted their quotas, Jews have made up more than half the enrollment. For the last ten years 70 percent of the editors of the *Yale Law Journal* have been Jewish—which suggests that they are at the top of their classes. Many Jews go to work for the government. Though it is impossible to determine to what extent they are actually making policy, they do have key positions in all the departments of the cabinet, even the formerly sacrosanct State Department. In the scientific world, a high percentage of Nobel Prize winners in chemistry, physics, and biology have been Jews. Einstein, Salk, and Sabin are known to all Americans.

And of course there's the Jewish doctor. In every area where Jews have been able to get into medical schools, Jewish doctors have been numerous. Of the 15,000 doctors in New York City, more than half are Jewish.[5] Among the specialties they are predominant in psychiatry, dentistry, and pediatrics, for the purely accidental reason that these specialties have been open to Jews for a long time. There are few Jewish surgeons because schools of surgery and surgical chiefs of staff have been notoriously anti-Semitic.

Jewish involvement in the intellectual professions is equaled by Jewish participation in the arts. Much has been made of the renaissance of Jewish writing in the last decade— Norman Mailer, Saul Bellow, Philip Roth, Bruce Jay Friedman, and so on. The truth is, there were just as many Jewish writers dealing with the life of contemporary Jews in the preceding decades. The twenties and thirties produced Clifford Odets, Irwin Shaw, Michael Gold, Tess Schlesinger, Henry Roth, Meyer Levin, Daniel Fuchs, Nathanael West, Jerome Weidman, Budd Schulberg; if nobody referred to them as a renaissance, it was perhaps because Jewishness wasn't nearly as fashionable then as it has since become.

Jewish musicians have also been prominent on the American scene for many years—particularly violinists, like Heifetz, Ellman, Stern; for the Russian custom, transplanted to America, was to teach boys to play the violin. But even though Jews haven't had the same monopoly on other instruments, they have made names for themselves as pianists (Horowitz, Rubinstein, Fleischer, Graffman), cellists (Piatigorsky, Feuermann), violists (Katims), and opera singers (Peerce, Tucker, Merrill, Resnick, Judith Raskin, Beverly Sills). Many of our leading composers have been Jewish too—from Aaron Copland to David Amram, from George Gershwin to Jerry Bock. The American musical comedy—whether it be cynical-sophisticated (*Pal Joey* by Rodgers and Hart) or slick-sentimental (*The Sound of Music* by Rodgers and Hammerstein)—sometimes seems to be largely the invention of Jews.

In the visual arts Jews arrived late. There is a *halakic* injunction against representations of the human form, and in the *shtetl* it was rigidly enforced; painters like Soutine and Chagall had to escape to Paris before they could draw pictures without fear of reprisal. The immigration to America weakened that injunction along with many others, and suddenly American Jews turned out to be painters and sculptors: Ernst, Lipschitz, the Soyer brothers in the twenties and thirties; Rauschenberg, Larry Rivers, and Helen Frankenthaler today. Chaim Gross, the great sculptor, who teaches regular classes at the Educational Alliance, estimates that 85 percent of his students are Jewish.

In the peripheral areas of the arts Jews are active too. The movie, theater, and television worlds are full of them. Many actors and even more comedians are Jewish; the percentage is very high among directors, designers, and producers. Sixty percent of the art dealers in New York and just under 50 percent of the major American book publishers are Jewish. Many of the leading concert managers are Jewish. There still aren't many Jewish museum directors and curators (the late James Rorimer of New York's Metropolitan Museum was a notable exception), but only because they have been excluded from this field.

Jews are even more prominent among the patrons and consumers of the arts. They buy more books—and Jewish parents are more likely to buy hardbacked books for their children, less likely to be satisfied with a Little Golden Book at the supermarket. Jews flock to concerts, operas, theaters, and nowadays, as soon as they can afford it, they buy paintings and sculpture. Not only do they enjoy the arts, they contribute money to them. One of the two big buildings in the new Los Angeles Art Museum is the Mark Taper Forum, named after a Jewish builder who contributed $1.5 million. The president of the Los Angeles Art Museum is Jewish, and so are many of the influential people on the symphony and museum boards of such cities as San Francisco, New Orleans, and Atlanta.

All in all, then, the American Jew does seem to be upholding the old tradition and passing his love of learning down to his children.

———●◆●———

It is sometimes said that Jews are better businessmen that other people. This is another generalization which smacks of anti-Semitism to the Jew, and which he tries to deny.

Yet the truth is that the strain of practicality, of *tachlis*—which might be translated as caution, realism, a feeling for prose and a distrust of poetry—is just as deeply rooted in Jewish tradition as the strain of intellectuality. In the *shtetl* the scholars were in the minority. Most people were butchers, tailors, peddlers, dairymen, other kinds of small tradesmen or artisans. They were on close terms with poverty; making a living was an activity they had to take very seriously indeed.

When the East European immigrants came to America, their practical know-how was considerably more valuable to them than their respect for learning. They had no money, skills, or experience. They had to start off as unskilled laborers on sewing machines, or as rag peddlers with pushcarts, in imitation of the Germans a generation earlier. Yet they had a big advantage over the Sicilian peasants and Irish potato farmers who shared the slums with them. The virtues that make for success in a middle-class world were already embodied in the

Jew's tradition. He was sober, saving, nonviolent. His orientation to life on earth, his conviction that he must improve his lot here and now, made him ambitious and hopeful, gave him the drive to work long hours, charge low prices, indulge in aggressive salesmanship.

Consequently, wherever Jewish businessmen were permitted to be successful, many of them have been successful. The fact that certain industries today are "Jewish" is almost completely accidental; in each case it can be explained by some external circumstance. Because the immigrants had very little capital and no place to store goods for any length of time, they could handle only movable merchandise that could be sold quickly; so scrap metal, pawn shops, and junk yards became Jewish businesses. The resistance of an entrenched establishment often forced the newcomers to go into businesses which were young and wide open; so Jews became small theater owners and then big movie producers (though the real financial control in the movie business has always been in the hands of the gentile banks). Anti-Semitism, real or imagined, made the Jew anxious to be dependent on nobody but himself, so he was attracted to businesses where he could be his own boss— small stores, small manufacturing, factoring, wholesaling. And if he couldn't really be independent, at least he could take a job that would give him the illusion of independence; this may be why so many Jews in New York became cab drivers. (Sixty percent of all New York cab drivers are Jewish even today, though the number is decreasing as more and more young Jews acquire college degrees.)

The prototypical Jewish business, of course, is the garment industry. From the start it attracted the immigrant because it offered him all the advantages at once. At the turn of the century it was just beginning to move into the mass-production age; there were many small factories, but no powerful monopolistic interests. The industry employed unskilled labor in large quantities; a man who had never seen a sewing machine before in his life could learn how to use one in a few weeks, while he was on the job. And after he saved a little money he could start a shop of his own—and if he had a little luck, he might make an overnight killing. A wild volatility characterized the needle trades in those early years; small companies were constantly springing up out of nowhere, and after a few months or a few years exploding into bankruptcy. But a few of these fly-by-night tycoons, the shrewder or the luckier ones, held on, grew, and eventually established substantial fortunes.

The influence of all those early factors is clearly reflected in the statistics today. According to studies which have been made in various large cities, about 50 percent of all American Jews are involved in wholesale or retail trades; 28 percent of the total white population are engaged in such trades.[6] Seventy-three percent of American Jews are white-collar workers of some sort, as against 33 percent of Catholics and 43 percent of Protestants. Forty-eight percent of all Jews are self-employed; the national percentage of self-employed is about 10 percent, and for white Protestants it's only as high as 19 percent. New York City is an exception in some ways; it has a higher percentage of Jews among skilled and unskilled laborers, clerical workers, and sales people. Many New York house painters, plumbers, and electricians are Jewish; the Brooklyn Plumbers Union, for instance, has 80 percent Jewish members. Also there are twenty-eight hundred Jewish policemen in New York, and about six hundred Jewish firemen. And nobody has ever made a survey of the number of Jewish waiters. No doubt the percentage is high; the union is hard to get into, and these are probably the highest-paid unskilled laborers in America. Yet even in New York there is a much greater tendency among Jews than among other groups to become proprietors of small businesses or to go into the professions.

There are many businesses and trades, of course, that Jews are hardly involved in at all. Few Jews are in banking, as we have seen, though many are on the boards of banks. Despite Jewish domination of the garment industry, the companies that make fabrics, particularly chemical fabrics, are largely gentile. There are no Jewish auto magnates in Detroit. Farm machinery, the central industry of much of the Midwest, doesn't have many Jews in it, nor are there many Jewish farmers. Big corporations are just beginning to hire Jews in management positions, though they have employed them for many years in their research and technical departments. There are many Jews in real estate, but few in the construction business. There are many Jewish insurance agents, but hardly any Jewish executives in the insurance companies. Historical accident seems to be the common factor. In every instance where the business has finally started opening its doors to Jews, the invitation is being accepted.

With all their activity on the American business scene, how much money are Jews making? On this subject it is almost impossible to find reliable statistics. The most educated guesses, however, suggest that American Jews are doing very well financially—but with certain limitations. A study made in Detroit a few years ago showed that the median income for Jews was $6,000 a year; for Protestants it was $4,800; for Catholics it was $4,650. (For Negroes, considered as a separate group because of their special problems, it was $3,500.) [7] This study and many others make it clear, however, that Jews seldom achieve the very highest incomes. Many Jews make good money, but the "real" money isn't Jewish. And this means that the real power isn't Jewish either.

There are hardly any Jewish poor left. Enough to keep the welfare agencies busy, but the number is decreasing all the time. Most of the Jewish poor are elderly people struggling along on small pensions and social security, civil service clerks who never got those crucial promotions and are caught now in the inflation squeeze, families where the father is ill and can't work. I have talked to many officials of Jewish welfare agencies in New York; not one of them has ever encountered a Jew whose income is so low that he qualifies for aid under the poverty program.

And so it would seem that the Jewish businessman has been no less successful in America than the Jewish intellectual. The tradition of *tachlis* is holding its own as strongly as the tradition of Torah.

Obviously many other ethnic groups in America contain a majority of businessmen and a minority of intellectuals. Except for the fact that the percentage of intellectuals is somewhat higher among Jews, they don't seem to be too different from anyone else. There *is* a difference, however. It lies in the peculiar and ambiguous relationship between the businessman and the intellectual in the Jewish community.

An old lullaby of the *shtetl* had this phrase in it: "Study Torah, darling. For Torah is the best merchandise." It isn't possible to be sure what these words really mean. Are Jews supposed to study Torah because they can use it as merchandise, barter their knowledge for a rich wife and a sinecure in the community? Or are they supposed to study Torah because it is on a higher level, purer, finer, than mere worldly merchandise? Either interpretation makes sense. The lullaby is ambiguous, like the Jewish attitude itself. Torah and *tachlis* are both valued, even when they conflict with each other. They stand for two divergent views of life which carry on a constant struggle within the Jewish community and inside each individual Jew.

In the *shtetl* there was no question of which came first. The scholar who knew Torah was given the greatest respect, even if people pitied him a bit for his impracticality and occasionally laughed at him behind his back. But in America the immigrant found a society in which it was easy to mix up these old values. Learning wasn't utterly rejected here; education was vitally important, just as important as it had been back in the old country, but the purposes of education were worldly rather than spiritual. You read and studied and acquired knowledge not for the glory of God but in order to get ahead. This American attitude was just close enough to the *shtetl* attitude, had just enough appeal to the *tachlis* in the immigrant's nature, to throw him off balance. To this day the American Jew hasn't quite succeeded in clearing up his inner confusion.

For this reason the words of the old lullaby—"Torah is the best merchandise"—haunt the businessman still. He prides himself on having all the characteristics of the typical American moneymaker. He is blatantly materialistic. He equates success with his big cigar, his chauffeured Cadillac, his yearly vacation to Miami Beach—or, if he belongs to a younger generation, with his pipe, his Jaguar, his yearly vacation to the Caribbean or the south of France. To buy these status symbols, he won't hesitate to be ruthless. In the garment industry there is a saying, "Nobody trades easy." The Jewish businessman takes this kind of hard trading for granted. He doesn't necessarily get angry when he becomes the victim of it. "That's business," he says. To protect himself he has an automatic attitude of suspicion toward others. When a bank in the Midwest a few years ago appointed its first Jewish vice-president, the only person to withdraw his money was its biggest Jewish depositor. "Excuse me," he said, "but I don't want Schwartz knowing so much about my business."

At the same time, however, the ruthlessness of the Jewish businessman often gets diluted with other contradictory traits that seem to belong to a different kind of person altogether. Most garment manufacturers, for instance, take genuine pride in the quality of their product. They are well aware of the great achievement of the industry, that it has given American women the best apparel in the world at the lowest prices. They may gouge their competitors and exploit their employees, but they seldom try to cheat on quality. Similarly, the Jewish businessman's pursuit of money doesn't seem to interfere with his generosity. We know how much he contributes to charity. Less publicized are his contributions to members of his family, or of his wife's family, who are down on their luck. Few Jewish firms of any size don't have at least one poor relation on the payroll, though his value may be dubious.

Another contradiction marks the behavior of the Jewish businessman. A certain independence of spirit, a cantankerousness, a fierce desire to be his own man, made him successful in business in the first place. Yet along with this he has always had a yearning to be conventionally respectable and dignified, to have "class." The struggle between both these impulses shows itself clearly in his attitude toward his son who has gone into the business with him. He feels contempt for the boy "because he doesn't have to do it all by himself, the way I did." Though he expects this son to take over for him some day, he fights bitterly to keep from delegating any responsibility to him. But he also feels pride, even a kind of awe, in the presence of this smooth, college-educated young man who, by some miracle, is his own flesh and blood. The owner of a large taxicab company told me that his greatest pleasure at the industry's annual meetings comes from watching the sons who are in their father's businesses. "The way they can get up on their feet and make a speech—so fluent, so intelligent! Mostly they talk a lot of impractical foolishness, of course, but what a delightful experience to listen to them!"

The sons are different from their fathers. They value their independence less and take their respectability for granted. They hide their ruthlessness under a smoother exterior. Nevertheless, the same conflict is going on in them. They too trade hard and give to UJA—and make sure that their offices have a highbrow tone by hanging up Picasso reproductions. They are further from the source of the conflict than their fathers, but they are still close enough.

This conflict produces in the Jewish businessman, young

or old, an ambivalent feeling toward the Jewish intellectual. On the one hand the intellectual is the enemy, the fool, the no-good. On the other hand he may be the one who has the right idea—he may be fulfilling the word of God. In the presence of an intellectual, few Jewish businessmen are entirely at ease. They always feel as if they're being judged, and they are, in fact; not by the intellectual but by themselves.

Their uneasiness gives rise to some strange forms of behavior. A movie executive on the coast announced in *Variety* that his studio doesn't intend to produce any "arty-schmarty pictures"; what's the good of winning awards and getting good reviews if you can't cover your negative cost? This same man regularly attends productions of Chekhov and Ibsen at UCLA and loves to boast about the presence of Stravinsky and Heifetz and Henry Miller in the Hollywood area. It is a curious paradox that Jewish movie producers are among the most prominent collectors of paintings and the biggest contributors to the Los Angeles Art Museum; yet they have so little respect for their own art that they have never founded a movie museum to preserve the best creations of Hollywood.

Alex Redein, a well-known painter who also serves as director of the garment manufacturers' association in New York, finds the same mixed attitude being shown to him by the businessmen for whom he works. Because he's an artist, they feel that he must be something of a nut. "Why do you do it, Alex?" they ask him. "Why don't you spend your free time playing gin rummy?" Recently he took a vacation to Florida in order to paint. A garment manufacturer offered him a free membership, during his vacation time, in his Miami Beach country club. When Redein refused the offer, the garment manufacturer was bewildered. "For God's sake, Alex, how can you go to Miami Beach and not play golf? Drawing pictures you can do here in New York!" Yet in spite of their bewilderment, the businessmen who employ him are curiously pleased that Redein is an artist. They don't want him to wear staid gray-flannel suits to their meetings; they prefer him to wear colored shirts and no tie, to look "artistic." He's a nut, but he's "our artist."

And so it is that the businessman with a son in the business may have another son who's living down in Greenwich Village and writing or painting. Publicly he may refer to this artist son as "that crazy kid," but nobody who has ever observed such a father can help but notice the undercurrent of pride and admiration. His kid is crazy, he'll never earn a decent living—but maybe that's the right kind of life for a good Jewish boy.

And then, of course, if his artist son should have the kind of success a businessman can understand—if he should write a best seller, if his pictures should bring fancy prices—the father no longer has to conceal his pride. The two halves of his nature don't have to be at war any more; he can have his cake and eat it too.

This ambivalence necessarily casts certain doubts on a phenomenon we observed earlier. While it is true that nobody takes as much interest in the arts as the American Jew, that nobody cares more deeply about education, we can't help wondering how much *tachlis* is mixed up in all this. Does the businessman buy paintings because he loves art or because he wants to show them off to his friends, and maybe even expects them to be a good financial investment? Does the Jewish mother force her son to study because she believes that knowledge is good, or because it would shame her if he didn't get into a top college? Do American Jews buy the books they want to read, or just the books that "everybody is reading"? Are Jews still the people of the book, or have they become the people of the Book-of-the-Month?

No certain answers can be given to these questions, because it's extremely difficult to disentangle the two contradictory motives in any given case. Take, for example, the millionaire Joseph Hirschhorn, one of the best-known art collectors in America. He was brought up in a poor, uneducated family on the Lower East Side, has made several fortunes, and today has one of the world's greatest collections of modern paintings and sculpture. He never had any formal training in art; he began by buying Bougereaus and Landseers, because he had seen them on calendars when he was a boy; he went into art collecting in a big way after reading a book which informed him that this was a favorite hobby of the great American millionaires. When he likes a painter's work, he often buys it in bulk and insists on a reduction in the price, just like any garment manufacturer buying fabrics. On the surface, Hirschhorn would seem to be the perfect stereotype of the ignoramus who collects art simply for the sake of show.

And yet if Hirschhorn were really this kind of man, it seems odd that he never collects anything else for show.

Yachts, race horses, jewelry, villas, automobiles—none of the
usual trophies of the status-minded have ever interested him.
And the same people who deplore his toughness in buying an
item for his collection admit that he has a kind of boyish
admiration for the artists themselves. "They're big people," he
says "They don't care about money! All they care about is their
work!" [8]

What kind of millionaire admires men who don't care
about money? The same kind who despises men who don't care
about money. A Jewish millionaire.

In the Jewish intellectual this conflict between *tachlis* and
Torah is a more painful and complex version of the same
conflict in the Jewish businessman. The businessman lives by
tachlis, but wonders if he shouldn't be living by Torah; he has
an inferiority complex which he appeases by occasional gestures of conciliation to the enemy. The intellectual lives by
Torah, but feels a strong temptation to live by *tachlis*.

He tries to appease this feeling by throwing himself into
the intellectual life with formidable earnestness and intensity.
It absorbs every moment of his time and every ounce of his
energy. He's constantly talking, writing, making points. All
right, he's an intellectual, but why does he have to work at it
night and day? The answer is, that's exactly what he has to do
—"work" at it. That's what they did in the *shtetl;* yeshiva boys
worked longer hours than butchers or shopkeepers. The life of
the mind must involve hard, constant, visible work, or else
someone might accuse the intellectual of loafing, wasting his
time, being an impractical good-for-nothing. Who might make
such an accusation? His businessman father, to start with; and
to follow, the whole Jewish community, with the combined
weight of thousands of years of tradition behind it; and to end
with, his own conscience. The Jewish intellectual, whatever
else he may do, seldom stretches under a tree and just thinks.

And then, the intellect can't be just a tool for him; it has to
be a weapon too. He doesn't use it simply to discover what the
world is like, or to create something beautiful, or to communicate his ideas. He must use it to beat down his competitors, to
prove his superiority. For him controversy is inseparable from
intellectual activity. Watch him at a party; note the vicious
delight with which he backs lesser intellects into a corner. He's

implacable; neither social decorum nor human compassion can soften his attack. If you want to observe this trait at a safer distance, read what he writes to the letters-to-the-editor pages. In all Jewish publications, from *Commentary* down to the most obscure Yiddish weekly, these pages bathe the reader in vitriol. Like his father, the garment manufacturer, the Jewish intellectual doesn't trade easy.

And above all he is very concerned about his "significance." He must always have something profound to say, even if he has nothing profound to say. There is nobody like a Jewish intellectual for making Important Statements. In its symposium called "Jewishness and the Younger Intellectuals," which *Commentary* conducted in 1961, many of the participants chose Freud and Einstein as their culture idols. This choice, it seems to me, is symptomatic of the Jewish intellectual's taste for complexity. The chances are that few of those who expressed admiration for Einstein have enough knowledge of mathematics to make any real sense of his work; what attracts them, I suspect, is the myth that only a handful of people can understand his theory of relativity. Freud, of course, has shown that the human mind is an enigma: we can never get to the bottom of it; no piece of behavior, not even a simple slip of the tongue, is what it seems to be. An ideal philosophy for the Jewish intellectual.

Not that he doesn't have a sense of humor. He has the Jewish sense of humor in abundance. Catch him with his guard down, and he can enjoy, and invent, Jewish jokes as heartily as his businessman father. But in his more intellectual moments he feels just a bit ashamed of his sense of humor; even when he has a natural comic talent, he often feels obliged to put it at the service of significance—or at least to convince himself that he's doing so. Abe Burrows, with all his success in the Broadway theater, is disturbed when people refer to him as a writer of comedy and ask him why he never does anything serious. "I *am* serious," he replied to a group of college students recently. "Everything I write has a serious purpose. It's just that my method is funny." [9] Bruce Jay Friedman, with a unique, priceless gift for bizarre humor, feels the need to turn out aphoristic short stories that make a "point"; fortunately he doesn't succumb to this temptation in his novels.

Manner as well as matter must be serious, and this often has disastrous effects on the Jewish intellectual's prose style. Its besetting fault is pretentiousness. It is characterized by long words, involved sentences, a pervasive heaviness of tone. A young Jewish inventor who has been experimenting with hearing aids produced this remark for the New York *Post:*

> My researches turned up very little evidence that anyone has ever tried to maximize the utility of the human ear.[10]

Lionel Trilling, in *Commentary,* made this evaluation of the thirties:

> The decade had never been thought of as a mere undifferentiated segment of the past, but now it was to be canonized as a veritable epoch or period, an entity with a beginning, middle, and end, and a style appropriate to the discernible logic of its events.[11]

It is not an accident that Jewish critics—Trilling, Philip Rahv, Leon Edel, etc.—have been among the leaders in the revival of Henry James. Maybe it serves that elegant old anti-Semite right.

But Jewish creative writers are just as guilty of this kind of pretentiousness as the scientists and critics. Here is a passage from Saul Bellow's novel *Seize the Day:*

> The flower and lights fused ecstatically in Wilhelm's blind wet eyes; the heavy sea-like music came up to his ears. It poured into him where he had hidden himself in the center of a crowd by the great and happy oblivion of tears. He heard it and sank deeper than sorrow, through torn sobs and cries towards the consummation of his heart's ultimate need.[12]

I find it curious that Irving Malin, in *Jews and Americans,* a detailed analysis of American Jewish literature, quotes this passage as an example of spontaneous, nonabstract writing.[13]

Abstractness is precisely the trap that lies in wait for Jewish writers. This is why they tend to be better critics than novelists. The art of the novelist consists in creating characters who are permitted to run wild and free, break the bonds of the novel's theme or philosophy, lead their own lives. Tolstoy and

Dostoevsky, Dickens and Thackeray all had strong ideas about religion, nationalism, social reform, which they never hesitated to put into their books; but they were also born novelists, and so their characters are constantly leaping beyond their ideas, behaving in ways which are irrelevant or even contradictory to those ideas. There is something essentially unserious about this trait. It makes playfulness and adventurousness just as important as significance—and it goes against the grain of the American Jewish intellectual.

In a lecture several years ago Saul Bellow stated that a writer must be a thinker. Alfred Kazin, in a *Commentary* article, praised contemporary Jewish fiction for its quality of 'intellectuality." [14] And conversely, Bruce Jay Friedman has been criticized by one leading Jewish critic on the grounds that he's "no intellectual." It seems to me that this compulsion to "think" is just what mars much Jewish fiction today. The novelist who theorizes too much seldom creates living characters; he creates blueprints instead. In *Jews and Americans* Irving Malin praises Bernard Malamud for "manipulating his characters into a final symbolic image." [15] Whether or not this truly applies to Malamud, it is nevertheless a strange compliment. It takes a Jewish intellectual to imagine that successful characters of fiction are "manipulated."

What this all means, of course, is that there is a terrible lack of spontaneity, a constant sense of constraint, in the Jewish intellectual's approach to life. He must watch and analyze his experience instead of simply having it. He is always in danger of substituting the word for the thing itself. And nobody is more aware of this than the intellectual himself. This urge to analyze rather than participate in experience has become one of the staple themes of modern Jewish literature. In the last ten years dozens of novels by Jewish writers have featured that same anxious, overearnest intellectual hero who just can't seem to break through to genuine emotion. A few of the better-known examples are Bellow's *Herzog,* Friedman's *Stern,* Markfield's *To an Early Grave,* Roth's *Letting Go,* Wallant's *The Tenants of Moonbloom.* And perhaps one reason for the success of these novels is that the country is full of Jewish intellectuals who like nothing better than to read their own case histories; it may be one of the symptoms of their disease.

The power, honesty, and moral force of these writers aren't in question. But these qualities make the basic weakness all the more disturbing. It seems a shame that men of such talent should be obsessed by this need to prove their importance, to establish over and over again their right to be intellectuals. The struggle between *tachlis* and Torah, between businessman and intellectual, has produced no greater tragedy.

And the end of this struggle is not yet in sight; for at the moment neither side is quite winning or quite losing. How can there be a clear-cut victory when no individual Jew knows for sure how deeply the enemy may be lodged in his own soul?

XVI.

Lay Religion

Jews pride themselves on their individualism, on the independence of their opinions, yet their political behavior can be predicted more easily than that of any other ethnic group in America. There definitely is a Jewish vote.

Among the East European immigrants, that vote was Republican (though a large minority voted Socialist). The Democratic party in New York in the first two decades of this century meant Tammany Hall, which was in the hands of the Irish; Jews felt they had no chance of exerting influence there. Furthermore, their great idol was President Theodore Roosevelt—after all, wasn't his signature on their immigration papers?

Woodrow Wilson was the first national figure to take a substantial portion of the Jewish vote away from the Republicans. Franklin Roosevelt brought all of it, or most of it, solidly into the Democratic camp, where it has remained ever since. In 1932 and 1936 the Jewish vote for Roosevelt paralleled that of the rest of the country. But in 1940 and 1944, when other minority groups and the working classes were beginning to have doubts about FDR, the Jews gave him 90 percent of their vote.[1] In 1948 the Jewish vote for Truman was far greater than that of the rest of the country. In 1952 and 1956 the Jews went for Stevenson while the rest of the country went strongly for Eisenhower. Other minority groups had become disenchanted with the Democrats, but not the Jews. In 1960, when Kennedy barely squeaked by, the Jews gave him well over 80 percent of their vote, more than any other ethnic or religious group.

Economic, social, and occupational differences don't have any appreciable effect on the Jewish vote. Most Americans change their political ideas as they move up the economic and social scale. The rich vote Republican, the poor vote Democrat. Jews have moved up steadily in terms of income and occupations; the group they most resemble today are upper-class Episcopalians and Presbyterians. Yet even the richest Jews continue to vote Democrat. Great Neck, Long Island, which has one of the highest concentrations of Jews in the United States, most of them prosperous, is in the middle of an old-guard Republican area; in the 1960 election this area gave 51 percent of its vote to Kennedy—but its Jewish sections gave Kennedy 61 percent of their vote.[2]

Another characteristic of Jewish voting that often bewilders political experts is that Jews don't vote for Jews. They don't vote against Jews either. The candidate's religious or ethnic background doesn't seem to matter to them one way or another. In the 1961 New York mayoralty race Robert Wagner, a Democrat and a Catholic, beat Louis Lefkowitz, a Jew and a Republican, and took a large majority of the Jewish vote. But even more significant, in the bitter Democratic primary which preceded that election—between Wagner and Arthur Levitt, a Jew—Wagner also had the Jewish vote sewed up. Apparently Jews won't necessarily vote for a Jew against a gentile, even when they're both Democrats.

If Jews don't vote for a candidate because he's Jewish, why *do* they vote for him? They vote for him because he's "Jewish." They like a candidate who, while not necessarily a Jew himself, can give them something "Jewish" to vote for. No Jew will admit that his Jewishness has any influence on his political choices, but the influence is there just the same.

Wherever there is a substantial Jewish population, for example, candidates can't go wrong if they use some sort of ethnic approach. This game is played mostly in New York, and to a lesser extent in Los Angeles and Philadelphia; but those cities contain more than half the Jews in America. The maneuver that always gets space in the New York newspapers is the candidate's ritual visit to the Jewish sections of town—to the Lower East Side, the garment center, the Grand Concourse—

where he shows himself to be on good terms with Jewish folkways. He buys a knish from Yonah Shimmel's store. He partakes of an egg cream. He stops for a lunch of blintzes and sour cream at a dairy restaurant. He goes out to Coney Island and accepts one of Nathan's Famous hot dogs; in some circles it is believed that a New York politician who doesn't get his picture taken eating a Nathan's hot dog can't be running legally.

And of course the candidate must appear at Jewish functions. The more dinners sponsored by Jewish organizations he goes to, the better the voters will feel about him. They've all been to such dinners themselves; they assume that any man who would voluntarily suffer through one of them must be a dedicated public servant.

One word of warning, though. Jews, as we have seen, are likely to have a double view of life. They constantly let themselves be bamboozled, but then, when you least expect it, they see through the deception. When a delicatessen owner sold a salami to Governor Rockefeller and charged him the cost price, a man in the corner of the store spoke up loud and clear, "To Rockefeller yet he gives discounts!" The candidates who think they can fool all of the Jews all of the time are well advised to keep their eyes on that little man in the corner.

A candidate might be able to get away with neglecting the egg creams, but he must somehow convey the impression that Jews are on his team. The Jewish voter can swallow a gentile candidate, but not one who has no Jews supporting him or involved in his campaign. The candidate who understands this will always have two or three recognizably Jewish personalities up on the speakers' platform with him, and a few unambiguously Jewish names on his list of backers. Political power is something that the Jew takes seriously: he knows from experience how effectively it can be used against him. He has no weapon except his vote to make sure that anti-Semites don't get into office; that's why a larger percentage of Jews exercise their vote than any other group in America. And he believes, rightly or wrongly, that a few Jews in the candidate's entourage, a little Jewish money in his coffers, will be some kind of insurance against his bad will.

For this reason the successful candidate who wants to get the Jewish vote when he stands for reelection will appoint a few Jews to responsible positions while he's in office. President

Grant made Jewish appointments in order to get the Jewish vote. Theodore Roosevelt appointed Oscar Straus his Secretary of Commerce and Labor, and admitted privately that if Straus hadn't been available, he would have chosen another Jew for the post. Wilson pleased the Jews of America by constantly calling Bernard Baruch to the White House for consultations. Franklin Roosevelt was careful to make Henry Morgenthau his Secretary of the Treasury. John F. Kennedy did him one better by appointing two Jews to his cabinet—Arthur Goldberg and Abraham Ribicoff. Eisenhower, on the other hand, confirmed the American Jew's suspicions of him by appointing no Jews to his cabinet during his first term. And every American President since Wilson has had at least one Jew on his Supreme Court. In the last thirty years, whenever a Jewish justice retires or dies, the custom has been to appoint another Jew to take his place. In certain cities, in fact, this principle has become part of the political way of life. In San Francisco, for example, all boards and committees are composed of one Jewish member, one Protestant member, and one Catholic member. In recent years this political version of pluralism has been extended, in many cities, to include one Negro member.

The Jewish voter does not automatically vote for Jewish candidates; indeed, he makes greater demands on them than he does on gentiles. Whatever form of Jewish affiliation is prevalent in his district, the Jewish candidate must be careful to abide by it. He must belong to a synagogue if his constituents do. He must involve himself in federations, defense agencies, pro-Israel groups. This sort of involvement, recommended for gentile candidates, is absolutely essential for Jewish ones. Otherwise the voter asks, "What kind of Jew is he, anyway?"

Above all, the Jewish candidate must be able to make the right sort of impression on the gentile world. This is vital to him, of course, if he has to get gentile as well as Jewish votes; but what gentiles want him to be, and what Jews *think* gentiles want him to be, are often quite different things. And so the Jewish candidate who is running in a statewide election, or from a district whose population is mixed, must learn how to perform a complicated psychological juggling act from which gentile candidates are exempt.

Styles in images change from generation to generation, of course. Thirty years ago two types of Jewish candidates were popular among Jewish voters. One was the Herbert Lehman

type—wealthy, dignified, aristocratic, rather pontifical in manner, as gentilized as he could possibly be, with only the faint-
est, subtlest whiff of Jewishness about him. He was valued
because he was "such a fine distinguished man, and he can talk
to the goyim in their own language." The other type of candidate continues to be sent to Congress from sections of New
York where older voters are in the majority. Congressman Leonard Farbstein of New York is an example: he is a mild-man-
nered little man; the Lower East Side in his accent is overlaid
by his CCNY education. What he projects is warmth, amiabil-
ity, and the homely, old-fashioned, down-to-earth family
virtues. One look at him, and the goyim know he wouldn't hurt
a fly; he'll make his sentimental speeches about Israel, but he's
absolutely safe. He is, in short, the political equivalent of the
gentle old pharmacist in *West Side Story*.

Among younger Jewish voters, and even among many
older ones, this type is out of style. One of the main reasons
why Abraham Beame lost the New York mayoralty election to
John Lindsay in 1965 was that Beame projects the old image
almost to the verge of caricature. New York Jews were very
well aware that he could have been their first Jewish mayor—
but he came along a generation too late; he was no longer the
kind of Jew they wanted for this distinction. It would be a
mistake to suppose, however, that Jews have stopped caring
how Jewish candidates look to the gentiles. They have simply
updated the image. Today the Jewish candidate mustn't pretend to be other than what he is. He must show that he's proud
to be Jewish, but he must also be able to serve as an ambassador to the gentiles, very much like the small-town rabbi.

The supreme Jewish politician, the one who combines all
the qualities that win votes from his fellow Jews, is Senator
Jacob Javits of New York. He was born on the Lower East Side,
speaks Yiddish, and worked his way through college and law
school. As one elderly lady said to me, "You have to give him
credit. His father was a janitor, and how could a Jew start off
any lower than that?" This is the Javits who appeals to the
older voters; but there is also a Javits who appeals to the
younger ones, the bright suburban executives who play handball in the synagogue gym. And just for good measure, Javits
has a sophisticated wife who buys pop art and goes to all the
first nights, and gives the Senator a toehold among the intellectuals. Javits exercising his power to be all things to all men is a

wonderful sight to behold. In addressing one kind of group he is the sentimental, warm-hearted self-made boy from the Lower East Side; with a different kind of group he effortlessly becomes the slick, hard-driving product of the 1960s. And if necessary—at a large gathering, with a mixed audience, for instance—he can project both these images at the same time.

Another essential quality which Javits possesses in abundance is energy. He isn't part of the Senate "club"—if he were, he would lose half his effectiveness with Jewish voters—but he makes up for this by being so knowledgeable on every subject that no important committee can get along without him. And his activities in the Senate seem like idle pastimes compared with the indefatigable, almost superhuman schedule that he maintains outside the Senate. Hardly a day goes by without Javits making at least one public speech, sometimes several; there isn't a topic before the public that Javits doesn't give an interview about, and always while it's still hot.

And the sheer number of organizations before which he appears is dazzling. In a period of one month in 1966 he attended a Jewish War Veterans banquet, the 135th anniversary of Temple Rodelph Sholem in New York, a party at a night club for Prince Philip of England, and a meeting of the Mt. Vernon Italian Civic Association; he marched in a procession to protest the treatment of Soviet Jewry, attended a dinner for Israel Bonds and another dinner for AJC, and incidentally went on a short good-will tour to South America. He did all this in addition to his regular routine of office appointments, letter writing, phone calls, and newspaper and magazine reading—and managed also to go strolling up Fifth Avenue on Sundays with his son, nodding and smiling at passers-by.

Nobody can deny the effectiveness of Javits' tactics. His continued vote-getting ability; his attraction to retired garment cutters in the Bronx, young advertising executives in Scarsdale, and the Loebs, the Warburgs, and the other German Jewish millionaires who provide 50 percent of his financial backing; the fact that he is the repository for all Jewish gripes, that he gets a dozen or more calls a week from ADL, AJC, and other Jewish agencies, that hundreds of people write to him every year when they have some specifically "Jewish" problem—all this suggests that Javits fills a real need. Even in the 1960s it would seem that the ancient function of the Jewish politician

—to provide his people with a champion in high places, to be "good for the Jews"—hasn't quite faded away.

———•◦•———

And yet it isn't really candidates that Jews vote for. With all his chameleonlike qualities, Jacob Javits would never get elected if he weren't able to satisfy the most important requirement of the Jewish vote, the common denominator that makes it so predictable: its consistent liberalism.

It is often said that liberalism is the American Jew's lay religion. The facts bear this out completely. The climate of opinion in every Jewish organization (with the exception of the American Council for Judaism) is liberal. The editorial policy of every major Jewish publication is liberal. The student body of every Jewish educational institution with an American orientation is overwhelmingly liberal; Yeshiva University rejected Barry Goldwater just as resoundingly as Brandeis, and has fewer supporters of the Conservative party than CCNY has. The Reform Democrats—the ultraliberal insurgents within the New York City Democratic party—are mostly Jewish. The Jewish War Veterans is in some ways the most conservative of all the mainstream organizations; yet its members join it, rather than the American Legion or the Veterans of Foreign Wars, because the conservative aura of those two groups makes Jews uneasy. (Many more Jewish veterans belong to the JWV than to the Legion and the VFW put together.)

American Jews have been predominantly liberal throughout the country's history. None of the conservative movements which have sporadically arisen in America ever drew much support from Jews. The Know-Nothings were opposed by Jews. Slavery was opposed by Jews, and many of the abolitionists were Jewish; Lincoln was the first great American folk hero among Jews. They supported Wilson's drive to get America into the League of Nations, though the rest of the country opposed him. Jews were against Prohibition. Jews have been in favor of unionism from the beginning; even Jewish businessmen, as most union leaders agree, are easier to deal with on this matter than gentile businessmen.

Many groups in America are liberal on certain issues but conservative on others. Jewish liberalism, however, cuts through all issues. Whether the question is economic or social, local or international, you can expect the vast majority of Jews to take the liberal side. Dr. John Bennett of the Union Theological Seminary, in a speech on reactionism among Protestants and Catholics, said, "I don't know anything about Jewish reactionaries. I never see any of them." [3]

They exist, of course. Some belong to the American Council for Judaism. Some write regularly for William Buckley's *National Review:* in a recent article Max Geltman expressed the view that Jewish liberalism was the chief enemy today of Jewish survival.[4] Jewish intellectuals like George Sokolsky, David Lawrence, and Eugene Lyons have achieved distinction among American conservatives. Nonetheless, they are not only in the minority; there is a feeling among most Jews that they are, in some unspecified way, "un-Jewish"—and even slightly ridiculous. When two Jews announced a couple of years ago that they were forming a branch of the John Birch Society, to be known as the Jewish Society for Americanists, the reaction from the rest of the Jewish community was a loud horselaugh; Dick Schaap, the New York *Herald-Tribune* columnist, spoke for almost everyone when he dubbed the new group B'Nai Birch.[5] Incidentally, it hasn't been heard from since.

The American Jew's devotion to liberalism is stronger even than his devotion to the Democratic party. A friend of mine, when he was asked to vote for John Lindsay, the first Republican mayor of New York, declared firmly, "I never voted anything but Democrat in my life." Nevertheless, like many other Jews, he finally voted for Lindsay, because he became convinced that Lindsay was the more liberal candidate. Republicans can get the Jewish vote—Javits, Lindsay, and many others have proved it—but only by being anomalies of a sort. In order to overcome the Republican stigma they must out-liberal the liberals.

Jewish liberalism has a double motive. Unquestionably there is a strong element of unselfish idealism in it. This shows itself in the deep-seated Jewish belief in social welfare. Jews are overwhelmingly in favor of social security, public health assistance, poverty programs; Jewish doctors are more likely to disagree with the American Medical Associations' anti-Medicare stand than gentile doctors; half the members of the Peace Corps are Jewish. Yet Jews on the whole, because of their affluence, get fewer benefits from social welfare than almost any other group. Their attitude is genuinely altruistic, and comes straight out of the tradition of *Zedakah*—the poor and the weak must be helped here on earth, not only with prayers and pious sentiments but with material things. Underlying the Jew's liberalism is his nonasceticism. "We are the inveterate secular Messianists," says Milton Himmelfarb. "We're always trying to create Paradise on earth."

But the second motive for Jewish liberalism is just the opposite from the first. Even when he's being most altruistic the Jew can't help asking himself that little question, "Is it good for the Jews?" Experience has taught him that liberalism is good for the Jews. For the last hundred years the political right in Europe, from Bismarck to Hitler, has traditionally been anti-Semitic. In America in the thirties it was Roosevelt and the Democrats who seemed, however lukewarmly, to oppose fascism, while Republicans were isolationists, unconcerned with Nazi persecution of the Jews. Today, too, liberals seem more prone to take the "Jewish" side on many issues; they worry about the resurgence of Nazism in West Germany and join with Jewish organizations in protesting against anti-Semitism in the Soviet Union.

The fear of anti-Semitism underlies another favorite Jewish liberal preoccupation—the defense of civil liberties. Jews on all levels of society were opposed to the activities of Senator Joseph McCarthy; the Gallup Poll of 1954 showed that 65 percent of American Jews disapproved of McCarthy intensely, compared to 31 percent of Protestants, 38 percent of Democrats, 45 percent of college graduates. Very few of these Jews were sympathetic with communism. What they feared in McCarthy was his disregard of due process, his willingness to make public accusations without legal proof and to use his Senate committee as a platform for character assassination. McCarthy wasn't anti-Semitic, but most American Jews felt that his methods would lead to anti-Semitism. They know that the abrogation of civil liberties usually opens the way to the persecution of the Jews.

For this reason Jews tend to oppose any form of censorship or repression, even when it doesn't appear to concern them directly. The society that suppresses free speech may end up forcing Jews to give up their religion. That is the real reason why, with few exceptions, they oppose laws which censor obscene literature or which prohibit abortion. Jews are not particularly given to reading obscene books, and unwed mothers are less frequent among Jews than among many other groups; but they get nervous when the law starts interfering in people's private lives.

Occasionally it happens that the Jew's predilection for civil liberties comes into direct conflict with his fear of anti-Semitism. Then he behaves in curiously ambivalent ways. Vicious anti-Semitism was the chief platform of the late George Lincoln Rockwell's American Nazi party, and the central refrain of all his speeches; surely the Jews had every moral right to try and muzzle this fanatic. Yet when many newspapers refused to cover Rockwell's activities, the Jewish publisher and editor of the *Northern Virginia Sun* in Arlington, Rockwell's home base, wrote, "As a person of the Jewish faith I find Rockwell's beliefs and activities profoundly offensive. However, I find the alternative to reporting them straight even more offensive." [6] And for many years, when Rockwell and his party were on the verge of bankruptcy, he was kept solvent by invitations to lecture, for fees and expenses, at college campuses; an overwhelming number of these invitations came from Jewish students, many of whom, I'm sure, heckled Rockwell unmercifully during his appearance.

Another inviolable tenet of Jewish liberalism in America has been the strict separation of church and state. This too has been based on the fear of anti-Semitism. A government which promotes the religious institutions of the majority ends up suppressing those of the minority. And so for the last fifty years Jewish organizations have opposed such violations of separation as enforced prayer, Christmas celebrations in the public schools, and government aid to parochial schools. Sometimes this opposition has been theoretical rather than actual. In the South, for instance, where many public schools can hardly be differentiated from straight Protestant parochial schools, Jews will hesitate to jeopardize their safety by making a fuss—but their belief in separation is no less intense on account of this.

This belief has no real basis in Jewish religious tradition. When the ancient Israelites were finally led into the Promised Land, they quickly turned it into a theocracy. The *shtetl*, within its limitations, was a theocracy too. And separation certainly doesn't exist in Israel today. "As a religious Jew," an Orthodox scholar told me, "I have an obligation to make other

Jews religious. And I believe the state must assist me—that's why Israel requires public observance of *kashruth* and of the Sabbath, though in private, of course, people can do what they please." His view is shared by many other Orthodox Jews. The leading advocates of separation, therefore, are the secular organizations, especially the American Jewish Congress, the most militantly secular of all. And within the religious establishment Reform rabbis believe in separation far more strongly than Orthodox rabbis. The farther you go from the heart of Judaism, the closer you get to belief in separation—a fairly good indication, I think, that this particular liberal ideal is based less on Talmud and Torah than on strategy in dealing with the gentile world.

And sure enough, as further confirmation of this, the Jewish solid front on separation has begun to crumble in the last few years. AJC is still officially in favor of separation, for example, yet *Commentary* published an article by Milton Himmelfarb, one of AJC's leading scholarly lights, in which he advocated a relaxation of the official position.[7] At its annual conference in 1967 the national leaders of AJC recommended that it reconsider its stand; many of the local groups opposed this recommendation, and there was a floor fight that lasted four hours and led to a compromise resolution. The Rabbinical Assembly, while it recently defeated a resolution favoring federal aid to church schools, approved such aid for transportation, lunches, and medical and dental services. And Senator Javits, who sometimes looks like a leader and sometimes like a barometer, supported the new New York State constitution, whose controversial plank permitted aid to parochial schools.

Die-hard separationists like the American Jewish Congress don't like to admit that these changes are taking place. Or if they do, they blame them on the increasing influence of the Orthodox who, with their commitment to more and bigger yeshivas, have something to gain from government aid to parochial schools. But in fact much of the new uneasiness about strict separation seems to be coming from secularists who were once firmly in favor of it. The key to their changed attitude, as Arthur Hertzberg has astutely pointed out, is the growing importance of interfaith dialogues.[8] Ten years ago Jews were allied with Protestants in opposing aid to parochial schools— the Protestants because they were anti-Catholic, and the Jews because they wanted to "get the Christians off our kids' backs."

But today the Protestants aren't nearly so anti-Catholic, and the Jews—especially the secular groups like AJC—are trying very hard to talk with the Catholics. How can they entertain Cardinal Bea and send Rabbi Tanenbaum to the Vatican, and still stand in the way of school prayers? A generation ago strict separation seemed like the best protection against anti-Semitism; today dialogue seems like a better protection. And the price of dialogue is the end of strict separation.

And so it would seem that all Jewish liberalism is nothing but enlightened self-interest, that self-defense is its only object and fear of anti-Semitism its only motivating force. So it would seem—until we turn it around again and look at it from the other side.

———————◆•◆———————

Many people would say that this ambiguity, though it may apply to the Jewish liberal, doesn't apply at all to the Jewish radical. In the last hundred years Jews have been deeply involved with all the radical movements, from socialism to anarchism to communism, and it must be admitted that nothing could be less parochial on the surface than this involvement. The Jewish radical, in fact, bends over backward to ignore that unspoken question, Is it good for the Jews? As a matter of principle he is interested in only one question: Is it good for humanity?

Nevertheless, Jewish radicals aren't quite like non-Jewish ones. In spite of themselves their Jewishness permeates their thoughts and feelings. It even gives a special cast to their radicalism.

In the early years of the century most of them rejected Judaism, not passively or indifferently but with fervor. Daniel DeLeon, the Lower East Side Communist, went so far as to invent a Catholic background for himself, and then boasted about despising it. Younger radicals used to make a point of eating ham sandwiches in front of the synagogues as the devout gathered for prayer; and they used to have wild parties on Yom Kippur to show how little this holiday meant to them. But while they rejected the religion, they never actually left the Jewish community.

On the contrary, they became the leaders of the community. The vast majority of East European immigrants were ignorant people. Their ambition was to succeed in America, and they knew they needed education to do it. They turned naturally to those among them who were most intellectual and closest to an urban industrialized society—and by and large these were the radicals. In their turn the radicals were willing to give the others what they wanted. The socialist dream would never be a reality, they felt, until the immigrants had shaken off the shackles of religion, and the best way to achieve this was to Americanize them—and incidentally, to secularize them. Ironically, the East European radicals took on the same task among their fellow Jews that the German Jewish million-aires were taking on.

The radicals created three institutions to perform this task. First there were the unions, and especially the Garment Work-ers Union. Second there was the Workmen's Circle movement, a loose network of semipolitical, semisocial clubs whose meet-ings were open to all Jewish laborers; these groups offered English lessons, some social welfare benefits, and political in-doctrination. Finally there was the *Jewish Daily Forward,* the largest of the Yiddish newspapers, founded by Abraham Cahan in 1897. It was owned by the Forward Association, whose members had, and still have, to prove their involvement in some kind of socialist organization. They served without pay; profits were put back into the paper (and later into the Yiddish radio station WEVD, which keeps the *Forward* going today). At its heyday, around 1917, the *Forward* had a circulation of 237,000 and an influence way beyond that. People used to settle arguments by saying, "It must be true. I read it in the *Forward.*"

Yet even then, with all the popularity of the *Forward* and the influence of Workmen's Circles, there was a difference between the radical leaders and their immigrant followers. The leaders looked on the followers with condescension, deplored their worldly ambitions, and hoped to turn them into better men. The followers accepted the benefits of socialist zeal but never really accepted the ideology. At most they sympathized with certain things the radicals said; to an immigrant who had just escaped from a pogrom, anybody who talked against the Czar couldn't be all bad. Later, in the thirties, an equally superficial sympathy was aroused in many American Jews by the fact that the leftists, through the Jewish Labor Committee, an umbrella organization of radical groups, were outspokenly antifascist long before almost anybody else was. But it was this antifascism, not a genuine belief in socialism, which made the Jewish working man support the Committee.

Anti-Semitism, in short, was the issue that enabled the Jewish radical to be a part of the total Jewish community. As long as radicalism could be equated with the fight against anti-Semitism, the Jewish radical was able to reject his religion without rejecting his people. He was even able to put his radicalism on a specifically Jewish basis. He gladly called attention to the similarity between his ethical ideas and the teachings of the Prophets. "You can't be Jewish without being radical" was the old Workmen's Circle philosophy. Abraham Cahan wrote about unionism in biblical terms and justified strikes with quotations from Leviticus; and the Talmudic injunction, "All Jews are responsible for one another," was used as a slogan for socialist fund raising. It was this atmosphere that produced a man like David Dubinsky—who quoted Yiddish proverbs, while a photograph of Morris Hillquit, the socialist congressman from the Lower East Side, smiled down from behind his desk. And it was this atmosphere that created a fabulous character like Tom Cook, who came to Ann Arbor in the twenties, was instrumental in starting a Workmen's Circle Hebrew school, built the local Negro church, and went to synagogue every Sabbath—though he always refused to read from the Torah because he admitted that he had no belief.

That atmosphere no longer exists. The decline of anti-Semitism, the defeat of fascism, dispelled it and revealed some hard truths about the landscape which it had been shrouding. The old radical was forced to see that his followers had never really shared his values. The average American Jew was happy to be part of the bourgeois, middle-class consensus. By all the laws of logic the old radical should now have rejected the Jewish community as he had rejected the Jewish religion, but in most cases he wasn't able to do it. He had been brought up a Jew, he had lived his life among Jews; it wasn't easy to stop being a Jew now, just because of an ideological accident. He had always thought he belonged to "mankind"—but for all practical purposes, as he now discovered, "mankind" had never been anyone except his fellow Jews.

The old radicals adjusted to this new state of affairs in several ways. The great majority settled down to being middle-aged liberals. The step wasn't really such a drastic one. As one of them has put it, "The Republican platform today supports all the things I used to fight for as a Socialist." And the labor movement today has become as entrenched an establishment as any we have in America. Young people aren't going into it; it isn't idealistic enough for them. But the young labor organizer of the twenties and thirties is quite content to be the labor lawyer, researcher, public-relations man of today; he doesn't have to face up to the fact that he might just as easily be performing the same job with a large corporation.

This new situation was vividly illustrated to an organizer for Histadrut, the Israeli labor organization, who came to a Midwest town a few years ago. He went straight to the local Workmen's Circle, where a board meeting was taking place. He asked the board to give him office space so that he could organize a Histadrut chapter in their town. They replied that because they were Socialists, they weren't pro-Zionist, and therefore they couldn't help him; but they suggested that he go to the Conservative synagogue on the following night and make his request of their board of trustees. He took the advice, and the Conservative board of trustees gave him his office space. "But the funny part of it was," he said, "the men I talked to at the synagogue were exactly the same men I had talked to at the Workmen's Circle the night before."

A minority of the old radicals haven't found it quite so easy to readjust to the postwar world. These men are now growing old and living in the past. The *Forward*'s circulation is down to seventy thousand; most of the readers are elderly people. Two thousand four hundred showed up at the seventieth-anniversary ceremony for the *Forward* in New York's Philharmonic Hall; they listened to speeches, sang old Yiddish songs, and ended the evening with a chant in memory of the Jews who were killed in concentration camps. Though the *Forward* still maintains the old format—the news from Israel, the "historical" novels, the stories of realistic workingman life, the "Bintel Briefe" column of advice (slightly psychiatric and Ann Landersish now)—it is a dying institution and knows it. "We'll be doing well if we last another twenty years," says its managing editor. And a sign over its front desk symbolizes what's happening to it and to the Lower East Side world which it is still located. "Se habla Yiddish," says the sign.

Yet many of the old radicals have passed on their ideas to their own children. Many of the Jewish young people who are part of today's New Left are "red-diaper babies," sons and daughters of parents who have long since ceased to belong to the left in any real sense. Michael Schwerner and Andrew Goodman, the two Jewish civil rights activists who were killed by the Klan in Mississippi, both came from old socialist families.

This new generation has turned the legacy into something quite different from what it was in the old days. Their parents were able to uphold their radicalism *as* Jews; the new breed must uphold it in spite of being Jews. Their parents fought against poverty and prejudice in the name of the dispossessed —and who was more dispossessed than their own people? But the young radicals today come from affluent middle-class families. They can't rebel against bourgeois values without rebelling against Jewish values too, for in their eyes Jews and gentiles are indistinguishable. That is why you don't find young leftist Jews in the synagogues, nor do you find them in the Hillels or the federations or the Zionist youth groups either.

Are they, then, identical with non-Jews in the leftist movement? Do they bring nothing with them, either ideologically or temperamentally, which could be called Jewish?

What they bring, I think, is a peculiar state of mind that can't be explained entirely in terms of leftist philosophy. Their parents had this state of mind too. It explains why the old Jewish radicals, despite their hot heads and flaming words and memories of Russian pogroms, seldom became Communists. In 1936 *Fortune* reported that there were 27,000 American Communists.[9] About 15 percent of them—3,500 to 4,000—were Jews. Yet the total Jewish population at that time was over 4.5 million; with all the poverty, exploitation, and radical activity among the immigrants, less than one out of every thousand turned to communism.

The rest of the Jewish radical movement, furthermore, was not indifferent to communism, but strongly against it. In the early twenties the *Forward* printed one of the first eyewitness reports from Russia that was critical of the Soviet government; despite pressure from within its own ranks it pursued a firm anticommunist editorial policy from then on. The ILGWU, like many other Jewish unions, rid itself of communist influence in the thirties, after a bitter struggle. The United Federation of Teachers fought the same battle shortly after the war, though most of its leaders came from a radical background.

Even those Jews who at one time or another flirted with communism soon turned against it. The reason lies in the Jewish character. What attracts Jews to communism in the first place is a kind of perverse anti-authoritarian streak. "I had it as a kid," one ex-Communist told me, "even when I was a Boy Scout. I raised a rumpus once because the Scoutmaster had too much power. I circulated a petition." The same streak is found in a number of Jewish college students who were recently interviewed by *The New York Times*. They were asked why they had joined the Students for a Democratic Society; their answers showed they were vague about the specific purposes of SDS, but they praised it for its "posture of protest," its "challenge to the power structure," its "insistence that drastic changes are necessary." [10]

Jews like to challenge the power structure. They like to go to lectures and read books on dangerous subjects; they have a curiosity about all opinions, even the most outrageous or explosive ones. This often makes them seem more radical than they really are. For the truth is, most Jews have an automatic safety device inside them; a little voice tells them that if they want to go on challenging the power structure, they had better live in a society where the power structure is flexible enough to *let* them challenge it. And so, however they may flirt with communism or other extremist movements, they usually stop short of putting themselves into the hands of complete authoritarianism. Jews are not fanatics; instinctively they realize that a world ruled by fanatics would probably be "bad for the Jews."

There is another, less obvious reason why the Jew makes a bad Communist. He feels sympathy for the poor and downtrodden masses, but he doesn't trust them very much. History tells him that populist movements generally turn out badly for the Jews. Tom Watson, the Georgia demagogue who whipped up public sentiment to lynch Leo Frank in the twenties, started off as a populist leader. So did Hitler. And so, as even Communist Jews are uncomfortably aware, did Stalin. It is no accident that the American Jew's political heroes in this century have been patricians, like Stevenson, John Kennedy, and Franklin D. Roosevelt, not folksy men of the people, like Harry Truman and Lyndon Johnson.

Populism divides the New Left today. The nonpopulist brand of radicalism is noisy, intellectual, ideological, and primarily Jewish. (Fifty percent of the members of leftist groups at Yale are Jews; at the University of Michigan the last two presidents of SDS were Jews. Most of the SDS members involved in the recent Columbia sit-ins were Jewish.) But a less urban, less sophisticated brand of radicalism has been growing stronger in recent years. It is pragmatic, anti-intellectual, and primarily gentile. Its basic philosophy—"Let's change things, and to hell with having a plan!"—has been described to me by a young Jewish activist as "left-wing Goldwaterism." As yet there has been no open break between the two factions, but sooner or later it must come.

The radicals of the last generation turned against communism when they discovered the combination of populism and authoritarianism at the heart of it. The young Jews in the New Left today will turn against the movement too, I think, and for the same reason. Many of them were disturbed by the New Left Conference in 1967, with its outbursts of mass hysteria and its destruction of democratic procedures—and its undercurrent of anti-Semitism, only slightly veiled as anti-Zionism. And even before that, a summer filled with more or less organized racial strife forced Jewish activists to do some hard thinking about the use of violence to achieve idealistic ends. "I think violence is necessary," said one young man, "and it frightens me." [11]

And so even the Jewish radical, though he may never be aware of it, eventually has to ask himself, Is it good for the Jews?

When you talk to young Jewish radicals about the Jewish community as a whole, they all say that they don't approve of it. Its so-called liberalism is phony, a façade. A lot of words, a reflex out of the past, but in terms of action it doesn't mean a thing. Jews aren't "really" any more liberal than other middle-class Americans. To test the truth or falsehood of this charge we must examine the behavior of the Jewish community in the face of the one crucial test of liberalism in America today—the problem of Negro rights.

The evidence in favor of the Jews has been given many times, but it is worth summarizing again. After the war, when the defense agencies switched from a passive to an active strategy on fighting anti-Semitism, they also began to take an interest in improving the lot of the American Negro. In the forties Alexander Pekelis of the American Jewish Congress established its Commission on Law and Social Action, and in collaboration with the NAACP it brought test cases on discrimination to the courts. In a few years AJC and ADL became involved in the same sort of activity. AJC was particularly effective in persuading Jewish businessmen around the country to provide jobs for Negroes, and in instituting training programs to prepare Negroes for those jobs. Then the other human relations agencies took up the cause. The National Council of Jewish Women ran strong pro-civil rights articles in the national publication, which shocked its southern chapters; the Jewish Labor Committee launched an intensive campaign to eliminate discrimination in Jewish unions. Then the synagogues joined in; the Reform movement began by forming a Social Action Committee, the Conservatives followed, and finally the Orthodox, though they tend to be less interested in social action than in religious activities. There is no question that the Jewish organizations were fighting for Negro rights long before any other white organizations, religious or secular, on the American scene.

Even before the organizations stepped in, however, many individual Jews were involved in this fight. For twenty-five years the president of the NAACP has been Jewish; the position is honorary (the executive director and the field representatives who actually do the work have always been Negroes), and simply indicates the heavy Jewish financial support which the organization has always received. As far back as 1923 Louis Marshall became a director of the NAACP and argued cases for it before the Supreme Court. And today the head of its legal defense fund is a Jew, Jack Greenberg.

Jewish activists and Jewish money were, until recently, the mainstay of all the other influential civil rights groups, particularly CORE and SNCC. The first organization at CCNY to stage a demonstration against segregation was the campus Hillel. In conjunction with Jackie Robinson they sponsored a huge Passover rally and sold buttons appropriate both to the Jewish holiday and the Negro cause; the buttons contained the legend, "Let my people go." At least half the whites who went to Mississippi in the summer of 1964 to encourage voter registration among Negroes were Jews; the two whites who got killed were Jews. Most of them went there as individuals, but some went as representatives of Jewish groups. Brandeis University sent a contingent. Rabbis representing every type of

Jewish congregation, from ultra-Reform to Young Israel, showed up in large numbers; there were more rabbis than any other kind of white clergy. The yarmulke, in fact, became a kind of unofficial symbol of the civil rights movement that summer. The JTS had to send two thousand yarmulkes down to Selma, Alabama. Everyone wore them on the march, whites and Negroes alike; they were known as freedom hats.

Up North Jews are almost always on the pro-Negro side of controversial local issues. They are active in neighborhood fair-housing committees. In Detroit and Kansas City they voted for open-housing laws; in Washington, D.C., they favor home rule, which will give political power to the Negro majority. In California Jews voted two to one against Proposition 14, a bill designed to discriminate against Negroes in housing; the total white vote was two to one in favor of Proposition 14. Jewish unions, on the whole, backed antidiscrimination rules before other unions, and have pioneered in extra training programs for Negroes. In the Midwest the Jewish owner of a large department store developed a highly successful program to train Negro buyers. Another Jewish department store owner became interested in starting such a program and asked if he could observe the operation. Permission was given, and he liked what he saw so much that he not only started a program of his own but pirated two of his competitor's best people.

Even in the touchy area of social life the Jewish record is outstanding. Jewish hotels in Miami Beach started taking Negro guests long before the non-Jewish hotels. The Catskill resorts have been open to Negroes for many years. The teen-age groups of several New York synagogues have been engaged for some time now on projects with teen-agers from the black Jews of Harlem. They have had joint dances and parties and spent several weekends together on kosher farms outside the city. And while there is no statistical proof of this, it is the impression of most observers that a majority of the white partners in interracial marriages are Jews.

Most revealing of all, I think, is the behavior of Jews in the South. Despite the most intense pressures from the Christian community—threats, charges of being "nigger-lovers," synagogue bombings—southern Jews have seldom been swept up in the all-out racism of other whites. The experience of a Reform rabbi, Malcolm Stern, in Norfolk, Virginia, gives a good idea of their behavior pattern. His congregation was wealthy and old, and its members tended to be less liberal than Jews generally are. They were disturbed when Rabbi Stern spoke too loudly about integration, especially if his words got to the ears of the gentiles. Then Norfolk had a crisis: the state legislature closed its public schools rather than integrate them. Twenty-three local parents sued the state to reopen the schools. Of those twenty-three only one was Jewish, and he wasn't a member of Rabbi Stern's congregation; most of them were frightened of reprisals and wouldn't make themselves conspicuous in the struggle for Negro rights.

Yet they sympathized with that struggle; the legal fees for the parents' suit against the state were largely supplied by the Jewish community. The suit was won, the schools were ordered to integrate and to reopen. The day before the scheduled reopening, as a means of avoiding violence, a full-page ad was run in the local newspaper; it urged all parents in Norfolk to send their children back to school in a peaceful fashion, and it was signed by the members of the Key Club, an honorary organization of high school seniors with top grades (many of them were Jewish). This full-page ad—which had the desired effect—was paid for out of the budget of Norfolk's Jewish federation, supported to a large extent by contributions from the wealthy members of Rabbi Stern's congregation. A few years later, when he left Norfolk, his congregation gave him a farewell dinner and presented him with a plaque commending him for "being in the forefront of the fight for integration."

This same pattern has repeated itself all over the South. In the fifties, when ADL was beginning to issue public statements in support of Negro civil rights, its southern membership was very upset. Some communities sent delegations up North to urge ADL to soft-pedal its stand. "Every time one of you makes a speech," said one woman, "I'm afraid my husband's store will be burned up." But ADL held firm, and today its southern chapters have not only stopped complaining but are among the best in the country at implementing its policies.

We could go on indefinitely, piling up evidence that American Jews are in favor of Negro rights. But there is also evidence on the other side of the question. The defense agencies, which took an early lead in the civil rights struggle, appear to have fallen behind in recent years. In poverty programs, street demonstrations, and other activist tactics the Christian churches are way ahead of the Jews; the implication is that the Jews withdrew from the fight as soon as it really became dangerous. Official Jewish support of open housing has been compared by certain skeptics to actual Jewish practice. When Negroes move into a neighborhood, the Jews move out; they don't have to riot, as the Poles or the Italians did, because they're wealthy enough to buy houses elsewhere. How many members of AJC or the American Jewish Congress are living in integrated neighborhoods?

The synagogues are as much a part of this recent withdrawal as the secular agencies. In 1964, when parents in Queens were picketing the public schools because Negro children were being bussed into them, liberal groups tried to get clergymen of all faiths to escort children through the picket lines. Every Protestant denomination sent somebody; many Catholic priests appeared; but no rabbi was available. In Kansas City, when Saul Alinsky instituted a program to improve the Negro slums, he was supported by most of the local churches—but the synagogues ignored him.

Furthermore, under certain circumstances Jews are just as capable of active anti-Negro behavior as anyone else. At a meeting on bussing in Long Island a Jewish housewife said, "The niggers should be sent South to be lynched!" She turned out to be a member of the local chapter of the American Jewish Congress. In Harlem the 125th Street Association, a powerful group dominated by Jewish store owners, refused until five years ago to allow any Negro store owners to join. Many southern Jews, though they avoid the Klan, do belong to White Citizens Councils, dedicated to stopping integration. They are just as given to vicious racist remarks as other southern whites. "When I first got here," said a southern Jewish boy at Ohio State University, "and I saw the blacks swimming in the same pool with the whites, I tell you I was *sick!*"

And on the personal level few Jewish parents would react with anything less than horror if their child married a Negro; few Jews have close Negro friends; few hesitate to sprinkle their conversation with words like "nigger" and "coon" or to tell anti-Negro jokes. And with all the indignation over restricted social clubs, Jewish social clubs are hardly ever open to Negroes. Much is made of the fact that a Jewish club in San Francisco recently accepted Willie Mays as a member; little is said about the bitter behind-the-scenes battle that went on.

But many examples of Jewish behavior toward Negroes

are so ambiguous that we can't be sure what they prove, whether they're evidence of good will or of prejudice. A perfect example is provided by a highly publicized incident that occurred in Mt. Vernon, a suburb of New York, a few years ago. A struggle over integration of the local elementary school culminated in a big open meeting of the school board. Tempers ran high; violent speeches were made, some of them by Jews who were associated with the local Parents and Taxpayers group that opposed integration. Finally a Negro representative of CORE, Clifford Brown, shouted out, "Hitler made one mistake—he didn't kill enough Jews!" His remark was reported in *The New York Times,* and when CORE didn't repudiate Brown immediately, the executive director of the American Jewish Congress, Will Maslow—an early and vigorous fighter for Negro rights—resigned from CORE's executive committee. His resignation was followed by many others.

I have talked to a dozen people who were involved in the Mt. Vernon fracas. Several of them were present in the hall when Brown made his notorious remark. Among these people there is sharp disagreement on the attitudes and behavior of the Mt. Vernon Jewish community. Charles Silberman, a *Fortune* editor and author of *Crisis in Black and White,* the best book yet written on the Negro problem in America, is a Mt. Vernon resident, heard Brown's remark, and participated in the school-integration fight that led up to it. His opinion is that the whole incident "stripped the veneer of liberalism from the Jewish community." He points out that although Mt. Vernon is controlled by the Italian majority, many Jews were active in PAT, its president was a Jew, and one of its leading Jewish members, Harvey Felton, later got elected to the Mt. Vernon school board. He believes that most of the Jews in Mt. Vernon were opposed to school integration and were waiting for an excuse to take the anti-Negro position; Brown's remark gave them that excuse. And Will Maslow's resignation from CORE gave many Jews outside of Mt. Vernon the excuse *they* needed to drop out of the whole civil rights movement.

One of the people whom Silberman excepts from his condemnation is Rabbi Leon Jick, now at Brandeis, who was spiritual leader of one of Mt. Vernon's Reform temples at the time of the incident, and who had been fighting hard for school integration. I talked to Rabbi Jick, and he disagrees with Silberman's view of the Mt. Vernon Jews. They were far more liberal, he says, than the rest of the whites. The Jews in PAT were loud and violent, but they were only a small minority, and none of them were respected by the Jewish community as a whole. When Harvey Felton ran for the school board, his opponent was a lady who serves as president of the Mt. Vernon JCC, and she got most of the Jewish vote; it was the Italians who elected Felton.

Half of the Mt. Vernon people I've talked to agree with Charles Silberman, the other half agree with Rabbi Jick. Who's right and who's wrong? It isn't possible to sort it out. This incident is simply a reflection of the ambiguity which cuts through every American Jew's feelings about the Negroes. He is sympathetic to them and he is hostile to them, often at the same time.

His sympathy is, first of all, a consequence of his belief in *Zedakah*. Every human being is equal before God, and equally entitled to the good things of life. The fact that Jews in America have been lucky doesn't exempt them from this belief; it gives them an even stronger reason for upholding it. Sometimes the American Jew carries this sense of fair play beyond reasonable bounds. When Le Roi Jones stands on a platform and says nasty things about "the Jew liberals," the chances are that his audience will be half Jewish.

The common bond of persecution is another reason why the Jew sympathizes with the Negro. Clifford Brown wasn't the only person to mention Hitler in connection with Mt. Vernon's Negro problem. In protest against Will Maslow's resignation from CORE, an elderly Jewish scholar wrote, "In the name of the six million martyrs, I demand school integration in Mt. Vernon."

To many Jews this isn't only a moral question but a practical one as well. The defense agencies pushed for Negro rights partly because they believed this to be the only way of achieving Jewish rights. In union there is strength; you can't expect a state legislature to pass a fair-employment law which applies to Jews alone. The help that Jews have got from Negroes never gets as much publicity as the help that Negroes have got from Jews, but it is substantial just the same. It was Negro pressure in 1948 which persuaded the U.N. delegates from Haiti and Liberia to vote for recognition of the state of Israel. And many Negro leaders today, including the late Martin Luther King, Bayard Rustin, Roy Wilkins, and James Farmer, have been active in the protests against Soviet anti-Semitism. Most anti-Semitic movements in America, including the Ku Klux Klan and Rockwell's American Nazi party, have also been anti-Negro—a fact which both minorities ought to keep in mind.

Against these reasons for sympathizing with the Negro, Jews have equally strong reasons for feeling hostile to him. Some anti-Negro feeling among Jews is, of course, the product of American mores. A young couple in Westchester, inspired by the American dream of moving up in the world socially, feels threatened by the appearance of Negroes in their neighborhood. The garment man's wife who objects to the civil rights movement because it's making her Negro maid "uppity" is keeping up with the Joneses, not with the Cohens.

The essential middle-classness of American Jews is another reason for their hostility to Negroes. For most Jews the only Negroes they ever meet are either domestic servants, menial employees, or delivery boys. The immigrant housewife used to refer to the Negro woman who helped her around the house as the *schwartse*—a Yiddish word meaning "the black one." It wasn't a term of hatred but of contempt, and its connotations remain in the minds of many Jews today.

But the most important reason why the Jew is hostile to Negroes is that he fears them. First of all, he fears them because they're gentiles. Negro anti-Semitism is more upsetting to him than white anti-Semitism. He doesn't think he deserves it, he feels he's been the Negro's best friend in the white world. The very existence of Negro anti-Semitism seems to prove that "it doesn't matter how good you are to the goyim, they'll always turn against you in the end." Deep in his heart the Jew harbors the suspicion that the "Negro revolution," if it ever succeeds, will simply result in a coalition of black and white Christians—and guess who they'll turn on then?

Connected with this is the Jew's feeling, which sociologist Nathan Glazer has analyzed in detail, that the Negroes are challenging the system of pluralism in America.[12] Each ethnic and religious group must keep to itself, live in its own neighborhoods, belong to its own clubs; in return nobody will be discriminated against, nobody will be prevented from enjoying all the material benefits of our society. But the Negro seems to think that this system isn't favorable to him. He *isn't* enjoying the material benefits, he's being left out of the game, and so he wants to change the rules. This frightens the Jew, for whom pluralism has been working very nicely; he has a feeling that the Negro's new rules will be disastrous for him.

And then, in certain practical areas of life he finds himself challenged by the Negro. The Jew believes in school integration, but he also believes in the vital importance of education. When lower-class Negro children without his training or motivation come into class, the educational standards drop, and his own child suffers. Many Jews hold jobs now in fields that Negroes are moving into—teaching, school administration, social work, other branches of the civil service. Jews went into these fields in large numbers in the twenties and thirties because they were prejudice-proof; promotion depended entirely on hard work and competitive examination. But Negroes today, not through their own fault but through the handicaps society has put on them, can't pass such examinations—yet they insist on recognition and promotion anyway. The Jew reacts against this strongly. "*I* worked hard for what I've got, so why shouldn't *they?*"

Finally, on the deepest level, almost on an unconscious level, the Jew fears Negroes because they seem, in one crucial way, to be the opposite of himself. His world is mental and theirs is physical: so the Jew often imagines. He believes in peace and they believe in violence. He works hard and saves his money, they hold up cabdrivers and mug elderly people on the street. Because their ancestors were "savages," because they're strange and irrational and unpredictable—and nevertheless gentile—they are a kind of apotheosis of the outside world, of the enemy, of "them."

It appears then that Jews have powerful reasons, some real and some imaginary, some calculated and some instinctive, for being hostile to Negroes. Does this prove the young radical's accusation that all Jewish liberalism is a fraud and a façade? I think it proves exactly the opposite. The real point about the Jew's hostility to the Negro is that it doesn't overwhelm him, it doesn't destroy every other impulse in him. The Negro threatens him in exactly the same ways that he threatens other white Americans, and in many extra ways that no gentile could possibly feel. It wouldn't be surprising if the Jew behaved worse toward the Negro than others do; but in fact he behaves better.

The ethical imperative within him, his sense of kinship with weak and oppressed people, is strong enough to hold out against the counterpressures. Not to *win* out—anti-Negro feelings continue to exist in him—but at least to put up a good fight. While it may be true that many Jews in Mt. Vernon used Negro anti-Semitism as an excuse to neglect their moral obligation, the fact is that they *needed* an excuse. There was no "copping out" for the other whites in Mt. Vernon because they had never been "in"; there was no clash of opinion within their community because they had never felt the moral obligation in the first place. Nobody knows this better than the Negro leaders themselves. "You can always talk to Jews about their obligations," one of them says. "Sometimes it won't do any good—but with most whites, you can't even talk."

In these difficult times the Jew finds himself in a painful bind: he hates prejudice, not fashionably or hypocritically, but with genuine passion; at the same time he recognizes that there is prejudice in himself. This is true of all American Jews, even of the young radicals—though they may find it more difficult than most to admit the existence of their prejudices. All of us, if we aren't too far gone in self-satisfaction or fear, could echo the words of an elderly Jewish businessman with whom I talked. "I always wanted that human beings should advance themselves," he said. "I gave money to the NAACP. I brought up my kids so they should be fair to everybody. But now, with the crime and the riots and the things some of them are saying about us, suddenly, after all these years, I believe I'm prejudiced. I hate myself for it. I wish somebody would help me."

XVII.

A Jew Has to Be Better

From the strictly theological standpoint both Judaism and Christianity demand that their adherents believe in God and lead good lives; you can't achieve salvation without fulfilling both these conditions. But from the practical standpoint Judaism makes works more important than faith. Obviously, since God Himself urges Jews to pay attention to this life and not trouble themselves unduly about the next, they must worry more about the second half of the Ten Commandments than the first half. With all their talk about relativism and unconscious motivations and "the new morality," Jews tend to judge people—and societies, institutions, political movements, ideologies—by how close they come to obeying the moral law.

The American Jewish community itself stands up to this test very well indeed, by all the usual standards. To begin with, Jews commit crimes less often than other citizens. We have no statistics for the country as a whole, but New York City provides a good indication. In 1906, when the waves of immigration from East Europe were at their highest, the New York police commissioner declared that most of the criminals in the city were Jewish. Nobody knows how impartial his opinion was, but by 1930 the situation had changed drastically. Approximately 3 to 4 percent of the people arrested in New York then were Jewish, though the total Jewish population was 27 percent. In the 1960s the percentage of Jews who appear before the criminal courts is still estimated at 3 to 4 percent.[1]

There is also a pattern in the kinds of crimes that Jews commit. Murder is much rarer among them than among any other ethnic or religious group, except the Chinese. Armed robbery, gang fights, assault and battery, and other crimes of violence are seldom committed by Jews. Larceny of various sorts is a bit more popular with them. There have been plenty of Jewish tax evaders, including the most famous of all, the Philadelphia publisher Moe Annenberg, who spent several years in prison for cheating the government out of $1 million. The courts in New York see many frauds by small Jewish businessmen. There were many Jews among the welfare workers and building inspectors recently suspended for taking bribes. Yet when these crimes are examined statistically, the incidence of Jews among the criminals is still much lower than would be expected.

Like all Americans in recent years, Jews have undoubtedly been afflicted by a cynical, careless attitude toward lawbreaking. They feel fewer qualms than they used to feel about cheating on their income tax, fixing speeding tickets, telling lies under oath. The kosher catering industry has been faced more and more since the war with the problem of pilfering; one of the reasons for skyrocketing costs has been that guests seem to be less reluctant nowadays to cram dishes, silverware, and glasses into their handbags during weddings or bar mitzvah parties. Recently the owner of a large catering firm caught a woman at this red-handed. "Haven't you forgotten something?" he asked her as she was about to leave the hall. "Don't you want to take some plates to go with that fork and spoon?" Her response was neither to hang her head in shame nor to deny the charge indignantly, but simply to draw herself up and say, "Big deal! What's a few forks and spoons, already?"

It is impossible to measure directly the extent to which this "big deal" attitude has infected American Jews. One indirect measurement might be provided by delinquency figures; when parents are dishonest, they usually pass this trait down to their children. All the available statistics indicate that delinquency is comparatively low among Jewish juveniles. It has increased slightly in the last ten years, but not nearly as much as the increase in the total population. The Hawthorne School for delinquent children, the largest Jewish institution of its kind in the New York area, receives about the same number of cases from the courts as it did in the 1950s. About 15 percent of its inmates are non-Jewish, because it can't fill its quota from among the Jews.

One form of delinquent behavior *is* growing more common among young Jews—drug taking. A New York judge said recently that he never used to see Jewish kids before him on such a charge; now he sees them every week.[2] This is disquieting, of course, but less so on closer examination than it seems at first. In the overwhelming number of cases the drug that the Jewish teen-ager or college student takes is marijuana; some, though not many, are also taking LSD; heroin and the other addictive narcotics are almost unknown among them. It would seem that young Jews, like young Americans generally, are taking drugs experimentally—in much the same way that their parents experimented with homemade booze during Prohibition—but hardly any of them are tempted to make this a serious way of life.

The legal or semilegal forms of immoral and antisocial behavior do better among Jews than the illegal ones—but not much better. Despite repeal, the war, and a vast change in drinking habits all over the country, alcoholism is almost as infrequent a Jewish vice as it was back in the *shtetl*. Even the prevalent local mores don't seem to affect Jewish drinking appreciably. In Minnesota, where the incidence of alcoholism is higher than in any other section of the country, it is almost nonexistent among Jews; in Hollywood, where Jews in the movie business have succumbed to every other local indulgence, where they get divorced more often and commit adultery more often, they still haven't become drinkers.

If Jews can be said to have a characteristic vice, that vice is gambling. Even back in the *shtetl* they were gamblers. Many psychiatrists have mentioned this phenomenon to me, yet nobody has been able to explain it exactly. Perhaps it's a symptom of Jewish anxiety, of the underlying feeling that life is a matter of luck at bottom and we're all helpless in its grip. Nevertheless, though Jews often gamble too much, they seldom gamble too high; they usually quit before they go broke.

Complete withdrawal from society is an indulgence that young Jews often have to get out of their systems. In the fifties a conspicuous minority were beatniks, and today young Jews have become hippies beyond their representation in the total population; 25 percent, including many of the leaders, are Jewish, according to a recent study. AJC in San Francisco has estimated that about 40 percent of the young people who migrate to the Haight-Ashbury section every year are Jewish. This comes to approximately seventy-one thousand of them, which is about equal to the whole Jewish population of San Francisco—a high enough figure so that a group of young rabbis plan to form a "mission" to them. But these "hippie rabbis" may be worrying themselves unnecessarily. Most of these young people come from respectable middle-class homes, and the average length of their residence in hippiedom is three to four months. Having had their fling at nonconformity, they will probably return to college, graduate, become doctors or lawyers or businessmen, and settle in the suburbs, just like their parents. But it may be a bit too soon to be sure about this.

On the subject of sexual promiscuity, the Jewish attitude has always been somewhat ambiguous. Adultery is a sin specifically prohibited in the Ten Commandments and as we have already seen, practically nonexistent among the Orthodox. At the same time Judaism has never suffered from the fundamentally disapproving attitude toward sexual relations that we find in Christianity; Jewish puritans and prudes are hard to find. Furthermore, Jews have an irrepressible urge to experiment, to try the latest thing. If the world is going through a sexual revolution, Jews don't intend to be left out. And so unwed pregnancy has unquestionably increased among Jewish girls since the war. For every Jewish child put up for adoption twenty years ago, twelve Jewish couples used to apply; today about three couples apply for every child. The reason is not that Jews have lost interest in adopting babies, but that there are more babies available.

Nevertheless, despite their prominence on the barricades, Jewish girls still produce far less than their share of illegitimate babies. Twenty years ago there used to be ten non-Jewish parents for each available baby; today the proportions are two to one, and often one to one.

Many people feel that the supreme Jewish crime is materialism. Jews, under the impact of their American experience, are said to have become money grubbers and turned away from the Almighty in order to worship the Almighty Dollar.

It certainly isn't hard to find instances which seem to bear this out. Half a dozen kosher resorts offer, along with the food and the golf and the high-priced entertainment, weekly lectures on how to invest in the stock market. A fourteen-year-old boy from the Bronx whose parents suddenly struck it rich has started reading the stock market reports in the paper every morning and saving money to make investments; his parents brag about this to everyone they know. A lady from Hadassah came out of a benefit performance of *Fiddler on the Roof* a while ago and said scornfully to her friend, "It couldn't have cost them much to put on that show. Did you see what rags they were all wearing?"

Not only do Jews want to make money themselves, they take an inexhaustible interest in those who have made it— especially in how much they've made and how much they've paid for everything. If I mention to one lady a novel I've just read or an actor whose performance I just admired, her instant question is, "How much are they making on that book?" "What do you suppose they pay him for a part like that?" She enters a friend's home for the first time and spends most of the evening feeling the drapes, peering at the rugs, turning over the plates and looking at the underside. What she wants to know is, "How much did all this cost them?" We may be sure that many of the other guests are carrying on the same investigation.

If anyone thinks this lady is an exception, let them study that dependable indicator of ordinary Jewish opinion, Leonard Lyons. His column appears in the New York *Post* six days a week, and hardly a day goes by when he doesn't let us know exactly how much some wealthy celebrity paid for something. In a period of a few months in 1966 we could have learned from him that Chagall sells a small canvas for $10,000, Deems Taylor got only $750 in royalties from one of his operas, Jean Arthur made $25,000 a week when she became a star, Joseph Levine bought a Monet for $100,000, Abe Feinberg donated $1.5 million to build a graduate school at the Weitzmann Institute, and the Jules Stein grants for medical research will involve larger sums than the Nobel Prize.

Spending money to make a splash, to achieve status with friends and relations, has become a common game among American Jews. Everyone makes jokes about the women at

Miami Beach with their mink coats and their jewelry, the women on Park Avenue with their wall-to-wall carpeting and their expensive furnishings in the style sometimes known as Brooklyn Renaissance, the men in their long black Cadillacs. ("Can your little boy walk yet, Mrs. Cohen?" "God forbid he should ever have to!") The popularity of these jokes itself is proof that they correspond to a reality—though the people who make them always insist that they refer to "those other Jews."

If you want to see that reality with your own eyes, spend a day or two at the Concord Hotel in the Catskills. One young man described his experience there: "I was standing in this big lobby the morning I got there. You know how it was decorated —strictly *nouveau* Scarsdale. Well, I was at the bottom of this huge red-carpeted staircase—like something they brought over straight from Buckingham Palace—when all of a sudden, at the top of the staircase, this ugly woman appears. She's sixty years old if she's a day, and her hair is rinsed orange, and she's wearing hip pads and toreador pants and a bikini bosom—and when she gets halfway down I see it! My God, attached to that bikini of hers is a diamond brooch! I went straight to the desk and checked out, and I've never been back there again!"

Even more horrible examples of lavishness and vulgarity are provided by many wedding and bar mitzvah parties. Extraordinary things occur—six-foot-high cakes; a catered buffet dinner, including guinea hen and caviar and Chagall's Jerusalem windows in aspic; friends and relations fighting to give the most expensive presents. (The parents of one bar mitzvah boy included this little rider on the invitation: "Please send savings bonds only.") And the ceremonies themselves don't escape from this desperate competitiveness. Weddings especially are often not held in the synagogue at all, but in the private banquet hall of a hotel (the posher the better) whose bandstand will be temporarily disguised as an altar. Or for those not released from the bondage of *kashruth* there are kosher catering halls with ornate, overdecorated "synagogues" on the premises, equipped with multicolored spotlights that follow the bride down the aisle.

This indictment could go on and on, but before we can understand what it really means we must see the American Jews in historical context. The great majority, immigrants or the children of immigrants, were brought up in poverty. The reaction they display today—the childish delight in mink coats, the curiosity about prices, the vulgarity and the ostentation—is surely neither particularly Jewish nor particularly American. It is something much more familiar and much more universal. It is, in fact, the pattern of behavior which has been associated with the *nouveaux riches* through the ages. Apuleius described it in *The Golden Ass,* and Molière in *Le Bourgeois Gentilhomme,* and Trollope in *Barchester Towers,* and Sinclair Lewis in *Dodsworth.* Every American immigrant group has followed this same pattern, the Irish and the Italians no less than the Jews.

Almost invariably the *nouveau riche* disease wears out in the third generation. The first generation fights like the devil to save enough money to give their kids a start in life; the second generation takes advantage of the start to make a fortune, let the world know they've made it, give their children "all the things our parents couldn't afford to give us"; the third generation uses those things, including an expensive Ivy League education, to rise above the naïveté and bad taste of the first two generations. This is precisely what is happening now in the American Jewish community. Caterers tell me that bar mitzvah and wedding parties have become much less lavish and expensive in the last ten years, mostly because the children themselves keep pulling the parents back. More and more young Jews insist on being married in the synagogue instead of in hotels or catering halls; this doesn't show a return to religion so much as a disgust with ostentation. Jewish girls don't wear nearly as much jewelry as their mothers do. There are even signs that the mink coat is no longer the all-purpose winter-or-summer day-and-night garment that it once was. And one of the great conspicuous-consumption symbols of the second generation has been almost completely shattered today: very few young Jewish mothers, no matter how wealthy, still hire "governesses," foreign or domestic, to take care of their children.

And so it is pointless to ask if Jews have been corrupted by their material success in America. Of course they have; the shock of moving from poverty to wealth is bound to have its effect. The important question is, Has this effect been any different on Jews than on other people? Is there any evidence that they have succumbed less enthusiastically to the corruption, or at least reacted to it differently?

"An anti-Semite," according to an old saying, "is someone who hates Jews more than necessary." This saying is Jewish, of course. Nobody who knows anything about Jews could have any doubts about that.

The truth is, no anti-Semite criticizes the Jew more vehemently than he criticizes himself. This has been going on since Moses caught the children of Israel worshiping the Golden Calf and destroyed it before their eyes, since Jeremiah and Isaiah inveighed against the godlessness of their people. Karl Marx was simply following in the footsteps of the Prophets when he declared that Judaism was nothing but moneymaking and exploitation. His anti-Semitism was so virulent that many editions of his works—often under the influence of Jewish editors with socialistic leanings—leave out the most offensive passages.

Today this habit of self-criticism is as intense as it ever was. The respondents in *Commentary's* 1961 symposium on "Jewishness and the Younger Intellectuals" made all the usual charges; the sentiments were those of Jeremiah, even if the language was that of Marx and Freud. An earlier symposium in 1951 and a still earlier one in 1944 sound as if they were written by exactly the same people. And every one of these fiery rebels sounds like Richard Wishnetsky, the central figure in a terrible tragedy which took place in 1966. Wishnetsky, a recent college graduate and the son of respected members of the congregation, jumped up on the platform during a bar mitzvah ceremony at Temple Shaarey Zadek in Detroit. He grabbed the microphone, made an impassioned speech, then pulled out a gun and shot Rabbi Morris Adler and himself. Both men died within a few days. What Wishnetsky shouted into the microphone was, "This congregation is a travesty and an abomination. It has made a mockery by its phoniness and hypocrisy of the beauty and spirit of Judaism. It is composed of people who on the whole make me ashamed to say that I am a Jew." In his diary was found a passage that carries the biblical tone of his condemnation even further: "Judaism in America does not need to worry about anti-Semitism destroying it from without. The American Jewish community is destroying itself from within. Shaarey Zadek is a synagogue which bears witness against God." [3]

Wishnetsky was a psychotic, of course, but somehow this doesn't make it easy to forget about him. Few Jews in America haven't been aware, at one time or another, of thinking very much the same thoughts.

The extraordinary thing is that these slashing indictments of American Jewish life come not only from the rebels but from the establishment itself. "The sudden move upward on the economic and social ladder has overwhelmed the American Jew, so that he has been mesmerized by the distorted values that sudden wealth brings, exposing him . . . to corrosive influences which he often has been unable to resist." [4] Who wrote that? One of the "younger intellectuals" in *Commentary*'s symposium? No, it was part of an address given by Rabbi Samuel Dresner of Springfield, Massachusetts, to the annual convention of the Rabbinical Assembly. And Rabbi Dresner was hardly saying something that shocked or surprised his colleagues. Within a few days I heard the same idea—that complacency, softness, too much love of material comfort, is the plague of American Judaism today—expressed by a leading Reconstructionist rabbi, an Orthodox scholar at Yeshiva, an official of UJA, and one of the directors of the American Jewish Congress.

The most astonishing aspect of Jewish self-criticism is that it is almost always unjust. No anti-Semite could exaggerate or distort the Jew's faults more cruelly than he does himself. The low incidence of crime among Jews is by no means a secret; it is certainly well known to members of the establishment. Yet this is what Max Frankel, the president of the National Association of Temple Educators, said in a speech in 1966: "We often hear that there is less delinquency, crime, divorce, and alcoholism among Jews than among non-Jews. But these statistics are changing; more and more we are becoming like the majority, and have a moral decay." The increase he refers to is so tiny that the statistical tables can't even record it; only a Jew could describe this as a "moral decay." [5]

Examples of this kind of unfairness present themselves constantly. A college professor climaxed an indignant condemnation of the Vietnam war with this rhetorical question: "And what about the Jews? Why aren't *they* stopping it?" Sholome Michael Gelber, in a 1959 essay, bitterly castigates Jewish hospitals because "there is jealousy, ambition, political in-fighting on the boards and among the doctors"—in other words, they're no different from non-Jewish hospitals. [6] Robert Alter, in a *Commentary* article, criticizes the immigrants on the Lower

East Side by quoting these words of Jacob Riis: "Over and over again I have met with instances of these Polish or Russian Jews deliberately starving themselves to the point of physical exhaustion, while working night and day at a tremendous pressure to save a little money." [7] A curious reason for criticizing someone—because he's so poor that he has to make sacrifices in order to save money. Another example is the contention, which Jews repeat among themselves all the time, that Jewish doctors charge higher fees than gentile doctors. New York Federation has made comparative studies which prove that there is no truth whatever to this—but Jews will go on believing it.

Self-hatred is the easy explanation which doesn't really explain anything. People who show none of the usual symptoms of self-hatred, who don't change their names or their noses, who neither fawn on gentiles nor shudder away from them, will join exuberantly in the swelling chorus of Jewish self-criticism. The common denominator that unites them all is the deep-seated conviction that Jews ought to be better than other people, that faults which might be forgivable in others are totally reprehensible in Jews.

This conviction is so strong that Jews continue to hold it even when they know how irrational it is, even when they are able to ridicule it. Thus a young civil rights activist, in an article about his experiences down South, writes, "I feel that Jews *are* different, that our history and our books, our hopes and sufferings have called us to special duties . . . I am caught in a tension between my rational estimate of Jews as ordinary people and my emotional insistence that Jews are special." [8] And in the same vein, the late Pearl Willen, the past president of the National Council of Jewish Women, cited studies which disproved the old prejudice that Jewish women treat their servants worse than other women do. But then she added, "It isn't enough! I expect Jewish women to treat their servants *better* than others! I know it's absurd, but I do expect Jews to be better than other people!"

This high expectation reveals itself clearly in the attitude of many Jews toward Israel. While fiercely sympathetic to Israel, and ready to rise to her defense at the smallest gentile imputation, they are also intensely critical of any fault, no matter how justifiable, that she may show. A young rabbi told me that in his opinion Israel shouldn't have an atomic bomb; even if her military defenses suffer, she ought to be "more moral than other countries." A Jewish American actor who played in the Israeli production of *West Side Story* was horrified at the way Israel discriminates against her minority group, the Yemenites. He admits that the Yemenites are treated much better than Negroes in America—"But that's not the point, Jews have no right to *any* prejudice at all!" This was the spirit which informed I. F. Stone's long article on the Israeli-Arab war in *The New York Review of Books* in 1967.[9] His case against the Israeli government, in a nutshell, was that it refuses to behave more nobly and altruistically than any other government in the history of mankind has ever done.

In his essay on Hannah Arendt, Norman Podhoretz refers to this Jewish characteristic. It fills him with exasperation. "The Nazis destroyed a third of the Jewish people," he writes. "In the name of all that is humane, will the remnant never let up on itself?"[10] His exasperation is understandable, but I must confess that I'm glad it isn't typical. The inability to "let up on itself" is, it seems to me, the emotional core of that ethical tradition of Judaism which we hear about so often. Without this constant itch to criticize himself, the Jew's ethical tradition would be barren, a set of abstract rules and regulations that living human beings had long since stopped paying attention to. But the fact is that Jews, because they expect more of themselves, get more out of themselves. They aren't born better than other people, but their tradition makes them less easily satisfied. Since the days of Moses the Jewish people have always been corrupt, and have always suspected that they were —and so have always been prepared to listen to the prophets among them who condemned them for their corruption.

It hasn't changed in America today. In an article entitled "An Atheist Looks at Judaism," Nat Hentoff tears into every aspect of Jewish life and finds nothing good to say about any of it from religious observance to philanthropy to politics; yet this article appeared in the official magazine of the Union of American Hebrew Congregations.[11] A couple of years ago a group of young activists picketed the Reform temple in Washington, D.C., on Yom Kippur eve; to the arriving worshipers they handed leaflets which accused certain prominent members of the congregation of owning property in the Negro slums; the leaflets urged these slum owners to search their consciences on the Day of Atonement. Instead of calling the police to remove the pickets, the president and the board of the congregation held a caucus in the lobby, and one of them was heard to say, "If I were their age, I'd be doing the same thing." Then the pickets were invited to come inside and join in on the services.

The corollary of all this is that nobody, no matter how reprehensible, ever gets completely read out of the Jewish community. Occasionally attempts are made to do this. A few years ago, for example, several rabbis suggested that B'nai B'rith and other large Jewish organizations should expel any member who owned slum property and was guilty of violations. Very few B'nai B'rith members are slum landlords, but the feeling of the vast majority of them—and of most Jews, I think—was strongly against any such disciplinary measures. The Jewish tradition is to persuade, influence, exhort, cajole, and even insult, but never to blackmail or intimidate people into virtue. Indignant tirades from the pulpit and dirty looks at the dinner dance are permissible; banishment into the void is not.

And what the Jewish community feels toward the individual, the individual usually feels toward the community. Even the man who rejects it most violently seldom does so totally. A part of him yearns for the community he has rejected, hopes for some miracle of reformation that will allow him to return to the fold. According to eyewitness reports, in the moment before he pulled the trigger Richard Wishnetsky looked into Rabbi Adler's face and said "Rabbi—" in a soft, almost tender voice.[12]

Jews are unconscionably hard on one another, and inevitably they forgive one another. This is as true of Jews in America today as it was of Jews in the *shtetl*, as it was of the children of Israel in the desert. This is, as it always has been, their greatest strength.

XVIII.

"Who Else Can You Count On—?"

The foundation of Judaism's moral strength, we are often told, is the Jewish family. No other aspect of Jewish life is so often praised, so shamelessly sentimentalized: the huge gatherings around the dinner table, Mama's chicken noodle soup, the tears and the laughter, the whole Sam Levenson syndrome. This urge to look at family life through rose-colored glasses is so strong in Jews that it even extends to the unpleasant parts, to the fights, the overpossessiveness, the boredom. All of these things are treated, in novel after novel and in personal reminiscences, as if they were affectionate little foibles without which family life somehow wouldn't have been as beautiful.

On the other hand, by a different kind of novelist and a different kind of person, family life is reviled and castigated as if it were an image of hell on earth. Such people blame their families for every misfortune that ever happened to them.

Both these reactions arise from the same source—the ambiguity of Jewish family life in America. Certain deeply felt attitudes, well adapted to the conditions of the *shtetl*, were brought here by the East European immigrant and transplanted in American soil. If this soil had been completely uncongenial to them, they would be dead and forgotten by now; but the soil was partly congenial, partly inimical. The attitudes were able to take root and grow, and all too often they produced some strange flowers.

The most important attitude of traditional Judaism is that the family is the sacred foundation of all life, the heart not only of daily living but of the religion itself. For this reason, in almost all Jewish religious holidays the home ceremonies are just as important as the synagogue ceremonies. The fundamental purpose of the Sabbath is to reinforce family solidarity. And Passover and Hanukkah take place entirely in the home; they don't require synagogue attendance at all.

This is what we might call the overt significance of Jewish family life. But it also has its secret significance, deeply felt but seldom openly acknowledged. This secret significance reveals itself in many curious forms of behavior. To take one random example: American Jews have pioneered in the development of family service agencies; Jewish parents who are having trouble with their children never hesitate to seek expert help from the outside. Yet as many studies have shown, they almost always seek this help from an agency which is at least nominally Jewish.[1] In actual practice it may have mostly gentile clients, administrators, and counselors: nevertheless, if it doesn't call itself Jewish, Jews with family problems won't go to it.

This fact tells us a lot, I think, about the secret significance of Jewish family life. In many of his other activities the American Jew has been able to overcome, or at least to mitigate, his ancient conviction that the world is divided into two groups, and that the gentiles belong to what Jerome Weidman, in his novel on the subject, called "the enemy camp"; but he clings tenaciously to this conviction when his family affairs are involved. Close family ties aren't merely an expression of love and warmth, belief in God and respect for old traditions; they are also a kind of protection against the outside world, the gentile world.

"Who else can you count on in this world except your own family?" When I was a child this phrase was dinned into my ears at every possible opportunity, and most other Jewish children have come to know it too. This feeling that one's family is one's only bastion against attack has many consequences in American Jewish life. The Jewish marriage rate is higher than that of most other groups.[2] A man isn't really a complete man unless he gets married, and an unmarried woman isn't much of anything. Old maids are rarer (and widows more frequent) among Jews than among other groups. Mothers don't breathe easy until their daughters of marriageable age have found mates for themselves. Unmarried sons are a source of worry too, though the concern isn't as desperate as it is for daughters. "For heaven's sake, get married!" my mother used to say to me. "What right have you got to go on being so selfish?"

Another consequence of this feeling—though it may not seem to be at first—is that Jews tend to get married somewhat older than other Americans.[2] The emphasis on education has something to do with this: "First finish college, then you can get married." But it also reflects the Jewish belief that marriage is a very serious business—not just fun and games, but a matter of life and death. A family isn't only a family, it's also a fortress.

The divorce rate is lower among Jews than among other Americans, with the exception of Catholics.[2] There is no firm injunction against divorce in Judaism; it is permitted, and even encouraged in cases of extreme incompatibility. Yet even among the non-Orthodox there is a vague, uneasy sentiment against it, a sense that the breaking up of a marriage, no matter what the circumstances, is a kind of tragedy. Many people have wondered why the Jews, with their comparatively low divorce rate, should always be in the forefront of agitation for the reform and relaxation of divorce laws. The answer is that to Jews divorce isn't really a moral issue, as it is to Catholics; it is a practical issue, a question of tactics. When you get divorced, you weaken yourself; by breaking up your family, you leave yourself defenseless. The vast majority of Jews who do get divorced remarry within a short period of time. And so do Jewish widowers, and widows who are young enough. Their instinct is to rebuild those defenses as quickly as possible.

This sense of solidarity exists not only with the immediate family, not only between husbands and wives, and parents and children, but with all the branches as well. The mere fact of a family relationship imposes an obligation. As we have seen, Jewish fathers not only take their sons into the business with them; if they have poor relations who aren't absolute idiots (and often even if they are), they'll take *them* into the business too.

All of this seems to be tied up with the idea of *Zedakah*—charity, after all, begins at home. And the same ambiguity which applies to *Zedakah* also applies to family relationships. I feel an obligation to the members of my family, but that doesn't mean I have to *like* them. I may, in fact, hate their guts; this doesn't for one moment relieve me of the obligation or weaken my sense of solidarity. Family fights are frequent among Jews, yet they seldom lead to permanent breaks.

On the contrary, most members of Jewish families, regardless of how they feel about one another, continue to get together socially. Relatives who live in the same city do a lot of visiting back and forth, and certain special occasions are always celebrated by large family gatherings. A Jew invites all his immediate family to weddings and bar mitzvahs; he runs the risk of giving grave offense to anybody he leaves out. Funerals will be attended by aunts and uncles and cousins that the deceased loathed and avoided whenever possible. The woman who has a baby is liable to be visited in the hospital by people who may never set eyes on the child again.

Holidays—and not just the religious ones—require family parties. Thanksgiving is big among American Jews. So is Christmas, though there may be no tree, no wreath, no presents, no overt reference at all to the significance of the day. Birthdays and anniversaries can seldom be ignored or celebrated quietly. If it's a "big" birthday or a "big" anniversary, the ordinary dinner-table festivities may be moved into a hotel banquet room, and your dreary Aunt Sylvia and your obnoxious Cousin Marvin, whom you thought you had seen the last of, will show up in your life again. In the last twenty years Mother's Day and Father's Day have become so popular among American Jews that many people seem to think they're mentioned in the Torah. As a matter of fact, it was a Jewish public-relations man who invented Father's Day, on behalf of the necktie industry.

The chief expression of the Jewish family spirit is eating. From the *shtetl* to the suburbs, food is the traditional symbol of love and solidarity. Families, as a rule, don't get together to "do" things. They don't go to the theater or listen to music. They don't even get together for conversation. A lot of competitive talking goes on—gossip, arguments, rich relatives boasting to poor relatives about their latest purchases—but the real business of the evening is the huge meal. Once it's over, the men gather at the TV set, the women play canasta, and the younger people excuse themselves and go somewhere else.

This emphasis on food and de-emphasis on conversation gives away the truth about the Jewish family party. It is a ritual, not a meeting of minds or a gathering of congenial spirits. The Jewish hostess says to her guests, "Eat, eat already!

Don't talk!" because she instinctively realizes that they have nothing to talk to one another about. Nobody really expects them to have similar tastes or ideas or interests. They have been brought together as symbols, not as human beings.

Yet the power of these symbolic occasions, these rituals of eating, can't be underestimated. Food has a way of arousing a sense of Jewishness in people long after everything else has lost its influence over them. Marc Chagall (who once announced to a group of friends, "You want my opinion of Judaism? I can say it in one word—fooey!") searches for a good kosher restaurant in every city he visits, because he's so fond of potato latkes. A nun in a Midwest hospital was converted from Judaism years ago and is perfectly content in the Catholic Church; nevertheless, whenever she's on night duty with a certain Jewish doctor, she likes to go off to an empty room with him and eat pastrami and pickles, and "enjoy being a Jew again." A prominent psychiatrist, who is married to a gentile and maintains no connections at all with the Jewish community, calls up a Jewish friend once a year and arranges to have lunch at a kosher restaurant. "It's my annual atavistic throwback," he says with a laugh—but he goes on doing it.

The psychological mechanism in such cases is clear. In the minds of many people food is equated with childhood, with festive gatherings around the dining-room table, with family life. And family life was and still is the chief means of imposing on the child a sense of his Jewishness.

The real reason for getting married is to have children. They are both the justification and the central concern of family life. In the *shtetl* a married couple who lived together ten years without having children was often compelled to get a divorce. No such barbaric measures are resorted to in America, of course, but something of the same feeling remains. Jews are more likely to adopt children than other groups, and the demand much exceeds the supply, because most states require the adopted child to be born into the same religion as his adopted parents.

The child-centeredness of Jewish family life is shown also, oddly enough, by the fact that Jews have fewer children: two per family, as compared to the national average of three per family.[3] The Hasidim believe that birth control is *halakically* prohibited, and their families average six children and often contain as many as fifteen children; but on the whole American Jews are on the side of family planning. They want fewer children because they want to give each one more attention, more personal care.

The key to this is the belief, which existed in the *shtetl* and exists just as strongly today, that one's child is an extension of oneself; what happens to him also happens to the parent. This is why Jewish parents are so intensely anxious about their children, so constantly overprotective. The outside world is hard, and the family exists to keep its members insulated; they are bound together in this nest, none of them quite separate from the others, for the common cause of self-protection.

With everything that's been written about this overprotectiveness, all the scorn that's been heaped on it, Jewish parents still indulge in it—and take their indulgence so for granted that they're often willing to speak about it without the least discomfort. Recently the bulletin of a Young Israel synagogue in New York announced that two of its members were moving to Flatbush, "in order to be closer to Brooklyn College, where their lovely daughter attends." [4] The extraordinary thing about this item is not that these parents felt the need to cross the Brooklyn Bridge for their daughter's protection, but that they cheerfully and unhesitatingly gave this reason to the synagogue bulletin.

The overprotectiveness shows itself most strongly in the concern that Jewish parents feel for their children's health. Jews are hypochondriacs generally—it's part of the atmosphere of anxiety in which they live—but they're even more hypochondriacal about their children than about themselves. This anxiety does have its good side, of course. In the early years of this century infant and child mortality rates were much lower among the Jews than among any other immigrant group—even though the majority of Jews, like the other immigrants, lived in the slums, where there was a high incidence of disease. But this doesn't mean Jews should blind themselves to the disturbing implications. For many Jewish parents, worrying about the child's health, though it may be an expression of love, is also a way of infantilizing him, keeping him helpless, preventing him from growing up.

The basic feeling of these parents is that their child is a fragile being, weak, incompetent, incapable of making decisions or doing anything for himself. One mother boasted to me that she had washed her son's hair until the day he went off to college. Another mother persistently referred to her youngest son as her baby; he was forty-two years old. A father retired from the garment business and turned over the whole operation to his thirty-year-old son; a year later, though the business was running more efficiently than ever, the father got practically hysterical because his son decided to move away from home and take an apartment of his own. "My God," said the father, "he's never been on his own before in his whole life! What'll he do for eating, for cleaning up? How's he going to get along?"

Parents who worry too much about their children and baby them as a consequence will inevitably spoil them too. "Everything for the children"—this old saying leads parents to lavish gifts, favors, and privileges on them. Cabdrivers don't make much money, yet I have met dozens of Jewish cabbies in New York who have put their sons through college and even medical school, and who brag about the big weddings they gave their daughters. Many of the hippies who congregate in the Haight-Ashbury section of San Francisco have been disowned by their parents, but not the Jewish ones. Most of these get regular checks from home, which they may or may not tear up. Jewish parents are just as exasperated at what the kids are doing, but it would never occur to them to cut their "babies" off without funds.

Home discipline is far less strict among Jews than among other groups. Jewish parents are naggers, screamers, nudgers—but not hitters. The child has to go pretty far before he'll get the back of his father's hand. And a lot more conversational freedom is tolerated. Jewish children are allowed to interrupt, contradict the grown-ups, be "fresh." Gentiles visiting a Jewish household for the first time are often horrified by the things they hear the children say—things which the parents and children themselves take for granted and are hardly aware of.

Sometimes parents recognize and deplore this, but they find it difficult to do anything about it. The American in them disapproves—because nice American children are supposed to be polite, well behaved, and respectful—but the Jew in them can't really agree. One Connecticut mother, after a long series of complaints about her son's laziness and ingratitude, said to me, "After all, why *should* we give him the car every time he wants it? What's stopping us from saying no?"

I asked her why, if she felt that way, she *didn't* say no. She gave a shrug and said, "Let's face it, it's hard not to be a Jewish mother."

———— •◆• ————

When Ambrose Bierce defined self-sacrifice as "the indulgence of a propensity to forego," he might have been writing about the Jewish parent. There is no clearer demonstration of this propensity, this belief that the role of the parent is to give and the role of the child is to take, than the Jewish attitude toward old age.

This attitude existed all the way back in the *shtetl*. A parent was supposed to take care of his child. A child wasn't supposed to take care of his parent; such a thing was against nature, an abortion. It happened from time to time, but nobody felt right about it, and often elaborate devices were used to pretend that it wasn't happening. For instance, an old man without a penny in the world, completely dependent on the bounty of his married son, would nevertheless be considered the legal owner of the house that he and his children and grandchildren were living in—so he could look people in the face and say, "I'm not living with my children, *they're* living with *me!*"

And so today the elderly Jew will do everything he can to keep from being dependent on his children. Unless he has a great deal of money saved, he will fight desperately against retirement. Jews live longer than other people, but they also go on working longer. Nobody is surprised at people like David Dubinsky, who "retired" from the presidency of the ILGWU at the age of seventy-three but still goes to all meetings, works a full day in his office, and issues statements of policy.

But even when he's forced to retire, even when his wife is dead and he's all alone in the world, the elderly Jew seldom goes to live with his children. If he has enough money, he will often go to Miami Beach or Arizona or southern California—partly because of the climate, but also because this takes him away from where his children are. He loves them dearly and looks forward eagerly to every visit from them, but the distance reduces any sense of dependence he might have on them. The chances are he's getting a check from them every month, maybe for extra luxuries or maybe to pay the rent; by keeping his distance he's better able to pretend that this check is coming from some anonymous, impersonal source.

If he has to live in the same city as his children, he will take a tiny apartment or a dreary hotel room rather than a room in their house. He prefers to remain on the Lower East Side or up on the Grand Concourse, feeling, "My children have their lives, and I have mine." He prefers a life of empty activity, of "passing the time" by sunning himself on Brighton Beach, where the old people fill the benches for blocks in a row; by being one of the "regulars" in synagogue every Friday night and Saturday morning, perhaps less out of religious conviction than a desire for human companionship; by going to the local Golden Age Club and playing cards and squabbling with others like himself.

And in the end he is often obliged to go into an old-age home. Jewish philanthropy gives a much higher percentage of its support to such homes than non-Jewish philanthropy does. The house with three generations under its roof is becoming rarer on the American scene generally, but it hardly exists at all among Jews. And even the old-age home is financed in such a way as to give its inmates the feeling that they are paying for it themselves. Sixty-five percent of the funds for Jewish old-age homes come from the old people themselves, mostly through their social security and other public benefits.

Many things are being done by Jewish organizations today to improve the conditions of old-age homes. Occupational therapy is given. The old people are encouraged to work, to read, to put on plays. They are allowed to leave the homes during the day, to take part-time jobs, to pay weekend visits to their relations. But nobody thinks of initiating a campaign to persuade their children to take them in, make them a useful part of the family again. Such a campaign would be opposed no more energetically by the children than by the old people themselves.

Although the Jewish child is overprotected, infantilized, spoiled, he is also pushed, hardened, forced to perform beyond his years. The same impulse which leads parents at one moment to one method of treatment leads them at the next moment to the opposite method.

To the Jew the child is an extension of himself. The silver

cord never gets broken, because this would weaken the family in its stand against the outside world. And so the Jewish parent not only worries about his child more, but feels more personally involved in his achievements. It's not only *tsouris*, trouble, which comes from a child, but also *nachis*, good fortune, satisfaction in the eyes of the world.

A father takes his son into the business with him not primarily to provide a comfortable future for the boy, but to enhance his own prestige. When he shows off the boy to his employees and his competitors, he is demonstrating his own status and ability. For the same reason mothers brag shamelessly about the accomplishments of their children; they bore everyone to tears with stories of "my son, the doctor," "my daughter, such a lovely-looking girl." On the Lower East Side this was the main form of competition among immigrant women, and I'm not so sure it's any different in Scarsdale or Shaker Heights today: "my son, the doctor" has simply turned into "my son, the nuclear physicist."

Studies have shown that Jewish parents are far more prone than others to praise their children for their achievements—and are much less hard on them for their mistakes.[5] But this can be deceptive. It's true that Jewish parents seldom hit their children when they fail, just as Jewish husbands seldom beat their wives, but psychological pressure can be just as relentless. In school, in business, in marriage, no parent can push his child harder than a Jewish parent—because his own ability to hold up his head at the next family gathering depends on his child's success.

The people who work in Jewish adoption agencies get to see this trait in its rawest form. In recent years there has been an increase in biracial babies, illegitimate offspring of Jewish mothers and Negro fathers. From the *halakic* point of view these children are unquestionably Jewish, yet the agencies find it almost impossible to get Jewish parents to adopt them. And this situation exists in spite of the shortage of Jewish babies for adoption, the liberal views of Jews on civil rights, and the establishment's constant warnings that they are losing Jews. The reason is other people's race prejudice. If you adopt a child who is half Negro, a child who has a "handicap" and isn't perfect, this will reflect badly on you: again, to the Jewish parent his child is an extension of himself.

This explains a parental ploy which all Jewish children are

bitterly aware of, but which seldom gets mentioned in the sentimental studies of family life. The Jewish parent may not use a strap to enforce obedience, but he uses an even more devastating weapon—guilt. "You're killing your mother," says the Jewish father when his child is doing something he doesn't want him to do. Instantly the rights and wrongs of the child's behavior become irrelevant; what matters is its effect on Mama. Thus, one mother I heard of threatened to jump out the window if her daughter refused to have an Orthodox wedding. And a father, whose daughter wanted to marry a Chinese boy, wrote the suitor a letter in which he never once mentioned his daughter's feelings, but repeated several times, "You don't know what you're doing to us! My wife is dying from her diabetes, and I'm under medication!"

This habit is so strongly ingrained in Jews that the very person who suffered from it as a child is likely to do it to his own children later on. I discussed this trait one day with a friend of mine. We traded examples of it from our own childhood. Then his little daughter started misbehaving, and he snapped at her, "Stop it, Lisa! Do you want to make Daddy ashamed of you in front of his guest?"

------◆◆------

Though they would have understood this device in the *shtetl*, they might have been surprised at its source. Traditionally it wasn't the father who snapped at the children. He was a figure of great dignity who sat silently at the head of the table or pored over his Torah in his chair. He was called upon by the mother only for the most serious breaches of discipline, and his method of punishment was simply to turn his eyes on the offender and glare quietly and sadly for a few seconds. This was enough to strike terror into any child's heart. It was the mother who ran things in the household; she not only did the cooking, the cleaning, and the punishing, but had charge of the accounts, dealt with the tradesmen, kept the money.

The young Jewish father in America today is very different from his grandfather or great-grandfather of the *shtetl*, but the connection between the two hasn't been snapped entirely. When the man of the *shtetl* arrived on the Lower East Side, he often found himself lost and bewildered in the new environment. His silent scholarly ways had value in the old country, but were superfluous in the American jungle. How could a cutter in a garment factory command the same almost religious respect as a patriarch in a pious East European household? The forms were often maintained—a middle-aged college professor described to me how the front room of his family's tiny apartment was always closed off during the week, no matter how crowded the rest of the place got, because it was meant to be occupied on Sundays by his father—but the spirit was gone.

Yet the point is that the forms *were* maintained. It was still the mother who dominated the family, the father who remained a shadowy but awesome figure. And this scarcely changed in the next generation, when the father became a successful businessman. His children still saw little of him; instead of being at the synagogue, he was at the office. The responsibility for their welfare and behavior was still the wife's. Many American Jews now in their forties or older can remember that remark which their fathers invariably made to their mothers when they were naughty: "Is *this* the way you're bringing him up?"

And that vaguely lost feeling which belonged to the earlier years in America still clung to the second-generation father, no matter how much money he might have made. Outside of his office he didn't quite seem to belong in the world. Dinner-table conversation didn't revolve around him and his interests. On vacations he always seemed to be a fifth wheel; he played cards with a few cronies or sat in the sun with a newspaper over his face, while the rest of the family enjoyed themselves together.

All of this seems to be very different today. Jewish fathers help with the dishes, diaper the babies, and take their sons to the ball game—just like all other American fathers. Yet something of the old feeling remains. I have talked with dozens of suburban teen-agers and have met only a few who didn't say that it was their mother who made the decisions in the family, who really ran the home. "Mothers are aggressive people," one girl said. "Not fathers—they're too busy listening to the mothers." I have run across many families where the women pay the bills, keep the accounts, make the important decisions about the children. Even in families where this doesn't occur, the woman is almost certain to be the one who makes the dates for herself and her husband—the implication being that his "real" life is in the office, and his social life is something over which he need have no control. Living in the suburbs and commuting to the city have given him less time to spend with his family. He sees them mostly on weekends, though nobody closes off the front room for him during the week.

It is often said that women are the ones who have really benefited from the changes in American mores during the last half-century. In a sense this is less true of Jewish women, because the Jewish attitude has always had a certain ambiguity in it. On the one hand, women are traditionally inferior; they must sit upstairs in the synagogue, they belong at the foot of the table, they aren't permitted to study Talmud as their brothers are. On the other hand, the Torah constantly urges men to treat their women with respect, even with a kind of worship, and *halakah* specifically states that the gratification of the woman is one of the prime purposes of sexual relations; the man who uses a woman sexually without giving her pleasure is commiting a sin, even if the woman happens to be his wife. She is definitely not to be considered either a plaything or a convenience or a beast of burden.

Much of this ambiguity remains in her position today. In Jewish clubs it's always the man who is put up for membership, not his wife. If he dies, she may inherit his membership—until she marries again, in which case she must qualify all over again through her new husband. Girls are sent to college now as well as boys, yet the feeling persists that it isn't fitting for a girl to be "too smart"; many Jewish mothers have urged their bright daughters to play dumb if they want to catch a husband. AJC's study of Wilkes-Barre teen-agers revealed that Jewish girls feel much less close to their parents than boys do—an indication, if not positive proof, that they are growing up in a boy-oriented culture.[6] Furthermore, when Jewish girls rebel against their families, they seem to do so in far more violently antisocial ways than their brothers do. They go out and get pregnant— and very seldom is the father a Jewish boy. A generation ago he was likely to be an Italian; today there seems to be a leaning toward Negroes. The point is that these girls choose boys who are as different as possible in background and tastes and appearance from their own families.

At the same time the domination of women in much of Jewish life is equally evident. The Jewish clubwoman type— involved in half a dozen organizations, presiding over meetings, writing letters to the newspapers—is about as different from an ineffectual, flowered-hat Helen Hokinson caricature as she could be. She's a formidable creature, and has been known to make strong men tremble. Any number of studies, in fact, have shown that Jewish women are more organization-minded than other women and go in more strenuously for all kinds of charitable and cultural activities outside of their homes. If you think this breed is dying, you need only visit any Sunday School class; the girls invariably have their hands raised a much as the boys, and their answers are liable to be just as bright and provocative.

The real difference between the Jewish woman in America today and her grandmother lies not in their fundamental character but in the effect that the American experience has had on it. The woman of the *shtetl* lived with her ambiguity; it created no conflict in her. The American Jewish woman is torn between the two sides of her nature, the aggressive and the submissive. She shares with other American women the problem of the "feminine mystique"—should she stay home with her family, or should she go out and get a job? But in her this is complicated by her doubts and confusion about her Jewish identity. If she neglects her family, will she also, in some mystical way, be betraying the Jewish people? And so, when she does leave the house, she often involves herself in some kind of Jewish organizational work; this relieves her conscience when she does the things she really enjoys, like shopping or playing mah-jongg.

And in the end she never stays away from her children too long. She knows that her place is by their side. Her Jewish blood tells her so—or maybe it's her Jewish anxiety. Anyway, who else is there to pamper them and worry about them and nag at them and make them feel guilty? The new mother's vocabulary is a bit more sophisticated than her own mother's was—she speaks of her daughter's negativism rather than her laziness, and instead of telling her son that his bad marks are killing her she says that they force her to wonder "in what way we've failed to motivate you"—but under her Radcliffe degree we know her for what she is—our dear old Jewish mother.

———•◦•———

Somebody or other is always bewailing the decline of the Jewish family. Along with the decline of prayer and the decline of morality, this is one of the most common subjects for sermons. The trouble with all this despondency is that it distracts attention from the interesting question: what does the Jewish family have to offer in this day and age? Do its virtues balance out its faults? Why *shouldn't* it decline?

Its defenders make two strong points in its favor. First, they ask us to look at the tremendous amount of happiness and satisfaction which Jewish parents, in spite of all the tensions, get from their children. You hear very few Jewish parents or grandparents saying, with a weary sigh, that they wouldn't have children if they had it to do all over again. Second, the pro-Jewish-family faction contends that Jewish children couldn't be brought up too badly since they usually turn out so well. Among all American ethnic groups only the Chinese, who also place great value on the closeness of family ties, have such a low rate of juvenile crime.

These points certainly indicate the strength of Jewish family life, but they don't really prove that it has no weaknesses. Delinquency, after all, isn't the only measure of failure or success. Children who get into bad trouble with the law are the ones who have been rejected by their families; society casts them out, so they strike back at society. Admittedly Jewish children are seldom cast out, but they seem to be up against exactly the opposite problem: how on earth can they *get* out?

But they *do* get out, the defender of the Jewish family will interrupt at this point. Comparative studies have shown that Jews are more willing to take jobs in cities where their parents don't live, that fewer Jewish couples live in the same neighborhood as their parents, that young Jews seldom ask their parents' permission to marry.[7] These facts prove that Jews are perfectly able to grow up and fly away from the nest.

On the surface this is certainly what happens. But what about beneath the surface? When the young Jew flies away from the nest, to what extent does he carry the nest along with him, a heavy burden that he can never quite get off his back? No statistics on juvenile delinquency can be of use in answering this question. We must turn instead to a subject about which Jews talk more and understand less than almost anyone else.

Ever since Freud invented psychoanalysis, Jews have been attracted to it in large numbers. I have seen no figures for the number of Jewish psychiatrists in America, but 84 percent of the psychiatrists in New Haven are Jewish, and in New York the percentage is only somewhat lower.[8] The Jewish theological seminaries were the first in the country to offer courses in pastoral psychiatry. In the early twenties Jewish agencies pioneered in the psychiatric approach to juvenile delinquency; Hawthorne was the first home for delinquents to transform itself into a residential treatment center, with individual and group therapy as a regular part of the program.

There is little question that a comparatively large proportion of the patients undergoing psychoanalysis in America are Jewish. It also seems to be true that Jewish parents are far more likely than equally affluent non-Jewish parents to send their children for psychiatric treatment. Those who can't afford analysis are just as enthusiastic about the blessings of less expensive psychiatry. According to one leader in the field, "If you open a mental health clinic and don't advertise, Jews will be the only people who flock to it." In some sections of the Jewish community, in fact, psychiatry has become a way of life, almost a substitute religion. In southern California it's hard to find a Jewish family that hasn't got at least one member in analysis.

Many different reasons have been given for the popularity of psychiatry among Jews. It doesn't conflict with the Jewish religious tradition, as it does with certain tenets of Christianity; Jews pamper themselves when it comes to their health and always want the best treatment for their illnesses; everything modern and up-to-date and experimental has an appeal to Jews; the intellectualism of psychiatry, and especially of psychoanalysis, makes it attractive to the Jewish mind. All these explanations are plausible, but they are secondary, I think, to the most plausible and most obvious explanation: Jews need certain kinds of psychiatry more than other people do.

To the extent that we have any statistics on the matter, they suggest a definite pattern in mental illness among Jews. In 1950 a study was made in New Haven of all patients under psychiatric care, both in and out of hospitals.[9] Jews were 9.7 percent of the total population of New Haven; 12 percent of all those under psychiatric treatment were Jews—slightly ahead of the rest of the town, but not startlingly so. The great discrepancy came when patients were categorized according to the type of disease they suffered from. Of those suffering from schizophrenia, affective disorders, and psychoses, approximately 11 percent were Jews—not significantly higher than their representation in the total population. But of those suffering from some form of neurosis, 24 percent were Jews.

A similar study was made in New York in 1962.[10] In mid-town Manhattan 1,660 people were chosen according to age, income level, and educational background; no attempt was made to restrict the sampling to those under psychiatric care. Each of these people was rated according to how many neurotic symptoms he showed; if he had comparatively few such symptoms he was rated "well." Protestants did best in this category; 20.2 percent of them rated "well." Then came the Catholics, with 17.4 percent. The Jews came last; only 14.5 percent of them were considered to be "well." Then the group was rated a second time according to how many severely crippling emotional disorders they had—psychoses, that is, rather than neuroses. Here the Jews did the best; only 17.2 percent of them had crippling disorders, compared to 23.5 percent of the Protestants and 24.7 percent of the Catholics. What this study suggests, aside from the fact that mental illness is hard to escape in our perilous society no matter what your religion may be, is that Jews seldom break down completely, but are more often afflicted with the kind of nagging, day-by-day anxiety and inner tension that enables a man to function even though he's miserable.

This is borne out by the personal experience of every expert observer I've talked to. Psychoanalysts don't see many Jewish schizophrenics or catatonics, homosexuals or paranoiacs —but they see a great many Jewish neurotics. The conditions of family life, both its virtues and its weaknesses, go a long way toward accounting for this. Jews seldom have the kind of brutal, shocking childhood experiences that result in psychosis. They aren't exposed nearly as often as other people to rejection, cruelty, parents who give them no love. On the other hand, they are exposed more often than other people to the kind of family atmosphere that makes for neurosis. Slowly and gradually their emotional growth is stunted by parents who give them too much love, who won't let them find their own way.

Not only in Jewish family life but in the whole Jewish attitude toward life—even in that sacrosanct "ethical tradition" —there is something which encourages the development of neurosis. Let's turn again to that aspect of the ethical tradition which is mentioned most often when Jews feel like congratulating themselves. Whatever else they are, they aren't alcoholics. Whatever sins and follies they are guilty of, they don't drink too much.

This fact has been the subject of much speculation by psychologists and sociologists.[11] After many years of questionnaires, interviews, and other methods for gathering data, here are some of the explanations they've come up with: the Jew is afraid of getting drunk because it might make him look bad to the gentiles; his experience of anti-Semitism has made the Jew wary, cautious, reluctant to lose control of himself for fear that a hostile world might use the opportunity to take advantage of him; in the Jew's mind, sobriety is a symbol of his moral superiority to the gentiles, and so he holds onto it as a way of looking down on them; sobriety is a symbol of his separateness from the gentiles, his unwillingness to relax and be friendly with them, and so he holds onto it as a way of maintaining the ghetto wall.

All these explanations express, in different forms, the same basic feeling—uneasiness in the gentile world. They make us wonder if the Jew has really made a deliberate, rational moral choice not to drink, or if he simply *can't* drink. Maybe his revulsion against liquor is as strong and as involuntary as the alcoholic's attraction to it. The people who have the closest regular contact with the subject seem to believe this. "I never knew a Jew who could drink," said a bartender who works for a catering establishment. "They're always trying to hang one on, but after three glasses they get sick." This is the plain fact which explains very much of the puzzling evidence: it explains why Jews drink very little more among gentiles than they do in their own families, why Jewish boys in college or in the army continue to be moderate drinkers even though they've been freed from the constraints of home, why Jews at business dinners will nurse one or two drinks throughout the evening despite their fear of offending their gentile clients.

In itself, of course, a man's ability to drink doesn't matter much. It is important, however, as a symptom of something deeper in his nature. To be a good drinker a man must be able to let himself go, throw caution to the winds, join in heartily and spontaneously on tonight's fun without thinking too much about tomorrow's hangover. Many Jews would say: who wants to be such a man? After all, there *is* a future. And hangovers are unpleasant things. And what do you gain by making a fool of yourself?

What do you gain by it? is the question the Jew asks himself at every stage of his life. He may not be talking about vulgar material gain at all. He may be talking about the highest, noblest ideals of culture or charity or public welfare. Nevertheless, he hesitates to do anything unless he can see the "point" of it. The experience of thousands of years of ghetto life —of carefully calculating what he was going to say to the goyim, because who knows how they might use it against him? —has turned his fear of instinct into a kind of instinct in itself.

Jews like to talk about how spontaneous they are, how natural, how warm-hearted. They are, in a way—for cold-blooded Puritanism is no more possible to them than hot-blooded hedonism—but there is always a safety valve on the spontaneity, it always manages to turn itself off before it goes too far. As one psychiatrist, referring to the promiscuity of Jewish girls, puts it: "Sure I believe the statistics, but what do they tell me about the feelings? I've seen plenty of these Jewish girls who do a lot of sleeping around, and I know they just don't get the same fun out of it that gentile girls get. They remind me of what Mark Twain said when he heard his wife swearing. 'You know the words all right, but you just can't carry the tune.'"

This was all true in the *shtetl*, of course, but the life people led there required a certain amount of cautiousness, calculation, repression. It isn't easy to be natural and spontaneous when you're starving in a mud hut with ten children, expecting a pogrom to descend on you at any moment. But what happens when these characteristics, essential for self-preservation in the *shtetl*, are carried over to America? Only one result is possible: that self-contradictory personality which confronts us no matter where we touch the American Jew. We hate and love our families; we shower charity on the poor, and we eat too much; we laugh at superstition, and we knock on wood; we believe in the brotherhood of man yet shy away fearfully from most of our fellow-men; we proudly proclaim ourselves to be idealists and individualists yet cling desperately to the safety of suburban conformity. And most of us never seem to resolve any of these contradictions, one way or the other, once and for all.

Furthermore, this split within us is wider today than it

was on the Lower East Side, because we *have* broken down the ghetto walls, we *do* live in the outside world. Yet not entirely in it—not freely, carelessly, with a sense of joy and adventure. We are halfway in and halfway out of the shell—and some of us are struggling to burst out all the way, and others are struggling to crawl back inside, and many are pulling in both directions at once. It is significant, I think, that the incidence of neurosis, according to every study, is higher among second-generation American Jews than it was among their immigrant parents—and higher still among their third-generation children.[12]

But few of us seem to be ready yet to admit that there is anything wrong. The magnificent edifice we've built for ourselves here in America has a serious flaw in its structure. But from this we carefully avert our eyes. We have become too adept at living with our self-contradictions. We even revel in them. We tell ourselves that the paradoxes make us "interesting," "colorful," "unpredictable." Like all the most successful neurotics, we are too smart for our own good.

This blindness, I think, could have grave consequences for our future.

Part Five

Dying?

XIX.

The High Cost of Survival

Everybody speculates about the survival of Judaism in America. There are the complete pessimists, like Professor Charles Liebman of Yeshiva: "I don't see any future at all for Judaism in this country." There are the cautious pessimists, like Rabbi Joachim Prinz, the president of the American Jewish Congress: "We can no longer say with any certainty that there will always be a Judaism, that we are an eternal people." [1] Are there any optimists? Yes, and they are very often the same people who at other moments are pessimists. Many of them echo the sentiments of an anonymous respondent to a survey that was made in the thirties: "I think that the Jews will maintain themselves in America, because my faith takes precedence over logic. I feel that there will always be Jews." [2]

With all the pessimism and optimism, however, there is great disagreement over what would seem to be the primary question: Why *should* Judaism survive in America? Why, in fact, should it survive anywhere as a separate and distinct entity? If in the natural course of things it seems to be dying of attrition, why bother trying to keep it alive?

The most frequently given answer might be called the Ethical Justification. Judaism embodies important ethical values—like monotheism, charity, love of peace—which are passed down from generation to generation through the organized Jewish community. Not only does Judaism pass down these values to its own people, but it preserves them for the rest of the world. As one man, a leader in the JCC movement, put it, "After the bombs drop, some moral force must be here to pick up the pieces. Historically this is what Jews have done. In the past, whenever other civilizations have lost their Jewish values, they disappeared."

The basic flaw in this Ethical Justification seems obvious. Assuming that Judaism *has* contributed certain indispensable values to Western civilization, the fact is that the contribution has now been made. Those values are now part of everyone's heritage, so why must Judaism continue to survive in its unique and separate form?

Many people reject the Ethical Justification and take a completely different tack, the Emotional or Aesthetic Justification. Judaism does have a splendid ethical content, but so do other religions—and even secularists can be honest, compassionate, and courageous. What Judaism offers uniquely is beauty—a warm, lovely feeling that brings the Jew serenity and satisfaction, that casts a glow over his life. Judaism must survive so that he can go on having that feeling.

This argument is difficult to deal with because it is so intensely subjective. We can only say to these people that, if Judaism gives them that warm, lovely feeling, they should go on practicing it by all means and try to pass it on to their children, if they can. But what about the growing number of American Jews who don't get that warm, lovely feeling any more? Their lives, though empty of Judaism, are full of color, excitement, stimulation, and yes, even warmth. Why should the survival of Judaism have any importance to them?

Sometimes the defenders of survival take a more belligerent, almost accusatory, tone. Out of this comes the Justification through Guilt. We must work for the survival of Judaism because so many throughout history have died for it. The six million martyrs to Hitler were only the last of the many billions of Jews who have been slaughtered or have sacrificed themselves so that Judaism might be preserved. To let Judaism pass away now would be an act of betrayal to our ancestors, and would show that we have no pride in ourselves.

The emotional content of this argument is so highly charged that we are in danger of overlooking its logical weakness. The fact that millions of people have sacrificed themselves to preserve a way of life doesn't necessarily mean that the way of life was worth preserving. And even if we assume it was, even if we agree that we would have sacrificed ourselves too in their position, why does it follow that such a sacrifice should be made when we *aren't* in their position? History is full of ideals, even religions, that men once fought and died for nobly and justifiably, but that nobody in his right mind would fight and die for today. If Judaism ought to survive, surely it must justify itself in terms of what it is, what function it can perform right now, and not in terms of what it used to be.

To one large segment of the Jewish community the justifications we've discussed so far are totally irrelevant. The Orthodox Jew may or may not agree with them; it's beside the point, for they are all subsumed in one larger fundamental justification. This we will call the Justification through Faith. Judaism must be preserved because Torah tells us so. We are not required to find a reason for the existence of Judaism any more than we are required to find a reason for the existence of mountains or mosquitoes; God's word is all the reason we need. As one of the girls from Stern College told me, "Should Judaism survive, should Judaism not survive? Big deal. That's not my worry, that's up to God."

This argument is unanswerable, of course. But it also begs the question. The people who use it are admitting, in effect, that they don't *know* why Judaism should survive and that they're not interested in probing the matter.

———◆———

Finally we come to what I feel is the most persuasive justification for the survival of Judaism, the only one that anybody presented to me which wasn't logically self-defeating. This might be called the Formal Justification; it is mentioned by Norman Podhoretz in his introduction to *Commentary's* symposium on "Jewishness and the Younger Intellectuals." He writes, "A man must have strong local or 'parochial' attachments before he can achieve a true universalism of spirit." The same idea was expressed in greater detail to me by a leading Zionist, an unusually undogmatic one. "I don't believe in Jewish values," he said. "That's all nonsense. There isn't a single so-called Jewish value which isn't also a universal value. But human nature is constituted in such a way that universal values have to take some specific form, or else they won't spread.

Universal values need a specific carrier—maybe a great many specific carriers—and Judaism is one of them."

There is a great deal of truth to this argument. It is the basis of all religious institutions and all political movements; rituals and slogans, prayer shawls and banners, are necessary in order to give concrete expression to abstractions, because otherwise they will never take root in the human heart. This is in fact the basis of the learning process itself. Children learn to think from looking at pictures—and Jewish children learn to value freedom and hate slavery from eating matzoh and bitter herbs during the Passover seder.

Nevertheless, this argument is not by itself a sufficient justification for the survival of Judaism. We must recognize that it has another side to it. Human nature does demand that abstract ideas be clothed in specific forms, but once that happens, human nature plays a dirty trick on those ideas. From the moment a ritual or a symbol is substituted for an abstraction, a process of subversion begins. In the course of time forms have a way of taking on a life of their own, growing stronger and stronger until they are strangling the ideas they were originally meant to support. At this point the forms must be discarded if the ideas are to be saved. New forms then are required, and the whole process begins all over again.

Does such a situation exist in American Judaism today? Are its formal aspects, and especially its institutional aspects, strangling the life out of it? Has the time come to save the essence by cutting away the dead wood?

There are indications of this. Much of the present talk about survival partakes ominously of a devotion to dead wood. In their desperation to hold onto the forms and shore up the institutions, members of the religious and secular establishments are showing themselves more and more willing to compromise, even to jettison, the universal ethical values of Judaism. For example, more and more rabbis have been saying that Jews should decrease their involvement in the civil rights movement. After all, this takes away time and money from the "real issue," the struggle for survival. In other words, Jews can't fulfill their moral obligation and improve Jewish education at the same time, so the moral obligation will just have to be neglected.

Similarly, a young Reform rabbi, a man of genuine taste and intelligence, recently rose to the defense of splashy, expensive bar mitzvahs and weddings. People who indulge in these folkways, he said, are expressing their Jewish identity and therefore contributing to survival. Vulgarity, it seems, is justifiable when it comes with a kosher label.

And even the great ideal of learning—that respect for "the book" which Jewish leaders are always congratulating us on having—can be sacrificed if it appears to stand in the way of survival. This, in fact, is the underlying reason why the Jewish intellectual feels estranged from Judaism and from the Jewish community.

There are always a few people, of course, who won't admit that he *is* estranged. When *Commentary* published its symposium on "Jewishness and the Younger Intellectuals"—in which most of the participants expressed their estrangement, many in harsh and bitter terms—a hue and cry went up immediately that the sampling wasn't really representative. It is impossible to believe this after an objective examination of American Jewry. Hillel Societies around the country report that only 10 percent of all Jewish students bother to identify with the organization. Studies show that Jews with college educations are more likely to intermarry than Jews without college educations, and the likelihood is increased among the children of college-educated parents.[3] In New Haven 64 percent of all the Jewish psychiatrists are intermarried.[4] In Washington, D.C., Jews who work for the government, with a few notable exceptions, don't identify with the Jewish community. And we could go on and on.

Intellectuals reject Judaism, I think, mostly because they don't see any point to it. Even if they have a growing need for mystical experience, as I.B. Singer believes, how irrelevant it seems to all those rituals, dietary laws, rabbinical posturings, holidays which celebrate events that no longer mean anything to anybody. And how excruciatingly dull they find it all! It provides no nourishment for the most important part of the intellectual's nature—his intellect. How could anyone who isn't a moron sit through the boring stuff that goes on in a synagogue, the long-winded sermons, the constant standing up and sitting down again, the bits and pieces of psalms thrown out in no particular order and with no sense of dramatic organization? Synagogue-goers invariably seem like the most inartistic, heavy-handed, ill-informed, narrow-minded people in the world. Rabbis as a rule are intellectually second-rate; the establishment won't admit this publicly, but within the rabbinical organizations there is constant discussion on how to attract a higher caliber of student to the rabbinate. Religious schools are hopeless; I have met dozens of intellectuals who withdrew their children after a year or two because the curriculum was so thin and undemanding. As one parent said, "What they gave him there was an insult to a kid."

In principle Judaism may not be anti-intellectual, but in practice it appeals, like the product of all other mass-communications media, to the lowest common denominator. And so, as Rabbi Arthur Hertzberg told me, "We're losing our bright kids when they're fourteen. And when they're twenty-five they write Philip Roth's novels."

The estrangement of the intellectual is further encouraged by another circumstance. He isn't the only kind of Jew who finds Judaism dull, but he has one big advantage over most of the others. He doesn't need the Jewish community; he has another world in which he can live. He is one of the few Americans lucky enough to be able to escape from the pluralistic system. With his enthusiasm for certain books, pictures, pieces of music, his closest bond, his deepest sense of solidarity, is with others whose lives revolve around the same things. This is why people on the faculty of a college are more likely to intermarry than people in the town: they don't think of it as intermarrying at all.[5] No six-o'clock shadow separates the Jewish professor from the rest of the academic community, the Jewish artist from other artists, the Jewish scientist from his fellow scientists. They are all intellectuals first, Jews second—if at all.

This is the problem, and it would seem obvious what the Jewish community must do about it. If it is interested in luring the intellectual back to Judaism, it must show him how Judaism can be exciting and stimulating to him. It must recast the values of Judaism in his own terms. And surely this shouldn't be an impossible task. After all, what other religion has such a strong intellectual tradition? Aren't Jews the people of the book?

Several major efforts are, in fact, being made in this direction. *Commentary* magazine was started by AJC in 1945, with the avowed intention of bringing about a rapprochement between the intellectual and the Jewish community. The idea was to get him thinking about things Jewish, in a deghettoized, nonparochial way; eventually he would come to value his Jew-ishness again. Brandeis University, supported by solid business elements in the Jewish community—the same people who support their federations and UJA—is another experiment along the same lines. It aspires to provide as complete, cosmopolitan, and nonsectarian an education as any other institution, but to do it under Jewish auspices, in a Jewish atmosphere; it purports to be Jewish in the same way that Yale is Congregation-alist or Swarthmore is Quaker. And the Jewish Museum in New York operates on the same principle; its property is owned and its board controlled by the Jewish Theological Seminary, but it attempts to mingle its exhibitions of religious objects, of old prayer shawls and menorahs, with the latest in *avant garde* art.

Each of these enterprises is highly successful: *Commentary* is one of our best magazines, Brandeis one of our best universities, the Jewish Museum one of the best places to see new art. And young Jewish intellectuals do have respect for them, do pay serious attention to them. It might be supposed, then, that representatives of the establishment would be well pleased. The intellectual Jew *is* finding common ground with the Jewish tradition—what could delight these representatives more?

But the strange fact is that, by and large, they aren't delighted. All three of these institutions are subjected to a constant barrage of criticism from leaders of the Jewish community. *Commentary* is taken to task for publishing articles that "fail to reinforce Jewish identification"; we are told in tones of horror that its editor, Norman Podhoretz, has publicly admitted that he can't think of any reasons for Judaism to survive.[6] Brandeis is continually under fire because it doesn't turn its students into "good Jews," because its campus Hillel is as sparsely attended as any Hillel in a non-Jewish college. The Jewish Museum is a steady target from elements at the JTS who want to know, "What's Jewish about pop art?" Board meetings invariably get around to an argument over which should be given the greater emphasis in the exhibitions, Jewish content or "universal" content. The recent resignation of Sam Hunter, the museum's director since 1965 and a vigorous champion of the universal against the parochial, suggests that the establishment forces have got the upper hand.

This continual sniping explains, it seems to me, why intellectuals aren't being drawn back into the Jewish community.

The community wants them on only one condition—that they give up their sense of belonging to a larger world, one which includes gentiles. To the establishment the ideals of "the book," the unrestricted pursuit of truth, the traditional Jewish devotion to learning, are less important than separatism, exclusivity, self-isolation—not the rigid physical isolationism of the Hasidim, not even the ideological isolationism of the liberal Orthodox, but a kind of confused, subliminal, half-admitted and half-denied isolationism. What the establishment says to the intellectual is this: "Paint your pictures and write your books, visit with your gentile friends, but always remember that your whole mind and your whole heart must *really* belong to us."

As further proof of this, observe the establishment's reaction whenever a Jewish writer objects to being pigeonholed as "Jewish." Many writers—Weidman, Bellow, Roth—have expressed this objection. Bruce Jay Friedman was speaking for all of them when he said to me, "All right, my work has a Jewish quality to it. Maybe it isn't possible for me to lose that—maybe it wouldn't even be desirable. But that quality is tangential, it isn't the heartbeat of my work." Let a writer express this point of view publicly, and members of the establishment will join immediately in howls of condemnation. The synagogual journals will break out in articles accusing the hapless writer of self-hatred, the Jewish community's great all-purpose putdown word.

The community simply can't understand the writer's real motive. It isn't self-hatred at all; it's the instinct of self-preservation. He feels a deep-seated fear of something which the community wants him to be and which is directly at odds with what he really is. The community wants to make him conform, turn him into a good Jewish boy, cut him off from the outside world—even if that means the betrayal of his intellectual freedom. He shudders away from this in revulsion, not because he's ashamed to be Jewish, but because he doesn't see himself as exclusively Jewish, or even primarily Jewish—which is what the community demands of him.

His revulsion is increased, of course, by his uneasy knowledge that a part of him yearns to conspire with the community in his own undoing. He himself, just as surely as those who attack him, hasn't quite escaped from the bondage of goy fear, the heritage of isolationism. But he *wants* to escape; he knows that he *must* escape if he is ever to write the best books that are in him. Every Jewish writer is obliged to work his way through this inner conflict; every Jewish writer must fight against the double temptation, either to put too much matzoh ball soup in his work or to bend over too far backwards to keep it out. And instinctively he knows that he has little chance of winning this fight unless he keeps his distance from the organized Jewish community. It has become a commonplace to say that the Jewish writer, and all other Jewish intellectuals, are alienated. But it is important to understand that their alienation is not the traditional Jewish alienation from the "outside" world. The world they reject—because it rejects them—is not Christian but Jewish.

And so with all its plausibility, the Formal Justification for the continued separateness of Judaism is ultimately as unsatisfactory as all the other justifications. It breaks down for exactly the same reason as the others do. At the heart of them you find that ancient Jewish obsession, fear of the gentiles. "They" will hurt us, "they" will corrupt us; we must keep ourselves apart from "them." If this is the best that the leaders of the community can do to justify the survival of Judaism, then we are forced to consider the alternative. Suppose Judaism *did* disappear. What effect, terrible or beneficial, would that have on the individual Jew? Are there any arguments *against* survival?

It isn't possible to answer that question unless we are willing to gather up our courage and take a hard, close, unprejudiced look at the Horror of Horrors—intermarriage.

———————◆◆———————

Many studies have been made of mixed marriages. Most of them are statistical; they tell us what percentage of the Jewish population in this or that community marry gentiles, how many convert to Christianity, how many bring up their children as Jews, and so on. A few of the studies have been psychological; they attempt to classify the reasons why people enter into mixed marriages. As far as I know, however, no full-scale attempt has been made to measure the success or failure of mixed marriages.

People who disapprove of mixed marriage have never had any trouble impugning the motives of those who enter into it. Why a gentile should want to marry a Jew is quite beyond them, but they know exactly why Jews want to marry gentiles.

It's all self-hatred, of course. The Jew is ashamed of being Jewish; he marries a gentile in order to escape from his identity. Even if he remains in the Jewish community, he thinks that his *shiksa* wife confers a kind of prestige on him, makes him somehow "less Jewish" than everybody else. Or if self-hatred isn't his motive, then it must be calculation; he marries a gentile in order to make business contacts, improve his social position, advance his career. Or if that isn't his motive either, then it must be "neurotic"; he had an unhappy childhood, he's rebelling against his parents, he marries a gentile in order to hurt them.

It would be absurd to say that no Jews have married gentiles for any of these reasons. In my own experience, however, I don't know of a single mixed marriage in which they figure to any important degree. Nobody can read another human being's heart, of course, but often there are outward signs which are reasonably convincing. In most of the mixed marriages I know of, for instance, the Jewish partner shows few of the usual symptoms of self-hatred. He doesn't conceal his Jewishness, drop his Jewish friends, make cracks about "kikes," or feel embarassed when his children talk with their hands; if anything, he seems a bit more relaxed about the whole thing than most Jews do. In only one mixed marriage that I know of did the Jew "move up in the world," either socially or financially; his gentile wife is the daughter of a socially prominent family and he is a distinguished scientist who brings quite as much prestige to the marriage as his wife does. As for neurosis, I suspect that many of the mixed couples I know got married for neurotic reasons; so did many of the Jewish couples I know.

Fortunately this is one area in which several dependable studies have been made. Every one of them, regardless of geographical variations, brings out the same facts.[7] Intermarriage is not a neurotic manifestation; there are indications, in fact, that people who do intermarry (both Jews and non-Jews) have emancipated themselves more successfully from infantile family ties than people who don't. Intermarriage is not an attempt to escape from Jewishness: there is far more of it in the third generation, among people who feel little shame about being Jewish, than there is in the second generation. Intermarriage is hardly ever a means of achieving social or economic status: the great majority of Jews who marry gentiles nowadays are on about the same social and economic plane as their partners. The conclusion that all these studies come to, and that everyone can check from personal observation, is that people enter into mixed marriages for the same conglomeration of reasons that they enter into any marriage. And one of the most common reasons—though the pious never mention it—is love.

Mixed couples do differ from other couples in one respect, however. Most of them, even after they fall in love, take longer to decide about getting married. They have greater qualms to overcome; all their lives they have been told about the special problems, the sinister difficulties, that lie in wait for those who marry out of their faith. Even when they manage to overcome those qualms, they may hesitate to reach a decision, because they know how deeply their parents (especially, according to many studies, the Jewish parents) will disapprove.

When the wedding day finally arrives, their parents' direst predictions often seem to be coming true. Somehow this event tends to arouse all the latent fears and hostilities of the family and the community. Few rabbis will perform the ceremony (for valid theological reasons, no doubt), with the result that the setting is almost always unsatisfactory and sometimes downright oppressive. If the wedding takes place in a Christian church, the Jewish relatives will shuffle uncomfortably all the way through, especially if the minister should be tactless enough to mention the name of Jesus Christ. If the wedding takes place at a registry office or in the bride's family living room, the young couple will feel that it's all rather antiseptic and unromantic. And no matter where the ceremony is held, all the tensions will come to the surface during the reception. As the guests drink more and more champagne, the dangers of an explosion will grow greater and greater. What if old Uncle Ed from St. Louis decides to tell one of his anti-Semitic stories, or Uncle Hymie from Chicago decides to tell one of his anti-goy stories?

And so the young couple goes off on the honeymoon in an atmosphere of hostility, misunderstanding, and doubt. And if this is what it's like in the beginning, what horrors must lie ahead!

But the strange part of it is that in the vast majority of cases no horrors lie ahead. The weeping parents, the uncles at the reception, the relatives making snide remarks in church— these turn out to be the end, not the beginning, of the "special problems." Certain bugbears about which anxious parents warn their children persistently simply don't appear. How many engagements have been broken off because the Jewish partner was afraid that his gentile wife, in the middle of an argument, would scream at him, "You dirty kike!" Thus in one moment, according to this cautionary tale which Jewish parents feed to their children, her "true feelings" will be revealed. But in actual fact that terrible moment never comes—or even if it does come, it turns out to be unimportant. She's furious at him, so she says the most awful thing she can think of, and he no doubt replies in kind. And when the argument is over, they both have enough sense to kiss and make up. Nothing has been "revealed" except that married couples, when they get into fights, will say precisely what they don't mean.

The same thing applies to all the other old-wives' tales with which Jewish parents try to frighten their children. "Gentile women are more likely to commit adultery than Jewish women." "A gentile husband won't treat you as well as a Jewish husband." But it doesn't turn out that way. It isn't true about any of the mixed marriages I have observed. If it were true generally, it ought to be reflected by the divorce statistics; but as far as I can tell (complete figures on this subject are not available), the rate of divorce among mixed marriages is no higher than among marriages between Jews.[8]

These bugbears, however, are merely the excuses that Jewish parents give to themselves for being opposed to mixed marriage. What really upsets them is their fear that the child who marries a gentile will turn against them, look down on them because they're Jewish, join up with "them" and never be seen in the family circle again. Even if their poor son doesn't want to behave in this outrageous way—after all, he's a good boy at heart—"that wife of his" will make him. And that family of hers—those cold fish! How can we ever have any warm, relaxed get-togethers with them, as in-laws ought to do? Our backgrounds are so different, we're a hundred miles apart, what on earth will we find to talk about?

None of these dreadful things ever happen either. Far from dropping his parents, the intermarried child has a tendency to stick closer to them than ever. And "that wife of his" usually encourages him in this; she is very sensitive to the reproach of "looking down" on her Jewish in-laws. As for the two sets of parents, their chances of getting along together are just as great, or just as slim, as if they were all Jews. The warmth which is supposed to exist between in-laws in a Jewish family is largely a myth; in most cases the relationship is purely formal, and goes no further than a display of joviality on certain official family occasions.

If a Jew who has married a gentile finds himself cut off from his parents, it is almost always their choice; they can't forgive him for what he did to them. But this seldom lasts very long. Reconciliation takes place, usually within twenty-four hours of the engagement announcement. What Jewish mother would deprive herself, for some piddling little theological reason, of the pleasure of arranging her daughter's wedding or crying at her son's? And by the time the first grandchild is on the way, all traces of coolness will have disappeared.

A friend of mind married a gentile girl over twenty years ago. His mother was terribly upset, there were hysterical scenes, and finally she accepted the situation; in a few months her gentile daughter-in-law was as much one of the family as if she had been born in the faith; and when my friend had children, the great joy of his mother's life was to visit them and bring presents to them. A few years ago my friend's younger brother also decided to marry a gentile girl. My friend called his mother to tell her the news, and she burst into tears over the phone. "But Mom," he said, "*I* married a gentile, and you're crazy about Peggy." "What are you talking about?" his mother cried. "Peggy's a gentile?"

But it is often said that mixed marriages are "bad for the children." They get emotionally torn; they lack the feeling of having roots which is so important for healthy development; they don't know who they are, and so they are unable to function normally. This is another old-wives tale. Emotional disturbance, according to many psychiatrists, is no more frequent or intense among the children of mixed marriages than among children whose parents are both Jewish. If they feel some confusion about who they are, it doesn't seem to affect them very seriously. "Are you Jewish, Mommy?" asked the child of one mixed marriage. "No, but Daddy is." "Then what does that make me?" "That makes you half Jewish." "When I grow up, will I be the whole Jewish?" Try as I will, I can't find any evidence of deep-seated anxiety in this child's question. Like most of the children of mixed marriages that I've observed, he seems to be reconciled to the ambiguity. Not because children like ambiguity, but because it doesn't seem very important to him. Being partly Jewish means about as much to him as having partly-brown hair.

This is what offends the opponents of mixed marriage more than anything else. These half-Jewish children aren't being given any religious training, any sense of belonging to the Jewish community. They are being lost to Judaism, as the phrase goes. And of course this is absolutely true. Most parents in mixed marriages talk a lot about "what to teach the children," and end up teaching them nothing. Or perhaps they settle on some kind of weird conglomeration—like one family I know, which includes a menorah in the crêche at Christmastime.

But what *are* these children being lost to, really? The forms and institutions of Judaism certainly; they don't learn the blessings, go to Sunday School, accompany their parents to a synagogue. But they definitely aren't being lost to those universal ethical values which the forms and institutions are supposed to preserve. The children of mixed marriages, as far as I can see, receive from their parents all those attitudes which we think of as belonging to the Judaic tradition. These parents have the same devotion to education, the same close family ties, the same standards of morality, the same belief in charity, the same liberal views in politics, that the Jewish community has. In every respect—except the formal and religious one— they are bringing up their children as Jews.

This really shouldn't surprise us. The very fact that two people have married outside their faiths, despite the opposition of family and community, suggests that they have more than an ordinary amount of courage, of dedication to what they believe. Who else has taken more seriously than they the central idea of monotheism, that all human beings are the children of one God and are equal in His sight?

Almost inevitably, then, the Jew who marries a gentile must be an idealist. And so he must pass the ideals of Judaism on to his children. And along with those ideals he gives something more.

———◆◆◆———

Rabbi Abraham Heschel, the leading philosopher of Conservative Judaism, has said that the Christian world is turning to the Jews today, trying to learn from Jewish values and experience. But Jews can't give them what they want, he says, unless they cast off the mediocrity and drabness of American life and return to Judaism.

Many others in the Jewish community, both secular and religious, have been saying the same thing. Jews must reassert their Jewish heritage, because the Christian world has much to learn from it. This is the kind of half-truth, I think, which could do more damage than an out-and-out falsehood. There is little point in Jews congratulating themselves on what the Christian world can learn from them unless at the same time they are willing to consider what they can learn from the Christians. I agree that Judaism has answers which humanity badly needs, but surely Judaism doesn't have all the answers. Is there nothing in the Christian tradition, in the non-Hebraic aspects of western culture, that can be of help to the Jews?

That they need help seems obvious to me. Years of suffering and persecution have enabled them to develop certain skills, certain sides of their nature, to formidable proportions. Their moral tradition, with its combination of idealism and tough-minded pragmatism, seems more relevant today than it ever was. Their intellectual attainments are the result of four thousand years of hard training. It is no accident that Freud, Marx, and Einstein—three Jews—have changed the face of the world. But it is also no accident that all three of these men, to a greater or lesser degree, not only turned away from Judaism but spent most of their lives outside the Jewish community. And the same thing is true of almost any distinguished Jew in our century whose achievement wasn't specifically religious or Zionist. There is a terrible irony in the fact that Jews today take so much pride in artists, scientists, statesmen, writers, most of whom have turned their backs on the Jewish world.

What the Jews must start recognizing is that the same history of suffering and persecution which made them strong in some ways made them weak in others. It gave them intellect and moral force, but deprived them of grace and spontaneity. It taught them to respect man, but kept them from loving nature. In a world which isolated them, which built ghetto walls around them, these weaknesses were inevitable. They could have turned out no better—and they are entitled to feel proud that they turned out no worse. But that world doesn't exist in America, and they cripple themselves severely by clinging to habits of self-defense that they no longer need.

The separateness and exclusiveness of Judaism were essential once—nothing else could preserve it from destruction. They are no longer essential; they have become the prime source of corruption.

The same thing is true of Christianity. It too has been essentially separatist and exclusionist. Its forms and rituals and institutions were designed, no less than those of Judaism, to keep it apart from the rest of the world. And it is suffering today much of the same erosion and attrition that Judaism is suffering. The most dramatic example is the revolution taking place within the Catholic Church, but the symptoms are widespread. The great men of the Christian world, its artists, scientists, philosophers, have turned away from Christianity just as surely as ours have turned away from Judaism.

The reason is not that people no longer believe in God, but that they can no longer believe in the God of Moses or of the Trinity, in a tribal God whose First Commandment creates a chasm between "them" and "us." It isn't that people are less mystical and more rational nowadays—just the opposite is true, I think—but that their sense of the mystery of life can't be contained within the strait jacket of what has come to be known as "organized religion." It isn't even that people have lost patience with forms and rituals, but that they are searching —often clumsily or comically or pathetically, sometimes disastrously—for new forms and rituals which will bring them closer to their fellow-men and which will encourage their drive toward being themselves.

Opponents of intermarriage often say that it serves ultimately as a means by which Jews turn into Christians. A Jew can't quite bring himself to convert to Christianity, but in marrying out of his faith he can open up the Christian world to his children—or at least to his grandchildren. Milton Himmelfarb, in a 1967 article in *Daedalus*, expressed this view, but significantly, his examples are all taken from the nineteenth century or the early twentieth century.[9] He mentions Mendelssohn and Heine—men who lived at a time when the treasures of Western civilization were suddenly available to a Jew, when he could become what he pleased in the social or financial or artistic world, but only if he converted to Christianity. Many Jews did convert—particularly intellectuals, who wanted what the modern world had to offer—and an aroma of dishonor does hang over what they did. But today the world is open to the

Jew with no strings attached. He doesn't have to go through the dishonorable ceremony of conversion. All he needs is the courage to reach out for his freedom.

If the majority don't have that courage yet, an increasing minority do. These are the people who marry gentiles—or don't marry gentiles—the people for whom the matter is irrelevant. No, not entirely irrelevant. The sociological studies show that many Jewish men who marry gentile girls are expressing a conscious preference, deliberately rejecting Jewish girls. But self-hatred has nothing to do with this rejection. What they feel in Jewish girls is what they saw in their own mothers—goy fear, the obsession of separatism, the desperate urge to turn marriage and the family and Judaism and life itself into a ghetto. And what they find in gentile girls is an acceptance of them for themselves, for what they are at heart and what they can become. When Jewish girls achieve this free and open attitude toward life—and more and more of them are doing so —the rate of intermarriage may decrease. But the official Jewish community won't benefit from this.

For this is the flaw in the argument that Milton Himmelfarb and many others have given. Intermarriage today is no more a passage from Judaism to Christianity than it is a passage from Christianity to Judaism. The vast majority of intermarried couples don't become either Christians or Jews and don't bring up their children to belong to either camp. They create for themselves a world which contains both Christians and Jews, yet which contains neither. And it is a world full of couples who *aren't* intermarried, full of Christians married to Christians and Jews married to Jews, but for whom the old categories have become unimportant. If Milton Himmelfarb and the B'nai B'rith and all the synagogual organizations and the whole UJA managed to get a law passed which prohibited any Jew from marrying any non-Jew, American Judaism wouldn't be any closer to survival. Attrition would continue no more slowly and no less inexorably than before.

What young Jews—a small but growing number—are moving toward today, I think, is a synthesis of Judaism and Christianity. They are not turning away from their tradition. Their pride in it is genuine; they feel themselves to be the heirs of a magnificent idea which has been upheld for four thousand years against persecution. But they feel also that to keep that idea separate and exclusive any longer would be to betray it. What it needs now is nourishment from other ideas, enrichment and renewal from sources which it has always disdained and feared. Unless this is permitted to happen, the idea will die. In this sense Jewish survival depends not on more separation but on less, not on the futile worship of the old distinctions but on the willingness to move beyond them.

This new synthesis hasn't found its form yet, and won't for a long time. And so it takes many different ones, all of them fluid and temporary. There are families, for example, who find it possible to express their identification with Judaism and Jewishness simply by lighting the candles at Sabbath—no blessings, no *kashruth,* only the simplest of symbolic actions to remind them of their past without committing them to a narrow restricted future. In one family of this kind the father, who married a gentile, established this custom when his son was small—and the son, also married to a gentile now, with children of his own, has established the same custom in *his* household. These three generations have Passover seders together too—and huge, joyous Christmas dinners—and all the grandchildren have been given Old Testament names. And nobody has been inside a synagogue or a church—or a UJA banquet hall—for many years.

People like this are a thorn in the side of rabbis and secular leaders alike. The usual reaction is, "What do they matter? There are such an insignificant number of them." Or else, "They're nothing but hypocrites! They want the credit of being Jewish without any of the inconvenience or responsibility!" It's easy to understand why the establishment is upset; the mere existence of such mavericks is a challenge. Yet they do exist, and calling them names won't exorcise them. When they finally find their voice and their direction, they may be the vanguard for a new Judaism—which probably won't be called Judaism at all. Or Christianity either.

———————

"And meanwhile," the establishment rabbi asks, "what becomes of our individuality, our unique Jewish identity? Are you really prepared to give that up because of some indefinable synthesis that doesn't even exist?"

I know the answer to this question. I know that something like this synthesis will happen to Judaism in America, that it ought to happen, that it doesn't mean giving up my identity at all but expanding it. Even so the rabbi's question shakes my confidence, makes me doubt my own knowledge. To be the kind of Jew I've been describing would mean to heal the breach within me, to bring together the two halves of the split personality. Am I ready to do that yet? The old doubts and fears—of "them" and of myself—still rise up in me, often at those moments when I have conclusively proved to myself how ridiculous they are.

But because I am Jewish I have hope, though I'm pessimistic. One important piece of equipment is in my possession —the Jewish imagination. Because I belong to a "people," not just to myself, I have always been able to think their thoughts, see through their eyes. There is no Jew I've described in this book whom I can't imagine being, whose feelings I can't make myself feel. I can sway and moan at an Orthodox funeral, weep with the aunts at a Conservative bar mitzvah, outrage my Reform congregation by marching in a protest parade for civil rights; I can hear my card being called at a UJA dinner, and sneer at the whole thing with the "younger intellectuals"; I can sigh sentimentally over Jewish mothers, and feel like strangling the next one who comes along; I can turn sick at the thought of Israel's destruction, and experience the anger and frustration and peculiar pride of those perverse crusaders in the American Council for Judaism. If my imagination can reach out to every Jew in America—just as theirs can reach out to me—why shouldn't I be able to stretch it just a bit further? With a little more training and exercise and determination, why shouldn't I be able to reach out to the gentiles too?

And if worst comes to worst and I don't succeed, I still don't have to give up hope. I have children, and I suspect that their imaginations are already wilder and freer than mine. Some day they will be able to say loud and clear what I can only mutter uneasily: "I am a Jew—and also I am more."

Bibliography and Notes

Most of the information and quoted opinions in this book have been drawn from personal interviews. In addition, the official publications and files of the various Jewish organizations, both religious and secular, have been extremely helpful—particularly *The American Jewish Yearbook,* an annual publication of the American Jewish Committee, and the many studies of Jewish life in selected communities which AJC and others have made through the years. Newspapers and magazines have been combed for pertinent stories and revealing quotations; those which yielded the most material are *The New York Times,* the New York *Post,* the late lamented New York *Herald-Tribune, Commentary, Midstream, Harper's,* and *The Atlantic.*

Many books have been used to provide background material. Only the most important—and the ones most likely to interest the general reader who might care to do further reading in the subject—are listed below.

Birmingham, Stephen, *Our Crowd,* New York, Harper & Row, 1967.
Gay, Ruth, *The Jews in America,* New York, Basic Books, 1965.
Glazer, Nathan, *American Judaism,* Chicago, University of Chicago Press, 1957.
Grayzell, Solomon, *A History of the Jews,* Philadelphia, Jewish Publication Society, 1947.
Halpern, Ben, *The American Jew: A Zionist Analysis,* New York, Theodore Herzl Foundation, 1956.
Herberg, Will, *Protestant-Catholic-Jew: An Essay in American Religious Sociology,* New York, Doubleday & Company, 1955.
Roche, John P., *The Quest for the Dream,* New York, The Macmillan Company, 1963.

Sklare, Marshall, editor, *The Jews: Social Patterns of an American Group,* New York, The Free Press, 1958.

Zborowski, Mark, and Elizabeth Herzog, *Life Is with People: The Culture of the Shtetl,* New York, Schocken Books, 1952.

CHAPTER I

1. Uriah Zevi Engelman, "Jewish Statistics in the U.S. Census of Religious Bodies," *Jewish Social Studies,* IX, 1947.

2. Bernard D. Weinryb, "Jewish Immigration and Accommodation to America," in *The Jews: Social Patterns of an American Group,* edited by Marshall Sklare, New York, The Free Press, 1958.

3. *Refugees in America,* a study directed by Professor Maurice R. Davie, 1947.

4. Harvey Swados, "A Sentimental Journey to the Lower East Side," *The New York Times Magazine,* September 18, 1966. (A superb example of the modern style of personalized journalism.)

5. Maurice Hindus, *Green Worlds,* New York, Doubleday, Doran and Company, 1938.

6. Quoted by Marvin Lowenthal, "Don't You Believe It," *Midcentury,* 1955.

7. Benjamin Disraeli, *Coningsby,* New York, G. P. Putnam's Sons, 1961. (Disraeli puts this phrase in the mouth of a character in the novel, but the context makes it clear that she is expressing the author's opinion.)

CHAPTER II

1. Quoted by Martin Buber, *Hasidism,* New York, Philosophical Library, 1948.

2. *Sports Illustrated,* March 5, 1962.

3. Ben B. Seligman, "Some Aspects of Jewish Demography," in *The Jews: Social Patterns of an American Group,* edited by Marshall Sklare, New York, The Free Press, 1958.

4. Alfred C. Kinsey, *Sexual Behavior in the Human Male,* Philadelphia, W. B. Saunders, 1948.

5. Quoted by Leonard Lyons in the New York *Post,* February 27, 1966.

6. In her obituary in the New York *Post,* February 10, 1966.

7. In an interview with Zero Mostel in the New York *Post,* March 20, 1966.

8. *The Essex County Jewish News,* April 7, 1967.

9. Irving Howe, "The Lower East Side: Symbol and Fact," *Midstream,* August–September, 1966.

10. W. Lloyd Warner and Leo Strole, "Assimilation or Survival: A Crisis in the Jewish Community of Yankee City," in *The Jews: Social*

Patterns of an American Group, edited by Marshall Sklare, New York, The Free Press, 1958.

11. *The New York Times,* February 17, 1967.
12. This story is told in Charles Liebman's extraordinary study, "Orthodoxy in American Jewish Life," *The American Jewish Yearbook,* 1965.
13. Mark Zborowski, "Cultural Components in Response to Pain," *Journal of Social Science,* 1952.
14. From an essay on Sholom Aleichem in *Age of Enormity,* edited by Theodore Solotaroff, Cleveland, The World Publishing Company, 1962.
15. Irving Kristol, "Is Jewish Humor Dead?" *Midcentury,* 1955.
16. "The Town of the Little People," in *The Old Country,* a collection of short pieces by Sholom Aleichem, translated by Julius and Frances Butwin, New York, Crown Publishers, 1946.

CHAPTER III

1. "The Extreme Jews," *Harper's,* April, 1967.
2. Quoted in an AJC pamphlet, *The Unequal Treatment of Equals,* by John Slawson and Lawrence Bloomgarden.
3. From a 1962 survey cited by John P. Roche, *The Quest for the Dream,* New York, The Macmillan Company, 1963.
4. John Young, "The Jewish Law Student and New York Jobs: Discriminatory Effects in Law Firm Hiring Practices," *Yale Law Journal,* March, 1964.
5. Lawrence Bloomgarden, "Our Changing Elite Colleges," *Commentary,* February, 1960.

CHAPTER IV

1. Milton Himmelfarb, "Negroes, Jews, and Muzhiks," *Commentary,* October, 1966.
2. "Germany through American Eyes," *The Atlantic,* May, 1967.
3. *The New York Times,* November 25, 1965.
4. In a speech to the Conference of Radical Theology at the University of Michigan, quoted in *The New York Times,* October 30, 1966.
5. Paul Lauter, "Reflections of a Jewish Activist," *Conservative Judaism,* Summer, 1965.
6. Pauline Kael, *I Lost It at the Movies,* Boston, Atlantic-Little Brown, 1965.
7. Manheim S. Shapiro, *As We See Ourselves: The Baltimore Survey,* conducted by AJC in 1962.
8. Harold Isaacs, "Americans in Israel," *The New Yorker,* August 27, 1966, and September 3, 1966.
9. Marshall Sklare and Marc Vosk, *The Riverton Study: How Jews Look at Themselves,* conducted by AJC in 1952.

10. Milton Himmelfarb, "Negroes, Jews, and Muzhiks," *op. cit.*
11. From a 1967 survey made by the Universalist Unitarian Association.
12. Kurt Lewin, "Self-Hatred Among Jews," in *Resolving Social Conflicts,* edited by G. W. Lewin, New York, Harper and Row, 1948.
13. *As We See Ourselves: The Baltimore Survey, op. cit.*
14. From *As We See Ourselves: The Baltimore Survey,* AJC's 1959 study in Dade County, Florida, and many others.
15. A resolution passed by the Rabbinical Council of New Jersey at its annual conference, December, 1965.
16. Erich Rosenthal, "Studies of Jewish Intermarriage in the United States," *The American Jewish Yearbook,* 1963.

CHAPTER V

In Chapter V through X all figures on membership, expenditures, etc., have been provided by the appropriate organizations, unless otherwise noted.

1. *The New York Times,* August 22, 1966.
2. From a survey made by the AJC office in the Los Angeles area: 29.5 percent of the Jewish population were affiliated with Reform temples in 1951, 19.4 percent in 1965; 20.5 percent were affiliated with Conservative synogogues in 1951, 35.3 percent in 1965. Between 1951 and 1965 Orthodox affiliation went down from 17.1 percent to 5.9 percent.
3. "Jewish Communal Services: Programs and Finances," The Council of Jewish Federations and Welfare Funds, June, 1966.

CHAPTER VI

1. From AJC's survey of Jewish attitudes in Kansas City, 1962, and others.
2. Charles Liebman, "Orthodoxy in American Jewish Life," *The American Jewish Yearbook,* 1965.
3. *Ibid.*

CHAPTER VIII

1. From a speech to the UOJC convention, Washington, D.C., November 25, 1966.
2. From an interview in *The Jewish World,* January, 1966.
3. Jacob Neusner, "The New Orthodox Left," *Conservative Judaism,* Fall, 1965.
4. Jacob Neusner, "Conservative Judaism in a Divided Community," *Conservative Judaism,* Summer, 1966.

CHAPTER IX

1. Arthur Hertzberg, "The Changing American Rabbinate," *Midstream,* January, 1966.
2. *Ibid.*

CHAPTER X

1. Manheim S. Shapiro, *As We See Ourselves: The Baltimore Survey,* conducted by AJC in 1962.
2. I am indebted here and elsewhere to Rabbi Samuel Rosenbaum's entertaining survey of synagogue bulletins, "As We See Ourselves," *Conservative Judaism,* Spring, 1965.
3. Quoted by Albert I. Gordon, *Jews in Suburbia,* Boston, Beacon Press, 1959.
4. Reported by Manheim Shapiro at the thirty-fourth General Assembly of the CJFWF, 1965.
5. *The Jewish Teenagers of Wilkes-Barre,* a study made by AJC, 1965.
6. "A Survey of the Political and Religious Attitudes of American College Students," *The Educational Review,* 1965.
7. A 1966 Gallup Poll, quoted in *Catholic Digest,* June, 1966.
8. "The State of Jewish Belief: A symposium," *Commentary,* August, 1966.

CHAPTER XI

All figures on fund raising, spending, etc. were provided by the Council of Jewish Federation and Welfare Funds, unless otherwise noted.
1. From a speech delivered by Max Fischer at the annual award dinner of the Reform Jewish Appeal, April 17, 1966.

CHAPTER XII

All figures on membership, fund raising, spending, etc. have been provided by the appropriate Zionist organizations, unless otherwise noted.
1. "Jewish Communal Services: Programs and Finances," The Council of Jewish Federations and Welfare Funds, June, 1966.
2. Marshall Sklare and Marc Vosk, *The Riverton Study: How Jews Look at Themselves,* conducted by AJC in 1952.
3. Harold Isaacs, "Americans in Israel," *The New Yorker,* August 27, 1966, and September 3, 1966.
4. *A Factual Study: The American Council for Judaism,* published by the New York Board of Rabbis, June, 1963.
5. *The Jewish Teenagers of Wilkes-Barre,* a study made in 1965 by AJC.
6. Arthur Hertzberg, "Israel and American Jewry," *Commentary,* August, 1967.

7. *Ibid.*
8. Harold Isaacs, *op. cit.*
9. *Ibid.*
10. Arthur Hertzberg, in a review of *The View from Masada* by Ronald Sanders, in *Book Week,* December 25, 1966.

CHAPTER XIII

All figures on membership, spending, etc. were provided by the organizations themselves, unless otherwise noted.
1. Isaac Levitats, "The Jewish Association in America," in *Essays on Jewish Life and Thought,* edited by Joseph L. Blau *et. al.,* New York, Columbia University Press, 1959.
2. Quoted in *This Is B'nai B'rith: A Story of Service,* a pamphlet published by B'nai B'rith for its members.

CHAPTER XIV

1. Rabbi Jack Schechter, "Primer for Revolution," *Conservative Judaism,* Winter, 1966.
2. "Jewish Communal Services: Programs and Finances," The Council of Jewish Federations and Welfare Funds, June, 1966.
3. Schechter, *op. cit.*
4. Jacob Neusner, "Conservative Judaism in a Divided Community," *Conservative Judaism,* Summer, 1966.

CHAPTER XV

1. William Dean Howells, "The Editor's Easychair," *Harper's,* 1915.
2. *The New York Times,* August 24, 1966.
3. *The American Jewish Yearbook,* 1964.
4. *The Jewish Teenagers of Wilkes-Barre,* a study made in 1965 by AJC.
5. New York Federation report on hospitals and philanthropy, March 25, 1960.
6. Ben B. Seligman, "Some Aspects of Jewish Demography," in *The Jews: Social Patterns of an American Group,* New York, The Free Press, 1958.
7. *Ibid.*
8. Quoted by Vivien Raynor, "Four Thousand Paintings and Sculptures," *The New York Times Magazine,* November 27, 1966.
9. Abe Burrows, quoted in the New York *Post,* December 28, 1965.
10. Interview with Sanford Greenberg, the New York *Post,* May 24, 1967.
11. Lionel Trilling, "Young in the Thirties," *Commentary,* May, 1966.
12. Saul Bellow, *Seize the Day,* New York, Viking, 1961.
13. Irving Malin, *Jews and Americans,* Carbondale, University of Southern Illinois Press, 1965.

14. Alfred Kazin, "The Jew as Modern Writer," *Commentary*, April, 1966.
15. Malin, *op. cit.*

CHAPTER XVI

1. Lawrence Fuchs, *The Political Behavior of American Jews*, New York, The Free Press, 1956.
2. L. S. Dawidowicz and L. J. Goldstein, *Politics in a Pluralist Democracy*, New York, Institute of Human Relations Press, 1963.
3. A speech before the annual meeting of the Conference on Jewish Sociology, May 17, 1967.
4. Max Geltman, "The Jewish Affirmation," *National Review*, October 4, 1966.
5. Dick Schaap in the New York *Herald-Tribune*, February 21, 1966.
6. A letter from Herman J. Obermayer, in *The Columbia Journalism Review*, Fall, 1965.
7. Milton Himmelfarb, "Church and State: How High a Wall?" *Commentary*, July, 1966.
8. A speech before the annual meeting of the Conference on Jewish Sociology, May 17, 1967.
9. "Jews in America," *Fortune*, 1936.
10. *The New York Times*, October 24, 1966.
11. *The New York Times*, May 7, 1967.
12. Nathan Glazer, "Negroes and Jews: The New Challenge to Pluralism," *Commentary*, December, 1964.

CHAPTER XVII

1. Sophia M. Robison, "A Study of Delinquency Among Jewish Children in New York City," *The Jews: Social Patterns of an American Group*, edited by Marshall Sklare, New York, The Free Press, 1958.
2. Quoted by Jimmy Breslin, the New York *Herald-Tribune*, April 1, 1966.
3. Quoted by T. V. LoCicero, "The Murder of Rabbi Adler," *Commentary*, June, 1966.
4. Rabbi Samuel Dresner, "Renewal," *Conservative Judaism*, Winter, 1965.
5. In a speech to the Jewish Educational Conference in Philadelphia, December 28, 1966.
6. Sholome Michael Gelber, "Does the Jewish Past Have a Jewish Future?" in *Essays on Jewish Life and Thought*, edited by Joseph L. Blau *et. al.*, New York, Columbia University Press, 1959.
7. Robert Alter, "Exhibiting the Lower East Side," *Commentary*, January, 1967.
8. Paul Lauter, "Reflections of a Jewish Activist," *Conservative Judaism*, Summer, 1965.

9. *New York Review of Books,* August 3, 1967.
10. Norman Podhoretz, "Hannah Arendt on Eichmann: A Study in the Perversity of Brilliance," *Doings and Undoings,* New York, The Noonday Press, 1964.
11. *American Judaism,* Winter, 1966–1967.
12. LoCicero, *op. cit.*

CHAPTER XVIII

1. "Jewish Social Work in the United States," *The Jews: Social Patterns of an American Group,* edited by Marshall Sklare, New York, The Free Press, 1958.
2. Ben B. Seligman, in *ibid.*
3. *Ibid.*
4. November, 1966, bulletin of Young Israel of Fifth Avenue.
5. Fred L. Strodtbeck, "Family Interaction, Values, and Achievement," in *The Jews: Social Patterns of an American Group, op. cit.*
6. *The Jewish Teenagers of Wilkes-Barre,* a study made in 1965 by AJC.
7. Fred L. Strodtbeck, *op. cit.*
8. A. B. Hollingshead and Frederick Redlich, *Social Class and Mental Illness: A Community Study,* New York, John Wiley and Sons, 1958.
9. Jerome K. Myers and Bertram H. Roberts, "Some Relationships between Religion, Ethnic Origin, and Mental Illness," in *The Jews: Social Patterns of an American Group, op. cit.*
10. Leo Srole *et al., Mental Health in the Metropolis,* New York, McGraw-Hill Book Company, 1962, Volume I.
11. Many studies have been made of Jewish drinking habits. The New Haven study, one of the best known, is described and analyzed by Charles R. Snyder, "Culture and Jewish Sobriety," in *The Jews: Social Patterns of an American Group, op. cit.*
12. Myers and Roberts, *op. cit.*

CHAPTER XIX

1. *The New York Times,* April 28, 1966.
2. W. Lloyd Warner and Leo Srole, "Assimilation or Survival: A Crisis in the Jewish Community of Yankee City," in *The Jews: Social Patterns of an American Group,* edited by Marshall Sklare, New York, The Free Press, 1958.
3. *Inter-Religious Dating Among College Students,* a study by David Caplovitz and Harry Levy, conducted by Columbia University. Also, Erich Rosenthal shows that the rate of intermarriage is 17.9 percent among those who haven't been to college, 37 percent among those who have.
4. A. B. Hollingshead and Frederick Redlich, *Social Class and Mental*

Illness: A Community Study, New York, John Wiley and Sons, 1958.

5. Rabbi Henry Cohen conducted a survey in Champaign-Urbana, where the University of Illinois is located. He showed that the rate of intermarriage was more than twice as high among the Jews on the faculty as among the Jewish townspeople.

6. Rabbi Samuel Dresner, "Renewal," *Conservative Judaism,* Winter, 1965.

7. Maria H. and Danel J. Levinson, "Jews Who Intermarry," *YIVO Annual of Jewish Social Science,* Volume 12, 1958–1959. John E. Mayer, *Jewish-Gentile Courtships: An Exploratory Study of a Social Process,* New York, The Free Press, 1961. Many other studies have been made of this subject. They are summed up and analyzed by Marshall Sklare, "Intermarriage and the Jewish Future," *Commentary,* April, 1964.

8. It used to be assumed, as a matter of course, that the rate of divorce and desertion was much higher in Jewish-gentile marriages than in marriages between Jews. Many studies seemed to confirm this. The occasional study that didn't (one is described by Henry J. Locke, *Predicting Adjustment in Marriage,* New York, Holt, 1951) were discounted. But in 1965 an analysis was done of the Iowa intermarriage statistics (Loren E. Chancellor and Thomas P. Monahan, "Religious Preferences and Interreligious Mixtures in Marriages and Divorces in Iowa," *American Journal of Sociology,* November, 1965) which dealt for the first time with a hitherto unnoticed factor. Many people who enter into mixed marriages have previously been divorced, often from partners of their own faith. A certain number of intermarriages, in short, are entered into by people who can be considered divorce-prone. If these people are left out of account, the discrepancy between the intermarriage divorce rate and the intramarriage divorce rate dwindles considerably. Applying this insight to a recent study of Jewish intermarriage in Indiana (*The American Jewish Yearbook,* 1967) Erich Rosenthal finds no appreciable difference in the two divorce rates. It also seems obvious that the more acceptable intermarriages become in the eyes of society, the more likely they are to succeed.

9. Milton Himmelfarb, "Secular Society? A Jewish Perspective," *Daedalls,* Winter, 1967.

Index

About the Author

JAMES YAFFE has written several novels, including *Mr. Margolies, What's the Big Hurry?* and *Nobody Does You Any Favors.* His play *The Deadly Game* (adapted from a story by Friedrich Dürrenmatt) was produced on Broadway in 1960 and off-Broadway in 1966. *Ivory Tower,* written in collaboration with Jerome Weidman, received the National Arts Foundation Grant in 1967 and was the choice of the American Playwrights Theater for production at colleges around the country. At present Mr. Yaffe is writer-in-residence at Colorado College and is at work on a new novel. He is married and has two children.